Developing European Internal Security Policy

The European Union (EU) is making strong inroads into areas of security traditionally reserved to states, especially into internal security, or Justice and Home Affairs. The Area of Freedom, Security and Justice (AFSJ), as it has been renamed in the Amsterdam Treaty, has seen significant policy developments since the late 1990s. In fact, there has been no other example of a policy-making area making its way so quickly and comprehensively to the centre of the treaties and to the top of the EU's policy-making agenda. After major treaty revisions in Maastricht, Amsterdam, Nice, and, finally the Lisbon Treaty, which entered into force on 1 December 2009, as well as an increased political impetus through the European Council Summits in Tampere (1999), the Hague (2004), and Stockholm (2009), the area appears as one of the most promising policy fields for integration in the EU in the foreseeable future. This process has deepened even more significantly after the terrorist attacks on 11 September 2001 in the United States, on 11 March 2004 in Madrid, and on 7 July 2005 in London.

This book is the first to analyse these hugely topical developments in European internal security at both the treaty and policy levels, as well as its implementation at the national level, from various disciplinary perspectives (political science, law, criminology, etc).

This book was previously published as a special issue of *European Security*.

Christian Kaunert is Senior Lecturer in EU Politics and International Relations at the University of Salford, UK and Marie Curie (Senior) Research Fellow at the European University Institute Florence, Italy.

Sarah Léonard is Lecturer in International Security at the University of Salford, UK and Marie Curie Research Fellow at Sciences Po Paris, France.

Developing European Internal Security Policy

After the Stockholm Summit and the Lisbon Treaty

Edited by
Christian Kaunert and Sarah Léonard

Routledge
Taylor & Francis Group

LONDON AND NEW YORK

First published 2012
by Routledge
2 Park Square, Milton Park, Abingdon, Oxfordshire OX14 4RN

Simultaneously published in the USA and Canada
by Routledge
711 Third Avenue, New York, NY 10017

First issued in paperback 2014

Routledge is an imprint of the Taylor & Francis Group, an informa business

British Library Cataloguing in Publication Data
A catalogue record for this book is available from the British Library

ISBN 978-0-415-68882-6 (hbk)
ISBN 978-1-138-79808-3 (pbk)

Typeset in Times New Roman
by Taylor & Francis Books

Disclaimer
The publisher would like to make readers aware that the chapters in this book are referred to as articles as they had been in the special issue. The publisher accepts responsibility for any inconsistencies that may have arisen in the course of preparing this volume for print.

Contents

INTRODUCTION

After the Stockholm programme: an area of freedom, security and justice in the European Union?

The European Union (EU) is making strong inroads into areas of security traditionally reserved to states, especially into internal security, or Justice and Home Affairs(JHA). The area of freedom, security and justice (AFSJ), as it has been renamed in the Amsterdam Treaty, has seen significant policy developments since the late 1990s (Kaunert 2005, 2007, 2009, 2010a, 2010b, 2010c). Monar (1999) underlines the fact that there has been no other example of a policy-making area making its way so quickly and comprehensively to the centre of the treaties and to the top of the EU's policy-making agenda. After major treaty revisions in Maastricht, Amsterdam, Nice, and, finally the Lisbon Treaty, which entered into force on 1 December 2009, as well as an increased political impetus through the European Council Summits in Tampere (1999), the Hague (2004) and Stockholm (2009), the area appears as one of the most promising policy fields for integration in the EU in the foreseeable future. This process has deepened even more significantly after the terrorist attacks on 11 September 2001 in the United States, on 11 March 2004 in Madrid and on 7 July 2005 in London. Some scholars have even suggested that these empirical develop-ments, and the resulting increasing involvement of the EU in internal security matters, have changed EU governance more generally. This special issue explores these significant developments in the AFSJ at both the treaty and policy levels, as well as its implementation at the national level, from various disciplinary perspectives.

The EUSIM project and the conference on 'internal security policies in the EU – after the Stockholm programme: an area of freedom, security and justice(AFSJ) in the EU?'

This special issue is derived from a conference on the AFSJ that took place at the University of Salford, Centre for European Security, on 28–29 January 2010. This conference is part of the EUSIM project, which is generously funded by the European Commission under the Jean Monnet programme/Lifelong Learning programme in 2009–12. Many thanks are therefore due to the European Commis-sion for this important financial support, without which the organisation of this conference would not have been possible. The main aim of the EUSIM project is to bring the study and research of the EU closer to students of a wide variety of backgrounds. Popular discourse in Britain often depicts the EU as an 'undemocratic and bureaucratic monster' imposing its will upon the unwilling and 'sovereignty-less' Member States. Consequently, students are often thought to be ideologically opposed to, or, at the very minimum, not interested in studying and researching the EU. This project aims to change this perception. It does so through the application of a problem-based learning (PBL) approach to the 'European Union Simulation' Jean Monnet module, which aims to support students in becoming independent, enterprising problem-solvers, through the examination of real-life EU policy problems. In addition to more traditional classes that introduce students to policy-making in the EU, students are given a policy scenario and negotiate in weekly sessions akin to Council meetings, before the culmination of the negotiations at a session modelled upon a European Council Summit. The scenario in 2009/10 was on the theme of the AFSJ, and all students were given free access to the latest cutting-edge research on their research topic by attending the conference and will gain further insights through the publication of this special issue. Bringing together students, researchers and practitioners considerably enhances the understanding and the enthusiasm of students who would normally not come into contact with the EU. The interaction between students, researchers and policy-makers has been of tremendous benefit to all involved.

From justice and home affairs(JHA) to an area of freedom, security and justice(AFSJ)?

One can distinguish two important arguments in the existing literature on the AFSJ. First of all, the development of European cooperation on JHA/AFSJ matters has often been explained as being the result of attempts by national governments to escape liberal constraints at the national level. According to Guiraudon (2000, 2003), which has developed this argument with respect to asylum and migration, governments have 'venue-shopped', that is, looked for a new policy venue more amenable to their policy preferences and found it at the EU level. In other words, Member States have attempted to circumvent domestic pressures and obstacles by 'escaping' to the EU level where they would be protected from these constraints (see Freeman 1998, Joppke 1998, 2001, Lavenex 2006). EU Member States, in this argument, have thus decided to enhance their cooperation in a process driven by national bureaucracies. These state-centred accounts emphasise the resilience of nation-states, which use the EU as a device for attaining policy objectives that are unlikely to be achieved at the domestic level alone.

Another important argument in the academic literature, which has also been developed by non-governmental organisations (NGOs), is that the development of the AFSJ has been mainly driven by security concerns. According to that perspective, security has become the dominant component in the 'security–freedom–justice' trio, at the expense of freedom and justice (Huysmans 2006, Baldaccini et al. 2007, Guild and Geyer 2008, Balzacq and Carrera 2008). Several scholars have argued that the terrorist attacks on 11 September 2001 have had a major impact in that respect. Levy (2005, p. 35), for example, has argued that 'the trend towards liberalisation seemed to be stopped dead in its tracks by the events of 9/11' (see also Guild 2003, Bigo and Tsoukala 2008).

How far have the academic analyses that have just been outlined come to explain the tensions, the contradictions and policy flows in this area? With the AFSJ being of crucial importance in the Lisbon Treaty, it is time to take stock of how far the EU has progressed towards creating this 'AFSJ'. The Commission, naturally, has analysed the achievements of the Tampere and the Hague programmes in a positive light. Although progress was perceived as patchy in some areas, there have been visible achievements, concerning amongst others the Common European Asylum System, the European Arrest and Evidence Warrants, as well as the development of the activities of agencies such as FRONTEX, Europol and Eurojust. Yet, it is precisely these achievements that have also been seen in a negative light by a large number of scholars and across the NGO community. The same mixed views exist in the European Parliament and at the Council level. At the end of 2009, a successor programme to the Tampere and the Hague programmes was adopted under the Swedish Presidency. Called the 'Stockholm programme', it was adopted at a special EU Council Summit on 10–11 December 2009. The following section will outline the changing environment in the AFSJ through the continuous provision of new competences and changes to old EU competences.

At the beginning stood the Intergovernmental Conferences (IGC) on Economic and Monetary Union and on Political Union, preparing the Maastricht Treaty, which established the new policy area of JHA. The Treaty on European Union (TEU) created a new legal concept, the so-called nine questions of 'common interest', which were: (1) asylum policy; (2) external border control; (3) immigration (entry, circulation, stay and fight against illegal immigration); (4) fight against drugs; (5) against international crime; (6) judicial cooperation in civil matters; (7) in criminal matters; (8) customs cooperation; and (9) police cooperation. Effectively, at the time, these areas of common interest only brought pre-existing forms of intergovernmental cooperation under the umbrella of the EU (Kaunert 2005).

Subsequently, the Amsterdam Treaty established the AFSJ, which replaced the policy area of JHAs. While the Maastricht Treaty had only described common areas of interest in which cooperation could happen in order to attain other Community objectives, the Amsterdam Treaty made the concept of 'Freedom, Security and Justice' an objective in itself for the EU. In addition, the notable achievement of the Amsterdam Treaty was the inclusion of Schengen into the framework of the EU. Regarding the use of legal instruments, the Amsterdam Treaty also brought about significant changes with the introduction of new legal instruments, much more closely modelled on EC instruments.

However, these new instruments needed to be given a purpose, which occurred subsequently with the start of the Finnish Presidency on 1 July 1999. Significantly, the Tampere Council summit gave the EU a policy direction to what had been hitherto a somewhat incoherent European approach. Until then, debates had mainly focused on whether national sovereignty should be preserved or, in contrast, could also be pooled at the EU level with respect to these policy matters. The Tampere Council marked the beginning of increasingly in-depth debates on the exact aims and purposes of European cooperation on these policy matters. Here, opinions ranged from considering the AFSJ as an add-on to the Single Market to envisaging it as a free-standing policy area (Kaunert 2005).

The terrorist attacks on 11 September 2001 had an important impact on the development of the AFSJ. The European Commission played a significant part in the construction of a role for the EU with regard to internal security matters through being a 'supranational policy entrepreneur' (Kaunert 2007, 2009, 2010a, 2010b, 2010c). Unsurprisingly, the Commission analysed the achievements of the Tampere and the Hague programmes in a positive light. 'The Hague Programme adopted a long term perspective, but it went further in that its strategic aims were accompanied

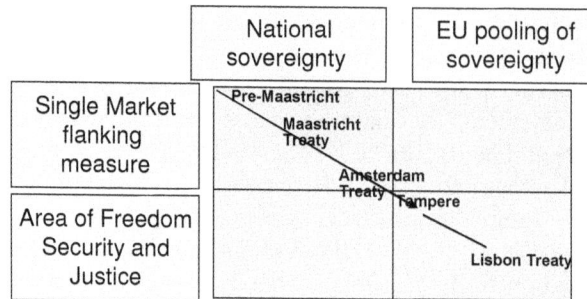

Figure 1.   The evolution from JHA to an AFSJ.

by a detailed action plan for delivering them. Progress has been mixed, but there have been visible achievements' (COM (2009) 263 final, p. 3). (Figure 1).

The future: the Lisbon Treaty and the Stockholm programme

Yet, as ever, the future may manage to contradict history. Although the EU is not a state, it has made strong inroads into various areas of security – including internal security matters – which have traditionally been seen as strongholds of national sovereignty. In that sense, the statement by Edwards and Meyer (2008) that '[the] governance of the European Union has been changed through its response to international terrorism' is correct. The actions of Osama Bin Laden and Al Qaeda seem to be achieving a clear response – the increased integration of European nations in response to a security threat. In the European Parliament, a political community is certainly in the making in response to this security threat, and familiar national faultlines emerge. The Stockholm programme provoked strong criticism from southern Europeans. Maltese centre-right MEP Simon Busuttil commented that 'the axis on security seems to have been watered down in the text', a point which was reinforced by a number of Italian MEPs. British Liberal MEP Diana Wallis countered this: 'We're beginning to see where the fracture lines in the house are [...] security is the main sticking point. Do we want to go further in terms of underlining security? Who knows what the final outcome will be in terms of immigration and migration? That could be difficult' (Euractiv 2009). The same political faultlines exist at the Council level. Sweden, that held the Council Presidency in the second half of 2009, pushed for as broad a programme as possible in order to achieve consensus in a EU of 27 Member States. Since the Council approved the Stockholm programme, the real political battles have started to emerge.

Outlines of the articles

Consequently, this special issue of *European Security* analyses recent and significant policy developments in this AFSJ in the wake of the ratification of the Lisbon Treaty and the adoption of the Stockholm programme, examining in particular: (1) the extent to which an AFSJ has been created; (2) individual AFSJ policies; (3) the roles of various political actors in the development of the AFSJ (EU institutions, Member States, civil society), and (4) the impact of the AFSJ on national policies. Policy areas to be discussed will go beyond a narrow understanding of 'EU internal security policy' and include issues such as border protection, the fight against terrorism and terrorist financing, and asylum and migration with its external dimension.

Dora Kostakopoulou examines the Lisbon Treaty changes to the EU institutional structure concerning the AFSJ, as well as the Stockholm programme. Her paper compares and contrasts the legacy of the Tampere and Hague programmes with the policy priorities and recommendations of the Stockholm programme. Her paper clearly suggests some light at the end of the Stockholm tunnel: less securitisation and control with a new 'citizen-oriented' and 'rights-based' perspective. In her view, this development, coupled with the Lisbon Treaty reforms, has the potential to shift the AFSJ policy area away from the securitisation paradigm.

Christian Kaunert shares this view on the Lisbon Treaty potential for the AFSJ. In his paper, he suggests that the Lisbon Treaty has the potential to push the AFSJ towards tremendous growth, and has provided the policy area with instruments that were unthinkable after the third pillar was created during the Maastricht Treaty negotiations. He investigates the role of the European Commission in this process of constructing an AFSJ. He argues that the Commission (through alliances with other institutional actors) managed to incrementally contribute to a shift in political norms towards an acceptance of EU pooling of national sovereignty. This manifested itself specifically during the negotiations of the Constitutional Treaty and the subsequent renegotiation of the Lisbon Treaty.

Ariadna Ripoll Servent investigates the impact of the significant Lisbon Treaty changes on the European Parliament, which has to contend with raised expectations due to its increased institutional role. In her article, she argues that the extension of co-decision increases the influence of the European Parliament on decision-making. Engaging with securitisation theory, Ripoll Servent poses the question of whether the extension of co-decision will transform the European Parliament into a new securitising actor, or, whether it will have the potential for de-securitising the agenda.

Eiko Thielemann and Nadine El-Enany analyse the substantive policy area of refugee protection. They engage with the so-called 'Fortress Europe' argument, which they counter substantively and reject, suggesting that Member States have been primarily interested in overcoming collective action problems amongst each other. In their view, this is the key driver for EU cooperation in this area. This argument is put forward convincingly through a thorough analysis of EU asylum laws, and comparing them with those of similar developed countries outside the EU. Thus, they suggest that 'there is no evidence to support the claim that European cooperation has led to uniquely restrictive refugee policies and protection outcomes'.

Sarah Léonard engages with the same securitisation argument in its application to EU border policies. Her paper examines the ways in which the activities of FRONTEX contribute to the securitisation of asylum and migration in the EU. It does so by applying a sociological approach to the study of securitisation processes, which, it argues, is particularly well-suited to the study of securitisation processes in the EU. Such an approach privileges the study of securitising practices over securitising 'speech acts' in securitisation processes. After identifying two main types of securitising practices in general, the article systematically examines the activities of FRONTEX and the extent to which they can be seen as securitising practices.

Vihar Georgiev focuses on the EU border policy from a complementary angle to the aforementioned paper. In his view, abolishing the internal borders of the EU has created a security deficit. While policy-makers intended for this to be compensated by guarding the external EU border, his article suggests this security deficit has not been fully resolved, primarily due to uneven policy implementation. Firstly, his article presents an overview of the various threats to the EU border security system. Secondly, he calls for a new approach to border security, i.e. the introduction of a common European border security policy.

Christian Kaunert and Marina Della Giovanna analyse the substantive policy area of counter-terrorist financing. In their paper, they examine the EU counter-terrorist financing (EU-CTF) regime since 2001, building on the notion of supranational policy entrepreneurship (SPE). While supranational institutions have rarely taken the lead in this area, their article suggests that, despite the centrality that Member States maintain in the policy-making process, European institutions, notably the European Commission and the Council Secretariat, have been significant in the development of EU-CTF cooperation. The paper outlines the different ways in which this occurred.

Javier Argomaniz examines the implementation of the EU counter-terrorism policy. He underlines the importance of examining this issue, as it has not been systematically analysed to date. His paper uses legal transpositions of counter-terrorism instruments into national law and highlights the presence of major implementation delays in this policy sector. Furthermore, it underlines the significant cross-national variation on this matter. The paper concludes with an assessment of the potential impact of the Lisbon Treaty on the implementation of the EU counter-terrorism policy.

Finally, Alexandra Schwell analyses the construction of the AFSJ at the national level by examining the anomalous case of the Eastern borders of Austria, which, since 1990, have been guarded by draftees of the Austrian army. This measure was first introduced in reaction to the Eastern European political transition process, and the resulting increase of cross-border crime. While this so-called 'support deployment' was initially planned for only ten weeks, it has since then continued. Her paper evaluates the political strategies of the various actors involved in what she considers to be securitisation practices, completely decoupled from the actual policing of the Schengen internal border.

References

Baldaccini, A., Guild, E., and Toner, H., eds., 2007. *Whose freedom, security and justice? EU immigration and asylum law and policy.* Oxford: Hart.

Balzacq, T. and Carrera, S., eds., 2008. *Security versus freedom? A challenge for Europe's future.* Aldershot: Ashgate.

Bigo, D. and Tsoukala, A., eds., 2008. *Terror, insecurity and liberty: illiberal practices of liberal regimes after 9/11.* London: Routledge.

Commission of the European Communities. 2009. *Communication from the commission to the council and the European Parliament – justice, freedom, and security in Europe since 2005: an evaluation of the Hague programme and action plan,* 10.06.2009. COM(2009) 263 final. Brussels: Commission of the European Communities.

Edwards, G. and Meyer, C., 2008. Introduction: charting a contested transformation. *Journal of common market studies,* 46 (1), 1–25.

Euractiv, 2009. *Parliament split on "Progressive" Swedish immigration programme.* Available from: http://www.euractiv.com/en/mobility/parliament-split-progressive-swedish-immigration-programme/article-186266 [Accessed 1 December 2009].

Freeman, G., 1998. The decline of sovereignty? Politics and immigration restriction in liberal states. *In*: C. Joppke, ed. *Challenge to the nation state: immigration in Western Europe and the United States.* Oxford: Oxford University Press, 86–108.

Guild, E., 2003. International terrorism and EU immigration, asylum and borders policy: the unexpected victims of 11 September 2001. *European foreign affairs review*, 8 (3), 331–346.

Guild, E. and Geyer, F., eds., 2008. *Security versus justice? Police and judicial cooperation in the European Union.* Aldershot: Ashgate.

Guiraudon, V., 2000. European integration and migration policy: vertical policy-making as venue shopping. *Journal of common market studies*, 38 (2), 251–271.

Guiraudon, V., 2003. The constitution of a European immigration policy domain: a political sociology approach. *Journal of European public policy*, 10 (2), 263–282.

Huysmans, J., 2006. *The politics of insecurity: fear, migration and asylum in the EU.* London: Routledge.

Joppke, C., ed., 1998. *Challenge to the nation-state: immigration in Western Europe and the United States.* Oxford: Oxford University Press.

Joppke, C., 2001. The legal-domestic sources of immigrant rights: the United States, Germany and the European Union. *Comparative political studies*, 34 (4), 339–366.

Kaunert, C., 2005. The area of freedom, security and justice: the construction of a 'European public order'. *European security*, 14 (4), 459–483.

Kaunert, C., 2007. Without the power of purse or sword: the European arrest warrant and the role of the commission. *Journal of European integration*, 29 (4), 387–404.

Kaunert, C., 2009. Liberty versus security?: EU asylum policy and the European commission. *Journal of contemporary European research*, 5 (2), 148–170.

Kaunert, C., 2010a. The external dimension of EU counter-terrorism relations: competences, interests & institutions. *Terrorism and political violence*, 22 (1), 41–61.

Kaunert, C., 2010b. Europol and EU counter-terrorism: international security actorness in the external dimension? *Studies in conflict and terrorism*, 33 (7), 652–671.

Kaunert, C., 2010c. *European internal security – towards supranational governance in the area of freedom, security and justice.* Manchester: Manchester University Press.

Lavenex, S., 2006. Shifting up and out: the foreign policy of European immigration control. *West European politics*, 29 (2), 329–350.

Levy, C., 2005. The European Union after 9/11: the demise of a liberal democratic asylum regime? *Government and opposition*, 40 (1), 26–59.

Monar, J., 1999. *Justice and home affairs in a wider Europe: the dynamics of inclusion and exclusion. ESRC one Europe of several?* Working Paper 07/00.

Christian Kaunert
Robert Schuman Centre for Advanced Studies,
European University Institute, Florence, Italy
Centre for European Security, University of Salford, Salford, UK.
c.kaunert@salford.ac.uk
Sarah Léonard
Centre for European Studies, Sciences Po Paris, France
Centre for European Security, University of Salford, Salford, UK.
s.leonard@salford.ac.uk

An open and secure Europe? Fixity and fissures in the area of freedom, security and justice after Lisbon and Stockholm

Dora Kostakopoulou

School of Law, University of Manchester, Manchester, UK

The Lisbon Treaty's depillarisation of justice and home affairs (JHA) cooperation represents a major break from the past. It opens the way for the full involvement of the Commission, the European Parliament and the European Court of Justice, an involvement that is bound to influence the substantive scope, and perhaps liberalise, legal and policy output in the years ahead. A different form of cooperation in area of freedom, security and justice institutionally and substantively is digging out its space within the present, security-oriented and traditionally executive-driven architecture. The Stockholm Programme and the proposed Action Plan are a reflection of this. Present in them are aspects of the Hague Programme and the logic of control and surveillance. But there also exist vessels of less ideology-driven policies, pragmatic responses to JHA challenges and respect for citizens' rights, human rights and the rule of law. Whether the latter paradigm, which is wrapped up within the logic of security, remains confined and crammed in the next five years or will be given room to grow remains to be seen.

The European Union's (EUs) area of freedom, security and justice (AFSJ; formerly known as justice and home affairs cooperation) has grown out of an institutional journey of remarkable experimentation and cautious trust-building among the Member States (MS) which has been both surprising and gripping. When the journey in the EU formally began in the early 1990s with the establishment of the so-called third pillar of the Treaty on European Union (TEU 2002) (in force 1 November 1993), nobody could have envisaged its road and turns in the 15 year period that followed.[1] Nor could one have predicted the incremental and quick transition from the TEU's diluted intergovernmentalism to partial Communitarisation at Amsterdam, via the insertion of Title IV EC for migration, asylum, third country nationals and civic law matters, and to full Communitarisation in the aborted Constitutional Treaty and the Lisbon Treaty (2007) (in force on 1 December 2009).

Given the fact that MS have not traditionally welcomed a possible loss of sovereignty in areas of high politics such as policing, judicial cooperation in criminal law, migration and asylum policy, the smooth depillarisation of the AFSJ appears to be a remarkable, albeit unforeseen, detour from the original itinerary. This detour has made secretive and national executive-driven decision-making a thing of the past thereby opening up new roads for better and more efficient law making in AFSJ matters. It has also made the EU more open and accountable by infusing the AFSJ with effective parliamentary supervision and judicial scrutiny. In the course of different, structured processes of cooperation, MS have finally realised not only the many things they have in common and that mutual trust results in enhanced capacity for action, but also the irrelevance of national borders and domestic frameworks of control for challenges that by definition cannot be confined within national borders, such as terrorism, drugs trafficking, international crime, refugee matters and increased human mobility (Walker 2004, Peers 2006, Kostakopoulou 2007).[2] Accordingly, the search for improved institutional arrangements and better law making and policy-making eventually led to the road that was not taken at the very beginning.

The 'circuitous' road to the ordinary Community method has also been accompanied by positive integration measures, that is, ambitious legislative initiatives, and the embedment of the principle of mutual recognition[3] in the Lisbon Treaty (see Chapters 3 and 4 of Title V on the Area of Freedom, Security and Justice). Notwithstanding the recent transformation of governance in the AFSJ which holds the promise of a more efficient, accountable, transparent and democratic decision-making (White 2003, Compare Peers 2004), a constant feature of justice and home affairs (JHA) cooperation in all its institutional forms thus far has been the prevalence of a security-centred paradigm. Institutional restlessness did not alter this underlying substantive logic. In the past, the fundamental principle of free movement characterising the first pillar was contrasted with the 'unfreedom' of the third pillar which had depicted asylum, migration and matters relating to third country nationals as security threats alongside terrorism and transnational crime. The removal of internal frontiers facilitated the spread of a number of discourses on Europe's alleged security deficit thereby enabling, among other things, the securitisation of migration and asylum, that is, their depiction as existential threats requiring measures beyond the bounds of ordinary politics (Weaver 1995, Buzan et al. 1998). The creation of a chain of equivalences among organised crime, migration and terrorism resulted in the creation of what Bigo and Leveau (1992) has termed an 'internal security field' in which irregular migration, crime and terrorism were placed on a single security continuum. It is true that most policy observers as well as scholars believed that the bifurcation between the free movement paradigm, on the one hand, and the security paradigm, on the other, was the by-product of the different institutional configurations of supranationalism characterising the first pillar and intergovernmentalism characterising the third pillar, respectively (Monar 1998, 2001, Kostakopoulou 2001). But as the third pillar began to dismember at Amsterdam first and later on in the aborted Constitutional Treaty, the security paradigm began to permeate the first pillar and to be promoted at the expense of freedom. Accordingly, not only was European citizens' freedom to cross borders (positive freedom) accompanied by a negative conception of freedom, that is, freedom from danger, risk or fear (including the perceived threat of irregular migration), but the latter, which presupposes security measures, was elevated into a precondition for the former (Huysmans 1998, 2002, Kostakopoulou 2000, Bigo 2004, Lindahl 2004, 2010) As freedom and security became closely aligned and the external environment became more uncertain and risk-ridden, the concept of security stretched both conceptually and geographically (Bigo 2002, Andreas 2003). Internal and external security also became closely linked, as attested by the presence of internal security objectives in EU external relations and the enhanced cooperation between the EU and third countries. Without any reservation, the EU sought to imitate the protective function of states thereby increasing its social legitimacy. Only a 'protective' Union would provide high levels of security for its citizens while making free movement in the internal market a reality (Kostakopoulou 2000, Kaunert 2005).

At the Tampere European Council (1999, pp. 2–3), the Heads of State and Government decided that 'the challenge of the Amsterdam Treaty [was] now to ensure that freedom, which includes the right to move freely throughout the Union, can be enjoyed in conditions of security and justice available to all. It is a project which corresponds to the frequently expressed concerns of citizens and has a direct bearing on their daily lives'. To this end, the Programme agreed at Tampere set out a number of ambitious policy orientations and priorities which would make the AFSJ a reality and prompted the articulation of a number of legislative initiatives in the fields of legal migration and asylum by the Commission.[4] By contrast, the Hague Programme (Council of the European Union 2004, European Council 2005), the five-year programme that succeeded the Tampere Programme (2005–10), lacked in ambition and had a more prominent security focus in light of the 9/11 terrorist attacks on the World Trade Centre and the Madrid bombing on 11 March 2004. Tackling terrorism, irregular migration and developing an integrated management of the Union's external borders became the central focus of the Hague policy agenda. In its Action Plan, the European Commission (2005, compare also 2006a, 2006b) attempted to strike a better balance between freedom and security and a similar effort can be discerned in its contribution to the process of the adoption of the successor of the Hague Programme, the Stockholm Programme (European Commission 2009) which is discussed below.

The discussion that follows examines the Lisbon Treaty's innovations concerning the AFSJ and the new phase of the EU's AFSJ by comparing and contrasting the legacy of the Tampere and Hague programmes with the policy priorities and recommendations of the Stockholm Programme that was adopted by the Brussels European Council on 11 December 2009. I argue that although the Stockholm Programme does not represent a well-reasoned retreat from the paradigm of securitisation and control that has characterised JHA cooperation since the very beginning, it would be a mistake to assume that the restrictive and security-based logic is unchanging, solid and fixed. The new 'citizen-oriented' and 'rights-based' perspective is a welcome development, and the 'reweighing' of freedom, which is reflected in both the order and number of the Stockholm Programme's policy priorities, coupled with the Treaty of Lisbon's new reforms, can set in motion a dynamic whereby the more national executives seek to return to the securitisation paradigm from which they set out, the further they move away from it. But more work remains to be done in designing and implementing common juridico-political frameworks in the AFSJ which are coherent, normatively sound and effective.

The ambitious transformation of the area of freedom, security and justice (AFSJ) in the Lisbon Treaty

The Lisbon Treaty, which was signed on 13 December 2007, was the by product of the process of 'structured reflection' on the future of Europe that followed the rejection of the Constitutional Treaty in France and the Netherlands in 2005. It entered into force on 1 December 2009 following the positive outcome of the second Irish Referendum (2 October 2009), its ratification by the Czech Republic (13 November 2009) and a favourable decision by the German Federal Constitutional Court (2009). The new Treaty in the main absorbed the Constitutional Treaty's innovations in the AFSJ.[5] One of the new objectives of the Union is to 'offer its citizens an area of freedom, security and justice without internal frontiers, in which the free movement of persons is ensured in conjunction with appropriate measures with respect to external border controls, asylum, immigration and the prevention and combating of crime' (Article 3(2) TEU). The insertion of this objective enhances the visibility as well as the constitutional status of the AFSJ, since it is no longer associated with the attainment of the internal market and the adoption of compensatory measures for the abolition of internal frontiers.

The New Title V on 'The Area of Freedom, Security and Justice' contains a chapter on General provisions (articles 67–76 TFEU) and chapters on policies on border checks, asylum and immigration (2), judicial cooperation in civil matters (3), judicial cooperation in criminal matters (4) and police cooperation (5). The unification of the institutional framework pertaining to migration related matters and judicial cooperation in civil matters, on the one hand, and police and judicial cooperation in criminal matters, on the other is the most significant innovation. Accordingly, qualified majority voting in the Council[6] and the ordinary legislative procedure (formerly known as co-decision procedure which transformed the EP into a genuine co-legislative body) become the norm[7] and the exceptional legal instruments of the Amsterdam Treaty are replaced by the Community instruments (Regulations, directives and decisions) which can now give rise to directly effective rights for individuals enforceable before national courts. In addition, the Commission has the right of initiative, be it exclusive in the areas of border checks, asylum and immigration and civic judicial cooperation,[8] and non-exclusive in criminal judicial cooperation, police cooperation and the ensuing administrative cooperation,[9] and the European Court of Justice (ECJ) can now exert its jurisdiction over all aspects of the AFSJ, with the exception of reviewing the validity or proportionality of police operations and measures taken by MS in order to maintain law and order and the safeguarding of internal security mentioned above (Articles 276 TFEU and 72 TFEU).[10] Without a doubt, the binding nature of the Charter of Fundamental Rights will aid the ECJ's scrutiny of AFSJ legislation and will ensure its compliance with fundamental rights across the EU, with the exception of the UK, Poland and the Czech Republic where the Charter is not applicable.[11]

The Treaty also formalises the institutional role of the European Council which shall 'define the strategic guidelines for legislative and operational planning within the area of freedom, security and justice' (Article 68 TFEU). The European Council's leadership role is thus enhanced and the election of a Council President for a period of two and half years, renewable once, will facilitate policy continuity. The effectiveness of decision-making in this field will also be enhanced by the separation between 'legislative' and 'operational' tasks and the reinforced coordination of operational collaboration by the new standing Committee within the Council on (broadly defined) 'internal security'. The new standing committee, which replaces the so called Article 36 TEU Committee, will facilitate the coordination of the action of MS' competent authorities (Article 71 TFEU), but does not have the power to direct the actions of national police and other authorities in relation to specific actions.[12] Notwithstanding the gains in terms of policy effectiveness, the all embracing concept of 'internal security' as well as the fact that the Committee will not be accountable to the European and national parliaments give rise to concern.[13] There exists a trend towards the securitisation of a number of policy issues and socio-economic problems, such as youth violence, road accidents, forest fires and energy shortages.[14] The application of a security-based approach to such policy areas augments civil society's anxieties about authoritarian policy-making and the adoption of a European security model characterised by a generalised focus on prevention and the neutralisation of the threat.

Having said this, however, the increase in democratic control, oversight and transparency in JHA matters cannot be underestimated. Greater transparency is also promoted by the amended text of Article 255 EC, now Article 15 TFEU. The latter article reaffirms the link between transparency and participatory democracy by stating that 'in order to promote good governance and ensure the participation of civil society, the Union's institutions, bodies and agencies shall conduct their work as openly as possible' and that the Parliament and the Council (when it considers and votes on a draft legislative act) shall meet in public. To this end, the right of access to documents applies to the Union's institutions, bodies and agencies. Although each institution, body or agency shall determine in its own rules of procedure-specific provisions regarding access to documents, Article 15(3) TFEU provides that Regulations will lay down the general principles and limits which govern the right of access and that 'each institution, body, office or agency shall ensure that its proceedings are transparent and shall elaborate in its own rules of procedure-specific provisions regarding access to its documents, in accordance with the aforementioned Regulations. And under Article 15(3) TFEU, the European Parliament and the Council of Ministers shall ensure publication of the documents relating to the legislative procedures'.[15]

Given the chronic lack of democratic control and oversight in JHA matters, the strengthening of the role of national parliaments in the European governance is a welcome reform. National parliaments are now involved in the political monitoring of Europol and the evaluation of Eurojust's activities and may 'participate in the evaluation mechanisms' for the implementation of Union policies in the AFSJ (Article 12(c) TEU). Although it is unfortunate that national parliaments' participation in the mutual evaluation of the MS' implementation of Union policies in the AFSJ is discretionary, the position of national parliaments in the EU legal order has been considerably strengthened as a result of their monitoring of compliance of legislation in the AFSJ with the principle of subsidiarity (Article 5(3) TEU, Article 69 TFEU) and the amended protocols on the role of the national parliaments in the EU and on the application of the principles of subsidiarity and proportionality.[16]

In addition to the above-mentioned reforms, the substantive scope of the AFSJ has also expanded. Article 67(1) TFEU, which replaces Articles 29 EU and 61 EC, states that 'the Union shall constitute an area of freedom, security and justice with respect for fundamental rights and the different legal traditions and systems of the Member States'. It also contains explicit references to the framing of 'a common policy on asylum, immigration and external border control, based on solidarity between the MS, which is fair towards third country nationals', the prevention and combating of crime, racism and xenophobia and the application of the principle of mutual recognition of judgments in criminal matters and judicial and extrajudicial decisions in civil matters. Article 75 TFEU creates a legal basis for administrative measures with respect to capital movement and payments for preventing and combating terrorism. But the maintenance of law and order and the safeguarding of internal security fall outside the EU's competence (Article 72 TEFU), thereby meeting MS' sovereignty concerns.

As far as migration law and policy is concerned, the new legal basis for the gradual introduction of an integrated management system for external borders is noteworthy, even though there is no explicit reference to the establishment of a European Border Guard which was mentioned in the Conclusions of the Seville and Thessaloniki European Council meetings in June 2002 and 2003, respectively. Although this provision builds on the momentum created by the incorporation of the Schengen acquis into the EC/EU and the Tampere conclusions, the suggestion that any measure in this area must give 'due regard to the necessary safeguards for democratic control and the rights of individuals' was not adopted. It is also interesting to note that Article 77(2)(e) TEU entails the possibility of the abolition of internal controls for third country nationals. But given national executives' anxieties, the third paragraph of Article 77 TFEU states that the Community's competence in this area shall not impinge upon MS' sovereign powers concerning the geographical demarcation of their borders, in accordance with international law.

A welcome development in the field of asylum is the reference to a uniform status of subsidiary protection for nationals of third countries requiring international protection. A provision that has given rise to many concerns, however, is Article 78(2)(g) which refers to measures concerning partnership and cooperation with third countries with a view to managing inflows of asylum seekers – a provision that was especially supported by the British Government. NGOs have argued that this may legitimise attempts to 'subcontract' the MS asylum obligations to third countries via the establishment of reception centres or even resettlement schemes. Explicit references to combating of trafficking in persons and readmission agreements have also been made in the Treaty.[17] In addition, the EU has now express power to act against unauthorised residence, in addition to illegal immigration, including the removal and repatriation of persons residing without authorisation (Article 79(2) TFEU). But the Tampere commitment to the equal treatment of long-term resident third country nationals has not found its way into the Treaty. Article 79(4) TFEU establishes a legal basis for EU supporting action in the field of integration of long-term resident Third Country Nationals (TCNs), 'excluding any harmonisation of the laws and regulations of the MS', while Article 79(5) TFEU specifically affirms the competence of the MS to 'determine the volumes of admission' of migrant workers from third countries. Furthermore, the embedment of the principle of solidarity and fair sharing of responsibility (including its financial implications) between the MS in the areas of immigration, asylum and border controls into the Treaty creates a specific legal basis for the adoption of appropriate measures in this area (III-268), thereby replacing the existing Community competence to adopt measures on burden-sharing related to asylum (Article 63(2)(b)).

While Chapter 3 of the AFSJ Title on civil judicial cooperation builds largely on the existing acquis in this area, the upholding of the principle of mutual recognition of judgements and decisions in extrajudicial cases, the development of measures of preventive justice and alternative methods of dispute settlement and the adoption of measures designed to ensure a high level of access to justice are noteworthy. The latter provision cannot but have implications for the future establishment of minimum standards guaranteeing an appropriate level of legal aid for cross-border cases throughout the Union and special common procedural rules in order to simplify and speed up the settlement of cross-border disputes concerning small commercial claims under consumer legislation or to establish minimum common standards for multilingual forms or documents in cross-border proceedings.

The principle of mutual recognition of judgements and decisions (negative integration) has been proclaimed to be the cornerstone for judicial cooperation in the criminal field, too, since Tampere. It works in tandem with measures of 'positive' integration, that is, the approximation of procedural and substantive criminal laws. According to Article 82(2) TFEU, directives may establish minimum rules, which take into account the differences between the legal traditions and systems of the MS – a reference that was inserted following pressure from the UK and Ireland which retain the option of not opting in, on: (a) the mutual admissibility of evidence among the MS; (b) the rights of individuals in criminal procedure; (c) the rights of victims of crime; and (d) any other specific aspects of a criminal procedure identified by the Council in advance. The EU's competence in this area applies only to the extent necessary to facilitate mutual recognition of judgements and police and judicial cooperation in criminal matters. It is envisaged that the adoption of minimum rules concerning (b) and (c) above will safeguard the rights of individuals who have been disadvantaged by the application of single market instruments in the field of criminal law.

A novelty of the Lisbon Treaty is the inclusion of the so-called 'emergency breaks' whereby, if a MS believes that harmonisation of certain elements of criminal procedure 'would affect fundamental aspects of its criminal justice system', it can request the referral of the draft directive law to the European Council (Article 82(3) TFEU). In this case, negotiations will be suspended and within four months the European Council can refer the draft directive back to the Council of Ministers for discussion. In case of disagreement, if nine or more states wish to go ahead, they can always activate the new simplified enhanced cooperation mechanisms by notifying their decision to the Parliament, the Commission and the Council. Although at first sight this provision can engender legal and political fragmentation in the EU, one should not also underestimate the extent to which the existence of such a mechanism can exert pressure for MS compliance. Otherwise stated, the emergency break mechanism has a Janus face: it appears to accommodate states' dissent and their anxieties about possible loss of sovereignty, while it simultaneously induces compliance.

The extension of the Union's competence regarding criminal procedural law also applies to substantive criminal law (Article 83 TFEU). As regards the approximation of substantive criminal law, directives may establish the minimum rules concerning the definition of offences and sanctions in 10 listed areas of serious crime with a cross-border direction, ranging from terrorism and trafficking in human beings to tackling computer crime and organised crime (Article 83(1) TFEU). However, Article 83(2) extends the EU's competence, if the approximation of criminal laws and regulations proves essential to ensure the effective implementation of a Union policy in an area which has been subject to harmonisation measures. In other words, minimum rules with regard to the definition of criminal offences and sanctions can be adopted irrespective of whether areas of crime have a cross-border nature. Article 83(3) also entails an emergency brake mechanism and the referral of a legislative measure to the European Council, thereby providing a safeguard of last resort. In addition, the new Article 84 TFEU gives specific legal basis for measures concerning crime prevention,[18] but Community action in this area excludes the approximation of legislation.

The remaining two articles of Chapter 4 focus on Eurojust and the establishment of a European Public Prosecutor (EPP), respectively. According to 85 TFEU, Eurojust can initiate criminal investigations, propose the initiation of prosecutions to be conducted by the competent national authorities, particularly those relating to offences against the financial interests of the Union, coordinate investigations and prosecutions and decide on conflicts of jurisdiction. Article 86 TFEU, on the other hand, envisages the establishment of a EPP's Office from Eurojust. Drawing on the Commission's green paper on the establishment of a EPP in the field of the Community financial interests,[19] the EPP shall be responsible for investigating, prosecuting and bringing to judgement, the perpetrators of and accomplices in offences against the financial interests of the Union and will 'exercise the functions of prosecutor in the competent courts of the MS in relation to such offences' (Article 86(2) TFEU). The establishment of a EPP requires a unanimous Council decision and the consent of the EP, as is the case with respect to the (future) extension of its powers.

The EU's powers concerning police cooperation, on the other hand, remain broadly unchanged. Article 87(2) TFEU envisages legislation concerning: (a) the collection, storage, analysis and exchange of relevant information; (b) support for the training of staff, and cooperation on the exchange of staff, on equipment and on research into crime detection; and (c) common investigative techniques in relation to the detection of serious forms of organised crime. The possible extension on Europol's functions in the area of implementing investigative and operational actions carried out jointly with the MS's competent authorities or in the context of joint investigative teams where appropriate in liaison with Eurojust is mentioned in Article 88(2) TFEU. The last indent of this paragraph ensures the accountability of Europol by stating that European laws shall also lay down the procedures for scrutiny of Europol's activities by the European Parliament, together with the MS' national parliaments. But according to the third paragraph of the same article, any operational action by Europol must be carried out in liaison and in agreement with the authorities of the MS whose territory is concerned. The application of coercive measures remains the exclusive responsibility of the competent national authorities (Article 88(3) TFEU).

Taking an overall view, although the Lisbon reforms are commendable, it is true to say that the overall effectiveness and dynamic development of an enhanced AFSJ cooperation are largely dependent on the implementation of the new multiannual Programme which defines the policy priorities and objectives for the period 2010–14, the so-called Stockholm Programme. It is also true that the Lisbon Treaty's commitment to a more open, democratic and participatory EU has fuelled expectations about a possible break with the security-driven logic of the Hague

Programme and the reframing of rights from obstacles to law enforcement to preconditions for security in the EU. To this end, the Stockholm Programme which is examined below makes a distinctive contribution.

The Stockholm Programme: the promotion of a citizens' Europe and elective affinities with Hague

The Stockholm Programme was adopted by the European Council (2009) in Brussels on 10–11 December 2009. Building on the previous AFSJ programmes, Tampere and Hague, it set out the policy priorities and objectives for the period 2010–14 (Council of the European Union 2009). In anticipation of the new programme, the Commission published a Communication on 'An Area of Freedom, Security and Justice serving the citizen' in June 2009.[20] The Communication highlighted the major successes of Member State cooperation during the last ten years as well as the challenges for the next five years and the main priorities. It recognised that ensuring the proper implementation of Community law by the MS remains a challenge, the need for an impartial evaluation of legislation and its implementation and the importance of improving the coherence of AFSJ policies with other Community policies, including external policy. Among the substantive highlights of the Communication was a clear effort on the part of the Commission to address the predominance of a security focus in the AFSJ and to make the policy priorities more balanced. To this end, it stated explicitly that the citizen must be placed at the heart of this project (European Commission 2009, p. 2). This approach was also echoed in the Stockholm Programme which has the subtitle 'An open and secure Europe serving and protecting the citizen'. The citizen-centred discourse which counterbalances the security-driven policy agenda of the Hague Programme is highlighted on page 3 of the Programme, too: 'The European Council considers that a priority for the coming years will be to focus on the interests and needs of citizens. The challenge will be to ensure respect for fundamental freedoms and integrity while guaranteeing security in Europe. It is of paramount importance that law enforcement measures and measures to safeguard individual rights, the rule of law, international protection rules go hand in hand in the same direction and are mutually reinforced'. Although the new 'citizen-oriented' approach is a welcome development in light of the restrictive and security-based focus of discourse and policy that prevailed in the past, the absence of references to 'Europe's Others', that is, migrants, third-country national border crossers, asylum seekers and refugees is puzzling. Surely, important principles such as fundamental rights, respect for diversity, protecting the vulnerable and data protection cannot be confined to EU citizens.[21] In addition, as the AFSJ strives to complement the securitisation ethos with citizen-friendly policies at the end of the first decade of the 21st century, progress cannot be made by looking backward and repeating the discourses and policies of the past. In this respect, the European Commission's Communication (2009, p. 5) sought to advance the journey towards an area of freedom, security and justice, by including four key policy priorities for 'building a citizen's Europe'; namely, (a) *promoting citizens' rights: a Europe of rights*, which included the realisation of the Lisbon Treaty's fundamental rights provisions including the accession of the EU to the European Convention on Human Rights (ECHR), the effective implementation of the Citizenship Directive (2004/38), respect for diversity, the protection of the rights of children, vulnerable people, including women who are victims of violence, and the Roma community, a comprehensive data protection scheme, consumer protection and promoting participation in democratic life by having a common election day for elections to the EP and making easier for citizens to register on the electoral roll; (b) *making people's lives easier: a Europe of law and justice*, which would facilitate people's access to the courts, improve legal aid schemes and utilise electronic resources (e-justice), further the implementation of the principle of mutual recognition and enhance judicial cooperation in civil and criminal matters; (c) *a Europe that protects*, which would advance a domestic security strategy, set-up an internal security fund, strengthen cooperation in police matters and law enforcement, the use of a European evidence warrant, develop an integrated border management and expand the operational capacities of Frontex, continue the development of the European Border Surveillance System (Eurosur), establish a European Schengen visa, combat human trafficking and the sexual exploitation of children and child pornography, intensify action against cybercrime, economic crime and market abuse and improve counterterrorism policy; and, finally (d) *promoting a more integrated society: a Europe that displays responsibility and solidarity in immigration and asylum matters*. As regards the latter policy priority, the formulation of a common immigration and asylum policy, based on the global approach to migration, partnership with third countries and respect for fundamental rights and dignity, features at the top of the future European policy agenda. The European Commission (2009, p. 32) assumed a leadership role by stating that the EU needs to 'promote a dynamic and fair immigration policy' based on a comprehensive, innovative and coherent framework (p. 23) which adapts to 'increased mobility and the needs of national labour markets' (p. 24). In this respect, it suggested the adoption of an Immigration Code which would end the present, fragmented and uneven approach to legal migrants' rights[22] by ensuring a uniform level of rights comparable with that of Community citizens. The development of a positive approach to migration was complemented by a preventive and law enforcement approach to irregular migration, the development of single area of protection in the field of asylum and the promotion of consistency among these policies and the Union's external policy. Overall, the Communication was ambitious and successful in reversing the long-standing tend towards security and infusing more fairness and dynamism in JHA cooperation.

Thanks to the Swedish Presidency's efforts to embark upon a wide-ranging dialogue with the civil society and various stakeholders and its prudent assumption that the next phase of the AFSJ must not compromise ambition, respect for human rights and the rule of law and the quality of legislation on the altar of security, the Stockholm Programme by and large did not alter the policy priorities identified by the Commission. It built on them, thereby creating a complex 'honeycomb' in whose cells an extraordinary amount of mandates for policy action have been placed. Some maintain the rights-based and citizen-friendly focus of the Commission's suggestions. Others increase the security dimension and surveillance on the Union, while others seek to improve coherence among the various Communities policies. Accordingly, the Commission's four priorities have now become six: the priority on 'a Europe that protects' has been subdivided into security and external border management while promoting the external dimension of the AFSJ now features as a general policy priority.

The first priority, *Promoting Citizenship and Fundamental Rights*, repeats the Commission's proposals on fundamental rights and Union citizenship, the protection of children, vulnerable groups, victims of crime, the rights of the individual in criminal proceedings, individuals' privacy and adds the realisation of the European citizens' initiative which the Lisbon Treaty introduced (Article 11(4) TEU), while the second priority, *a Europe of law and justice*, focuses on the promotion citizens' access to justice, the promotion and extension of the principle of the mutual recognition of judicial decisions and judgments, the setting up of a comprehensive system for obtaining evidence in cases with a cross-border dimension, the adoption of new legislation on combating trafficking in human beings and the enhancement of cooperation among public professionals.

The main security-based priority, namely, *A Europe that protects*, focuses on the development of an internal security strategy and greater cooperation in law enforcement, criminal judicial cooperation, border management, civic protection as well as the development of a proactive intelligence approach (Council of the European Union 2009, 35 et seq). The development, monitoring and implementation of the internal security strategy will be one of the core tasks of the Internal Security Committee set-up under Article 71 TFEU (see the Section above). In addition, the European Council considers it important to implement an EU information management strategy which includes the development of large scale IT systems. Interestingly, the EU information management strategy will be based on a 'business vision for law enforcement, judicial cooperation, border management and public protection' (Council of the European Union 2009, pp. 37–38). Other proposed measures that fit the grid of security include the proposal for an EU Passenger Names Record System, a European Police Records Index System, a register for third country nationals who have been convicted by the Courts of the MS, more effective European law enforcement cooperation, the development of a Police Cooperation Code and more effective crime prevention and combating interventions. Although with respect to security and surveillance the logic is the same as in the Hague Programme, the fourth priority of the Stockholm Programme, namely, access to Europe in a globalised world, fuses the extension of the logic of surveillance and control with the replacement of the 'Fortress Europe' image (Geddes 2000) with that of an 'open Europe in a globalised environment'. The former is reflected in the proposed enhancement of the role of Frontex, the development of an electronic system recording entry to and exit from the MS, an electronic system of pre-entry authorisation, the use of automated border control gates and the development of a common visa policy, which could be based on personalised assessments of risk in addition to the presumption of risk associated with one's nationality. Europe's openness, on the other hand, is manifested in the explicit commitment that 'the Union must continue to facilitate legal access to the territory of the Member States' (Council of the European Union 2009, p. 55), thereby lending credence to the argument that 'open Europe' represents more rhetoric than a substantive policy commitment.

The fifth priority, which deals with migration and asylum laws and policies, has been adjusted in ways that accommodate national executives' beliefs and interests. It is expressly stated that the European Council reaffirms the principles set out in the European Pact on Migration and Asylum (European Council 2008) as well as the Global Approach to Migration (European Commission 2006a, 2006b). The Commission Communication's reference to 'a fair migration policy' and the adoption of an Immigration Code have been replaced with references to 'well managed migration', flexible admission systems that take into labour market requirements and optimising the link between migration and development (Council of the European Union 2009, 59 et seq). At the same time, the law enforcement and preventative approach to irregular migration that featured in the Commission's Communication has been preserved.[23] As far as asylum law and policy are concerned, the Stockholm Programme entails policy mandates for the development of a common European Asylum System based on a common asylum procedure and uniform status for those granted international protection in accordance with Article 78 TFEU by 2012 at the latest and for developing the external dimension of the European Asylum System in partnership and cooperation with third countries. Finally, with respect to the rights and status of TCNs in the Union legal order, the Swedish Presidency did manage to resurrect the Tampere mandate of 'ensuring fair treatment of third country nationals who reside legally on the territory of its MS. A more vigorously integration policy should aim at granting them rights and obligations comparable to those of EU citizens' (Council of the European Union 2009, p. 64). This objective would have to be realised by 2014 and its implementation would require the consolidation and amendment of the four directives on legal migration and the 'evaluation and, where necessary, review of the directive on family reunification, taking into account the importance of integration measures' (Council of the European Union 2009, p. 64). Although the contours of the precise action are uncertain at the moment, it is, nevertheless, the case that the 'Stockholm' discourse on 'proactive policies for migrants and their rights' has brought forth the alignment of the templates of intra-EU mobility and citizenship, on the one hand, and extra-EU migration, on the other. The same trend can be observed in the area of migrant integration; there exists a subtle discursive shift away from the 'common basic principles' and mandatory regimes of language and civic orientation classes and tests towards the development of indicators that monitor the results of integration policies in the fields of education, employment and social inclusion and more consultation with civil society.[24] The final policy priority for the next five years emphasises the importance of the external dimension of the AFSJ and the integration of the latter into the general policies of the Union, thereby replicating the Hague Programme.[25] It identifies six thematic priorities for EU external cooperation (migration and asylum, security, information exchange, justice, civil protection and disaster management) as well as a number of key partners in Europe, the Mediterranean area and beyond.

The Commission's Action Plan, which was published in April 2010 (European Commission 2010), entails a clear discursive shift away from restriction and control towards affirming migrants' fundamental rights and the values of human dignity and solidarity. Under the heading of 'delivering an area of freedom, security and justice for Europe's citizens' (European Commission 2010, p. 3), it emphasises the EU's duty to 'protect and project' the values of respect for the human person and human dignity, freedom, equality and solidarity and to ensure that 'citizens can exercise their rights and fully benefit from European integration'. In a clear attempt to reverse the downgrading of individual rights owing to the predominance of internal security concerns, it states that 'the Union must resist tendencies to treat security, justice and fundamental rights in isolation from one another. They go hand in hand in a coherent approach to meet the challenges of today and the years to come' (European Commission 2010, p. 4). To this end, it entails a number of measures to ensure the protection of fundamental rights, including a 'zero tolerance policy' with respect to violation of the Charter of Fundamental Rights, the enhancement of data protection, the promotion of citizens' mobility, participation in the democratic life of the Union and access to justice, the approximation of procedural and substantive criminal law and the establishment of a Public Prosecutor's Office from Eurojust.

Under the heading 'ensuring the security of Europe', the Action plan contains a number of actions and legislative proposal on Passenger Name Record data, the evaluation of the Data Retention Directive 2006/24/EC, a European register of convicted third country nationals, firearms legislation, a regulation on Europol, a proposal for information exchange among Europol, Eurojust and Frontex, a proposal on the establishment of an observatory for the prevention of crime, actions against trafficking in human beings and the sexual exploitation of children as well as the combating of economic crime and corruption. The counter-terrorist legal framework, including the definition of terrorism and terrorism lists, unfortunately remains unamended, and only two new legislative proposals are envisaged on precursors to explosives and security vetting of persons having access to chemical, biological, radiological and nuclear substances or explosives, respectively.

Under policy priority 6 on 'putting solidarity and responsibility at the heart of our response', the Commission observes that 'robust defence of migrants' fundamental rights out of respect for our values of human dignity and solidarity will enable them to contribute fully to the European economy and society. Immigration has a valuable role to play in addressing the Union's demographic challenge and in securing the EU's strong economic performance over the longer term. It has great potential to contribute to the Europe 2020 strategy, by providing an additional source of dynamic growth' (European Commission 2010, p. 7). In this respect, the Action Plan refers to the design of a common immigration and asylum policy 'within a long-term vision of respect for fundamental rights and human dignity and to strengthen solidarity, particularly between Member States as they collectively shoulder the burden of a humane and efficient system' and resurrects the suggestion for an Immigration Code which was omitted in the Stockholm Programme (European Commission 2010, p. 7). The latter would consolidate 'a uniform level of rights and obligations for legal immigrants comparable with that of European citizens' (European Commission 2010, p. 7). There also exist references to the congruence of a preventative irregular migration policy with the Charter of Fundamental Rights and respect for the fundamental right to asylum, including the principle of 'non-refoulement'.

In sum, the Action Plan has set out a principled and ambitious legislative agenda, comparable to the Tampere one. Internal security is no longer the primary driver of EU legislation and action as it has been acknowledged that ensuring rights protection and engaging European citizens are essential for the legitimacy and credibility of enhanced cooperation in the AFSJ. As the Commission states, 'the active, informed citizen for whom, all this being done is a key driver and actor in the whole process' (European Commission 2010, p. 9). In this respect, it comes as no surprise that in its meeting on 3 June 2010 the Council noted that 'some of the action proposed by the Commission are not in line with the Stockholm Programme and that others, being included in the Stockholm Programme, are not reflected in the Communication of the Commission' (Council of the European Union 2010, p. 2). And it urged the Commission to 'take only those initiatives that are in full conformity with the Stockholm Programme in order to ensure its complete and timely implementation' (Council of the European Union 2010, p. 2). Accordingly, the

AFSJ may have been infused with more freedom and a citizen-oriented approach, but the extent to which the new 'normative order' will take hold remains to be seen. The shifting nexus of security and power, on the one hand, and rights and citizenship values, on the other, remains under negotiation.

Conclusion

Incremental integrationist efforts have brought surprises and unforeseen change in the AFSJ. The Lisbon Treaty's depillarisation of JHA cooperation represents a major break from the past. It opens the way for the full involvement of the Commission, the European Parliament and the ECJ, an involvement that is bound to influence the substantive scope, and perhaps liberalise, legal and policy output in the years ahead. In addition, it marks a change in culture; we are witnessing less competition and strife among the supranational and intergovernmental institutions of the EU and more willingness on their part to remedy existing deficiencies and to work together to provide solutions to the multifarious challenges facing the Union. Obviously, disagreements and entrenched institutional interests still exist and domestic as well as international exigencies may preclude a wholesale agreement on many issues. But it is equally true that openness to experimentation and gradual trust-building has yielded fruits. A different form of cooperation in AFSJ institutionally and substantively is digging out its space within the present, security-oriented and traditionally executive-driven architecture. The Stockholm Programme and the proposed Action Plan are a reflection of this. Present in them are aspects of the Hague Programme and the logic of control and surveillance. But there also exist vessels of less ideology-driven policies, pragmatic responses to JHA challenges and respect for citizens' rights, human rights and the rule of law. Whether the latter paradigm, which is wrapped up within the logic of security, remains confined and crammed in the next five years or will be given room to grow will depend on interventions from both the Commission, the EP and the ECJ as well as on pressure from below, that is from civil society, NGOs and Europe's citizens and residents.

Notes

1. For a discussion on the origins of JHA cooperation (1985) and the advanced intergovernmental cooperation (1985–92), see Kostakopoulou (2007, pp. 156–158).
2. For the role of other conjectural factors in this process, see Donnelly (2008).
3. The principle of mutual recognition was first included in the Presidency Conclusions of the Cardiff European Council in June 1998, was explicitly endorsed by the Tampere European Council (1999) Compare Joint Cases C-187/01 and C-385/01 *Gozutok and Brugge* (2003) ECR I-1345 at para 33.
4. The first initiative was the proposal for a Directive on Family Reunification; COM (1999) 638 final, amended by COM(00) 624 final.
5. Provisions III-257–277 became Articles 67–89 TFEU in the Lisbon Treaty. For a discussion on the Constitutional Treaty's provisions, see Kostakopoulou (2007).
6. Interestingly, measures concerning border checks, a common European asylum system, and a common immigration policy have been removed from the domain of unanimity. The areas that still require unanimity are EU measures concerning passports, identity cards, residence permits and other documents necessary for the free movement of persons (Article 77(3) TFEU); family law (Article 81(3) TFEU); the establishment of a EPP and the future extension of its powers (Article 86 TFEU); measures concerning operational police cooperation (Article 87(3) TFEU); decision on the conditions and limitations under

which law enforcement and judicial authorities may operate in the territory of another MS (Article 89 TFEU). Qualified Majority Voting (QMV) now requires the support of 55% of the MS representing at least 65% of the population of the Union.

7. The traditional consultation and consent procedures are now 'special legislative procedures'. In the AFSJ consultation still applies to measures concerning passports and other documents (Article 77(3) TFEU), the adoption of temporary measures in case of an emergency situation caused by a sudden influx of third country nationals (Article 78(3) TFEU), measures on family law (Article 81(3) TFEU), operational police cooperation and rules on the conditions and limits of the operation of law enforcement and judicial authorities in other MS. The European Parliament's consent is required for the identification of new areas of Euro-crime (Article 83(1) TFEU), the establishment of a EPP's Office and the extension of its powers (Article 86 TFEU), measures concerning operational police cooperation (Article 87(3) TFEU); decisions on the conditions and limitations under which law enforcement and judicial authorities may operate in the territory of another MS (Article 89 TFEU).

8. The Commission already had an exclusive right of initiative in judicial cooperation in civil matters under the Treaty of Nice.

9. In these areas, a quarter of the MS can initiate a legislative proposal (Article 76 TFEU). The Convention's Working Group X had suggested the introduction of a threshold of either 1/3 or 1/4 or even 1/5 of the MS for a MS initiative to be admissible. Following this suggestion, the Constitutional Treaty (Article III-264) stated that a quarter of MS can bring forward legislative initiatives in criminal matters including the operational cooperation between administrative and police bodies of the MS. The imposition of this threshold is designed to prevent governments from taking politically expedient decisions which do not reflect a wider European interest.

10. A transitional phase of five years is envisaged by Protocol 36 annexed to the Lisbon Treaty: polices and judicial cooperation measures already in place before the Treaty entered into force will be reviewed by the ECJ under the pre-Lisbon regime during the next five years.

11. Protocol (No. 7) on the Application of the Charter of Fundamental Rights to Poland and to the UK. The Protocol will be amended to include the Czech Republic in the next treaty of accession. On the Protocol and its implication for the UK, see House of Lords, Constitution Committee's 6th Report of Session 2007–08, *EU Amendment Bill and the Lisbon Treaty: Implications for the UK Constitution*, 28 March 2008, HL Paper 84.

12. According to Article 4(2) TEU national security remains the sole responsibility of the MS.

13. Internal security is not confined to police matters; it includes operational cooperation in the event of a major catastrophe, natural and man-made disasters as well as terrorist attacks.

14. The Council approved an 'Internal Security Strategy for the EU' on 25 February 2010; 6870/10 (Presse 44), Brussels, 25 February 2010.

15. The Amsterdam Treaty required the Council, when acting a legislator, to publish the results of its votes, but not its deliberations (Article 207(3) EC). The Seville European Council (June 2002) obliged the Council to open its legislative meetings to the public. Implementing the conclusions of the Seville European Council, the new rules of procedure for the Council state deliberations on acts to be adopted in accordance with the co-decision procedure shall be open to the public.

16. National parliaments have witnessed an incremental increase in their involvement in EU affairs initially by Declaration 13 appended to the TEU and later on by the Amsterdam provisions concerning the prompt forwarding of consultation papers and legislative proposals or a proposal for a measure to be adopted under Title VI TEU to national parliaments within six weeks before the item is placed on the Council's agenda for decision (subject to exceptions on the ground of urgency).

17. The Hague Programme envisaged the appointment of a Special Representative for a common readmission policy.

18. Notably, crime prevention was mentioned in Article 29 EU, but it was not included in the specific legal bases of Articles 30 and 31 EU.

19. COM(2001) 715 final.

20. For a reflection, see Guild and Carrera (2009).

21. Guild and Carrera also suggest the replacement of the term citizen with that of individual; p. 10.
22. This is due to the four Directives on TCNs: Directive 2003/109/EC of 25 November 2003 *concerning the status of third country nationals who are long-term residents*, OJ L 16/44, 23.1.2004; Directive 2004/114/EC of 13 December 2004 *on the conditions of admission of third country nationals for the purposes of studies, pupil exchange, unremunerated training or voluntary service*, OJ L 375/12, 23.12.2004; Directive 2005/71/EC of 12 October 2005 *on a specific procedure for admitting third country nationals for the purposes of scientific research*, OJ L 289/15, 3.11.2005; Directive 2009/50/EC of 25 May 2009 *on the conditions of entry and residence of third country nationals for the purposes of highly qualified employment*, OJ L 155/17, 18.6.2009.
23. 'In order to maintain credible and sustainable immigration and asylum systems in the EU, it is necessary to prevent, control and combat illegal migration'; European Council (2009, p. 11).
24. Compare the Common Basic Principles on Integration adopted by the JHA Council of 19 November 2004; Justice and Home Affairs Council Meeting 2618, 14615/04 of 19 November 2004.
25. Compare The Hague Programme: Strengthening Freedom, Security and Justice in the EU, Council of the EU, Brussels, 22 October 2004, 13302/2/04 REV2, p. 37.

Notes on contributor

Dora Kostakopoulou is Jean Monnet Professor in European Law and European Integration.

References

Andreas, P., 2003. Redrawing the lines: borders and security in the twenty-first century. *International security*, 28 (2), 78–111.

Bigo, D. and Leveau, R., (1992). *L'Europe de la securite interieure* [Internal Security in Europe]. Paris, France: Foundation Nationale des Sciences Politiques, 75.

Bigo, D., 2002. Border regimes, police cooperation and security. *In*: J. Zielonka, ed. *Europe unbound: enlarging and reshaping the boundaries of the European Union*. London and New York: Routledge, 213–239.

Bigo, D., 2004. Criminalisation of 'Migrants': the side effect of the will to control the frontiers and the sovereign illusion. *In*: B. Bogusz, R. Cholewinski, A. Cygan and E. Szyszczak, eds. *Irregular migration and human rights: theoretical, European international perspectives*. Leiden: Martinus Nijhoff, 90–127.

Buzan, B., Weaver, O., and de Wilde, J., 1998. *Security: a new framework for analysis*. Boulder, CO and London: Lynne Rienner.

Council of the European Union, 2004. *The Hague Programme: strengthening freedom, security and justice in the European Union*. Brussels, 3 December, 16054/04.

Council of the European Union, 2009. *The Stockholm Programme – an open and secure Europe serving and protecting the citizens*. Brussels, 2 December, 17024/09.

Council of the European Union, 2010. *Council conclusions on the Commission Communication 'Delivering an area of freedom, security and justice for Europe's citizens – action plan implementing the Stockholm Programme (COM (2010) 171final)*. Luxembourg, June 10.

Donnelly, B. *Justice and home affairs in the Lisbon Treaty: a constitutionalising clarification*. EIPASCOPE 2008/1.

European Commission, 2005. *Communication to the Council and the European Parliament, 2005. The Hague Programme: ten priorities for the next five years – the Partnership for European Renewal in the filed of Freedom, Security and Justice*. Brussels, 10 May, COM(2005) 184 final.

European Commission, 2006a. *Implementing the Hague Programme: the way forward*. COM(2006) 331 final.

European Commission, 2006b. *The global approach to migration one year on: towards a comprehensive European migration policy*. Brussels, 10 November, COM(2006) 735 final.

European Commission, 2009. *Communication. An area of freedom, security and justice serving the citizen: wider freedom in a safer environment.* Brussels, 10 June, COM (2009) 262/4.

European Commission, 2010. *Communication. Delivering an area of freedom, security and justice for Europe's citizens – action plan implementing the Stockholm Programme.* April, COM (2010) 171. Brussels.

European Council, 1999. *Tampere Presidency conclusions.* Brussels, 15–16 October, SN 200/99.

European Council, 2005. *The Hague Programme: strengthening freedom, security and justice in the European Union.* 3 March, OJ C 53/1. Brussels.

European Council, 2008. *The European pact on immigration and asylum,* Brussels, 16 October.

European Council, 2009. *Conclusions.* Brussels: 11 December, EUCO 6/09.

Federal Constitutional Court, (2009). (BVerfG), 2 be 2/08 vom 30.6.2009, Absatz-Nr. (1-421), Judgement of 30 June 2009. Available from: http://www.bverfg.de/entscheidungen/es20090630_2bve000208en.html [Accessed 1 November 2009].

Geddes, A., 2000. *Immigration and European integration: towards fortress Europe.* Manchester: Manchester University Press.

Guild, E. and Carrera, S. (2009). *Towards the next phase of the EU's area of freedom, security and justice: the European Commission's proposals for the Stockholm Programme.* CEPS Policy Brief, No. 196/20, August. Brussels: Centre for European Policy Studies.

Huysmans, J., 1998. Security! What do you mean? From concept to thick signifier. *European Journal of international relations,* 4 (2), 226–255.

Huysmans, J., 2002. The European Union and the securitisation of migration. *Journal of common market studies,* 38 (5), 751–777.

Kaunert, C., 2005. The area of freedom, security and justice: the construction of a European public order. *European security,* 14 (4), 459–483.

Kostakopoulou, D., 2000. Protective union': change and continuity in migration law and policy in post-Amsterdam Europe. *Journal of common market studies,* 38 (3), 497–518.

Kostakopoulou, D., 2001. *Citizenship, identity and immigration in the European Union: between past and future.* Manchester: Manchester University Press.

Kostakopoulou, D., 2007. The area of freedom, security and justice and the European Union's constitutional dialogue. *In*: C. Barnard, ed. *The fundamentals of EU law revisited: assessing the impact of the constitutional debate.* Oxford: Academy of European Law, European University Institute, Oxford University Press, 153–191.

Lindahl, H., 2004. Finding a place for freedom, security and justice: the European Union's claim to territorial unity. *European law review,* 29 (3), 461–484.

Lindahl, H., ed., 2010. *A right to inclusion and exclusion? Normative fault lines of the EU's area of freedom, security and justice.* Oxford: Hart.

Monar, J., 1998. Justice and home affairs in the Treaty of Amsterdam: reform at the price of fragmentation. *European law review,* 23 (4), 320–335.

Monar, J., 2001. The dynamics of JHA: laboratories, driving factors, costs. *Journal of Common Market Studies,* 39 (4), 747–764.

Peers, S., 2004. *The EU constitution and justice and home affairs: the accountability gap.* London: Statewatch.

Peers, S., 2006. *EU justice and home affairs law.* 2nd ed. Oxford: Oxford University Press.

Treaty Establishing a Constitution for Europe, 2004. 29 October, OJ C 316/1.

Treaty of Lisbon amending the Treaty on European Union and the Treaty establishing the European Community, 2007. OJC 306/1, 17 December.

Treaty on European Union, 1992. 29 July, OJ C191.

Walker, N., 2004. In search of the area of freedom, security and justice: a Constitutional Odyssey. *In*: N. Walker, ed. *Europe's area of freedom, security and justice.* Oxford: Hart, 3–40.

Weaver, O., 1995. Securitisation and desecuritisation. *In*: R. Lipschutz, ed. *On security.* New York: Columbia University Press.

White, S., 2003. *European constitution: what is new in the area of judicial cooperation in criminal matters and police cooperation.* Federal Trust Online Constitutional Essay, 27/2003. London: Federal Trust.

The area of freedom, security and justice in the Lisbon Treaty: Commission policy entrepreneurship?

Christian Kaunert[a,b]

[a]Centre for European Security, ESPaCH, University of Salford, Salford, UK; [b]European University Institute, Florence, Italy

Scholars may rightly claim the European Union's (EU) area of freedom, security and justice (AFSJ) has become one of the most significant developments in the European integration process. The Lisbon Treaty (LT) has the potential to push the AFSJ towards tremendous growth, and has provided the policy area with instruments that were unthinkable after the third pillar was created during the Maastricht Treaty negotiations. This article investigates the role of the European Commission in the process of constructing an 'AFSJ'. It argues that the Commission (through alliances with other institutional actors) managed to incrementally contribute to this shift in political norms. This shift derived from the policy-making level from 1999 onwards. It manifested itself specifically during the negotiations of the Constitutional Treaty (CT) and the subsequent re-negotiation of the LT. Here, the Commission acted with the support and the use of other supranational actors during the Convention, without which this result would have been difficult, if not impossible, to obtain. Firstly, the article will deal with the main advances of the CT which resulted in the LT. Subsequently, the role of the Commission and other EU institutional actors will be examined, resulting in an overall evaluation.

Introduction

When final result showed 67.1 per cent of Irish voters in favour of the Lisbon Treaty (LT), with 32.9 per cent voting against, the Irish Taoiseach Brian Cowen celebrated that 'today we have done the right thing for our own future and the future of our children' (Euractiv 2009). This article focuses on the LT celebrated by the statement above, specifically its advances regarding the area of freedom, security and justice (AFSJ). In particular, the article investigates the role of the European Commission at the treaty level in the process of constructing an 'AFSJ'. Obviously, given the interactions involved in both treaty- and policy-making, it is evident that other European Union (EU) institutions also feature in this analysis. However, the main of this article is to investigate the reshaping of the inter-institutional balance in the AFSJ.

The road to the entry into force of the LT was very long and hard. It evolved out of the rejected 'Treaty establishing a Constitution for Europe' and is part of what is commonly referred to as the process of treaty reform. This includes all EU treaties from the Treaty of Rome (1957) to the Single European Act (1986), the Maastricht Treaty (1992), the Amsterdam Treaty (1997) and the Nice Treaty (2001). Very soon after the latter, the so-called 'Post-nice Process' was launched to start a debate about the future of Europe (Christiansen and Reh 2009). The outcome of the 'future of Europe' debate was first included in the Convention on the Future of Europe, which provided the blueprint for the Constitutional Treaty (CT). The Convention, led by former French President Valery Giscard d'Estaing, was composed of national governments, members of the European Commission and members of national parliaments and the European Parliament. Its members were allocated in different sectoral working groups (Christiansen 2008, p. 40), it started in February 2002, and finished its work by 10 July 2003.

Yet, despite the fact that the Convention managed to set the agenda decisively for the Constitutional intergovernmental conference (IGC), with arguably increased input by civil society, the CT was rejected on 29 May 2005 by 55 per cent of the electorate in France, and on 1 June 2005 with 62 per cent in the Netherlands. Subsequently, the UK froze ratification of the Treaty on 6 June 2005, resulting in a decision by the European Council summit of 17 and 18 June 2005 to create 'reflection period' until 2007. This was meant to enable a re-negotiation and entry into force of the new 'Reform Treaty' before the June 2009 European Parliamentary election. Accordingly, the LT was signed by the Heads of State or Governments in December 2007, and entered into force on 1 December 2009, after the aforementioned successful (second) Irish referendum. While the precise AFSJ content of the signed LT will be discussed in the next section, it is notable that the vast majority of provisions of the CT were also included in the LT. This is especially remarkable for the AFSJ (Donnelly 2008).

This article conceptualises the Commission's political role on two levels which are dependent upon one another: (1) the treaty level, most notably the LT and (2) on the policy-making level of the AFSJ more generally. In agreement with Christiansen (2002), treaty-making in the EU is a process dependent on the policy level, and not separate from it. The treaty level provides the legal tools required at the policy level. Yet, without policy change, there is no need to alter the existing tools or to provide new ones. Christiansen (2002) explicitly challenges aspects of Moravcsik's (1998) theory of liberal intergovernmentalism in this context. He explains the limits of 'intergovernmental bargaining', as the process of treaty reform includes a wider process of issue-framing, agenda-setting, decision-making, as well as implementation and legitimation. This implies that the whole policy process prior to the IGC can be seen as part and parcel of the bargaining itself. Thus, given that one level depends on the other, this article will analyse the role of the Commission at the treaty level taking into account how policy-making itself frames the bargaining environment for treaty negotiations. In other words, this article will analyse the role of the European Commission in the adoption of the institutional framework for the AFSJ as per LT, i.e. the negotiating 'procedure' for the AFSJ, and the way in which its role, formalised within the substance of the previous treaties themselves, influenced the bargaining environment of the Commission during the LT negotiations.

Yet, 'can faceless bureaucrats, unelected and without power of purse or sword really influence the decisions of powerful nation-states? Are we seeing the emergence of a "new statecraft" grounded in international networks managed by supranational political entrepreneurs'? (Moravcsik 1999a). Moravcsik (1999a) certainly questions whether unelected bureaucrats without financial and legal enforcement powers would actually be able to influence political decisions made by national governments. Yet, this debate has produced different outcomes (Haas 1958, 1964, 1967, Lindberg 1963, Lindberg and Scheingold 1970, 1971, Hix 1994, 1998, 1999, Pollack 1997, 2003, Stone Sweet and Sandholtz 1997, Moravcsik 1999a, Stone Sweet *et al.* 2001, Tallberg 2002, 2003, 2006, 2008, Beach 2004, 2005, Kaunert 2005, 2007, 2009).

When examining the role of European institutions in detail, notably through the prism of supranational policy entrepreneurship (SPE), this article builds on the conceptual framework put forward by Kingdon (1984). The article further argues that the Commission in particular (through alliances with other institutional actors during the Convention phase) managed to incrementally contribute to a shift in norms. This shift derived from the policy-making level from 1999 onwards. It manifested itself specifically during the negotiations of the CT and the subsequent re-negotiation of the LT. Here, the Commission acted with the support and the use of other supranational actors during the Convention, without which this result would have been difficult, if not impossible, to obtain.

The structure of the article unfolds as follows. The first section provides an overview of the new AFSJ institutional architecture, firstly within the CT which subsequently was maintained by the LT. The second section examines the debate on the political role of the European Commission as a SPE, and the precise framework used for this analysis. The third section will outline the empirical findings, and thereby the role of the supranational actors, namely the Commission, in this process. In the final section, the article will conclude that the European Commission has been influential in this process of European integration, which has implications on how scholars need to regard the powers of these supranational institutions in the AFSJ more widely.

The Lisbon Treaty and the area of freedom, security and justice

This section examines the changes of the LT in the AFSJ in order to provide a comprehensive picture of achievements in the treaty negotiations, as well as providing the spectrum of legal competences in the AFSJ since 1 December 2009. With the entry into force of the LT, the policy area will be one of exponential future growth and development of EU action (Carrera and Geyer 2008). Thus, Monar (2005) might have correctly identified that future historians are likely to regard the EU's creation of the AFSJ as one of the most significant developments in the European integration process.

Whatever the achievements of the treaty in other areas, the main focus of this section is on the relevant parts of the AFSJ institutional architecture in the LT. The following section will analyse the finally agreed text of both the CT and the LT together. It will substantiate the argument that the LT remained substantially the same 'beast' as the CT, at least regarding the AFSJ. Equally, the final draft of the CT relied very significantly on the report produced by the Working Group X of the Convention (2002a, CONV426/02), which provided the rationale for the draft treaty section. The final outcome (Conference CIG 87/04 2004) was not significantly different from the draft. Thus, the end result of the AFSJ provisions in the LT were to a very large extent already the same as provided for by the Constitutional Convention AFSJ working group.

General provisions

The LT amends two separate bodies of treaties (1) the Treaty on European Union (TEU) and (2) the Treaty on the Functioning of the European Union (TFEU). Article 3(2) TEU (formerly Article I-3 CT; Conference, CIG 87/04 2004, p. 15) elevates the 'AFSJ' to become an objective with the same status as the Internal Market (Article 3(3) TEU). 'The Union shall offer its citizens an AFSJ without internal frontiers, in which the free movement of persons is ensured in conjunction with appropriate measures with respect to external border controls, asylum, immigration, and the prevention and combating of crime'. The EU legal competences in the AFSJ are now also clarified. Article 4(2j) TFEU (formerly Article I-13 CT; under B. Specific amendments, 46/47) puts the area as one of shared competences.

Furthermore, the LT creates a simplified decision-making procedure. Firstly, the pillar structure is formally abolished, which results in the advanced, but incomplete, communitarisation of the areas of criminal justice, policing and terrorism, albeit with drawbacks in the form of 'emergency brakes' and 'accelerators'. Secondly, the standard decision-making procedure in the AFSJ is co-decision according to Article 294 TFEU (formerly Article 251 TEC) and qualified majority voting (QMV) in the Council. This gives the European Parliament joint decision-making power. The Commission will be given the exclusive power to propose legislation. In criminal justice and policing legislation, the latter power is shared with a quarter of the member states. Thus, this is in line with the stipulations in the CT (Article III-396).

Thirdly, the disappearance of the pillar structure leads to a commonality of legal instruments between titles that were formerly Pillars 1 and 3. In the LT, this is achieved under the name 'ordinary legislative procedure'. It is important to note that for the first time the Union can use the 'ordinary legislative procedure' in principle for the whole area. Nonetheless, instead of using the new terms of the CT, i.e. European laws, European framework laws, European regulations, the LT retains the traditional community instruments, i.e. regulations, directives, decisions, etc. The previous legal instruments in the AFSJ, i.e. framework decisions, common positions, conventions, etc. disappear. Judicial control is expanded by applying the normal court rules on the European Court of Justice's (ECJ) jurisdiction to all AFSJ matters in all member states (including the possibility for all national courts or tribunals to send questions to the ECJ).

Fourthly, the legal status of the Charter of Fundamental Rights of the Union is clarified for the majority of member states. By virtue of the first subparagraph of Article 6(1) TEU, the Charter has the same legal value as the treaties. This article provides a cross-reference to the Charter on Fundamental Rights, which renders the Charter directly legally binding for the European institutions, Union bodies, offices and agencies, as well as member states when they implement Union law (except those that have exceptions to various degrees, such as the UK, Ireland, Poland and in principle, soon the Czech Republic). This has the following significant implications: (1) EU institutions and other EU agencies and bodies can be held to account on the basis of the fundamental rights contained in the Charter and (2) member states can be held to account on the basis of the same rights, generally when implementing EU legislation, but possibly also when adopting national legislation with an EU dimension (depending on the ECJ interpretation). This will put EU actors and member states under a clear legal obligation to ensure that fundamental rights are respected and will thus strengthen the freedom dimension of the AFSJ.

Finally, these institutional changes may have very strong implications to the role of EU institutions in the AFSJ. The LT provides for a very clear potential reshaping of the inter-institutional balance in the area. In general, the supranational institutions have been greatly strengthened. This implies an even stronger role for the European Commission, as its role as an initiator of legislations has been clearly reinforced. However, even more importantly, the European Parliament has been given the generalised role as a co-legislator in the area, which has the potential to greatly influence the future balance of power between the different EU institutions. Nonetheless, while this supranational dimension in the EU institutional structure has been strengthened, the role of the European Council as a strategic decision-making institution in the AFSJ has also been reinforced and strengthened. Overall, this might very well lead to a diminished influence for EU interior ministers, who had been widely seen as driving forces in the AFSJ before the entry into force of the LT.

Asylum, migration and border controls

In the areas of asylum, migration and external border controls (Articles 77–80 TFEU), significant new competences are transferred to the EU level. Legally, according to the previous treaties, it is only possible to legislate on minimum standards for asylum measures. The LT (as well as the CT) provides the competence to adopt, acting in accordance with the ordinary legislative procedure, laws for a uniform status of asylum valid throughout the Union, a uniform status of subsidiary protection, a common system of temporary protection, common procedures for the subsidiary protection, standards for reception conditions (formerly only minimum standards) and partnership and cooperation with third countries for the purpose of managing inflows of people. The areas of migration and illegal migration bring similar new competences for the EU. In addition, according to the LT (and previously the CT), incentives for integration measures for third country nationals can now be legislated by the EU. Both treaties also provide for a burden-sharing mechanism within the EU member states. Similarly, the competences of the Union in civil law matters have increased.

Criminal justice and counter-terrorism

The LT (as well as previously the CT) constitutes a big step forward towards the communitarisation, i.e. the full transfer of the competences to the Union level, for the area of criminal justice and counter-terrorism (Articles 82–89 TFEU), albeit with a number of drawbacks attached to this in the form of 'emergency brakes and accelerator procedures'.

The provisions regarding procedural and substantive criminal law, often mentioned as a cornerstone in developing mutual trust among member states, stipulate the following: Article 82 (1a, b, c) TFEU opens up the legal possibility to establish rules and procedures to ensure the recognition of all forms of judgements and judicial decisions throughout the union, to prevent and settle conflicts of jurisdiction and to support the training of the judiciary. Article 82 (2 a, b, c, d) TFEU provides the competences to establish minimum rules in criminal matters with a cross-border dimension. Article 83 TFEU opens up the legal possibility for the union to establish minimum rules concerning the definition of criminal offences and sanctions. It then lists the areas where these definitions would fall into, which is significantly more inclusive than the previous treaties. In addition, the Council can adopt a unanimous European decision to include more crimes to this list. Consequently, the area of criminal justice has been communitarised to a large extent, but with certain drawbacks attached to this, which come in the form of the so-called 'emergency brake' and 'accelerator' procedures – two of the compromises of the CT IGC, which have been slightly modified for the LT (less brake and more accelerator). Paragraph 3 of Articles 82 and 83 TFEU provides the 'emergency brake' in both the aforementioned articles. Paragraph 4 provides for the so-called 'accelerator'. De facto, this means that the national veto will no longer exist in the area of criminal justice. Instead of a veto, this paragraph creates a de facto 'opt-out' possibility for every member state.

Furthermore, the LT (as well as the CT) creates the legal possibility of establishing a European public prosecutor out of Eurojust under Article 86 TFEU. Initially, the competences of such a prosecutor would be related to crimes affecting the financial interests of the Union. However, Paragraph 4 provides the legal possibility to amend the competences by a unanimous European decision to include serious crimes with a cross-border dimension. This paragraph was added in the CT IGC and did not feature in the original Convention draft. The function of such an office would include the investigation, prosecution and bringing to justice the perpetrators and accomplices of serious crimes. It would exercise the functions of a prosecutor in a national court. The establishment of this institution needs a unanimity decision by the Council with the consent of the European Parliament. However, the LT goes even beyond the CT; in Paragraph 1 (Article 86 TFEU), two new paragraphs have been added to circumvent the unanimity requirement through the 'accelerator procedure' in order to establish this European Public Prosecutor. Again, as in the paragraphs above, in the absence of unanimity in the Council, nine member states may send this measure to the European Council, which needs to send it back to the Council after four months. In case of continuing disagreement, nine member states may then proceed on the basis of enhanced cooperation, and the authorisation for enhanced cooperation is deemed to apply automatically. This means the likelihood of establishing a European Public Prosecutor is much increased with the LT compared to the CT. Thus, the LT is a significant advance in this area.

Finally, the introduction of an explicit principle of solidarity, i.e. a solidarity clause modelled on NATO Article 5 (mutual defence clause), within the AFSJ is one of the most significant innovations of the LT. The clause stipulates that in the case of a terrorist attack or a natural or man-made disaster, the Union shall act jointly to mobilise all instruments at their disposal. Firstly, the procedure would require a European decision by the Council on a proposal from the Commission, and the High Representative for Foreign Affairs for cases with military implications. In addition, the European Council acquires the legal responsibility to regularly assess the threats facing the Union. In conclusion, the normative question has now been conclusively answered as a political consensus of decision-makers; the EU should be legislating in the AFSJ. The AFSJ is the 'big winner' of the LT arrangements.

The European Commission as a supranational policy entrepreneur?

This article suggests a framework of SPEs, which is often referred to by the academic literature that discusses the role of institutions in European integration (Pollack 1997, 2003, Stone Sweet and Sandholtz 1997, Moravcsik 1999a, Stone Sweet *et al.* 2001, Tallberg 2002, 2003, 2006, 2008, Beach 2004, 2005, Kaunert 2005, 2007, 2009). The SPE model that aims to explain policy change in the EU. It is an evolutionary policy-making model starting with the identification of a problem (first stream), which is then followed by a search for alternative solutions (second stream) and a decision among these alternatives (third stream). Policy entrepreneurs, 'advocates [...] willing to invest their resources – time, reputation, money' (Kingdon 1984, p. 188), stand at a policy window in order to propose, lobby for and sell a policy proposal. In order for policies to become adopted, it is necessary for a policy entrepreneur to do this as otherwise policy inertia takes over. While the SPE model does not specify who the policy entrepreneur could be (which could range from the Commission, the European Parliament or individual member states in the Council), it assumes that an entrepreneur will be present in order for a policy to be adopted. In this article, this model is used as a benchmark against which the political behaviour of the Commission, and indeed that of the other EU institutional actors, is measured against as laid out by Kingdon (1984) and further developed by Kaunert (2007, 2009).

The model is grounded in the works of Kingdon (1984, p. 173) within the context of US politics. In this model, the aforementioned agenda-setting process narrows the set of alternatives for different policies due to the fact that only a certain number of issues can potentially be considered simultaneously. Kingdon stresses two factors which influence agenda-setting and the specification of alternatives: (1) the participants who are active and (2) the process by which agenda items and alternatives come into prominence. He foresees three potential mechanisms of how issues arrive onto the 'formal' agenda. This is described either (1) through the mobilisation of the relevant public by leaders; (2) through diffusion of ideas in professional circles and bureaucrats; or (3) from a change in party control (Kingdon 1984, p. 17). On some occasions, a 'policy window' opens for the adoption of certain policies. Policy entrepreneurs (Kingdon 1984, p. 188) stand at this window in order to propose, lobby for and sell a policy proposal.

Sandholtz and Zysman (1989) and Sandholtz (1993) have been one of the first scholars to draw on Kingdon's model. Sandholtz, Stone Sweet and Zysman have all contributed significantly to the conceptualisation of policy entrepreneurship. Yet, since these studies, European integration has moved on into other significant policy areas, for instance the AFSJ. But how is the Commission characterised by this conception? A priori, institutions matter (Stone Sweet and Sandholtz 1997, p. 310). Rules define roles (who is an actor) and norms matter. Actors behave in self-interested, rationalist–materialist ways. Therefore, institutions like the Commission work to enhance their own autonomy and influence within the European polity. Thereby, it acquires legitimacy by promoting the interests of transnational society.

In their book 'The Institutionalization of Europe' (Stone Sweet *et al.* 2001), the authors built upon this theme again. Emphasising that institutions are human artefacts which are made by humans, they also introduce a notion of institutional change, which should counter the static vision of institutionalist path-dependency. Reasons for change are (1) exogenous shocks; (2) the fact that rule innovations are endogenous to politics; (3) diffusion of organisational behaviour and models of action; and (4) policy entrepreneurship. Institutional entrepreneurs (Stone Sweet *et al.* 2001, p. 11) are conceptualised to construct and revise 'policy frames' (i.e. the collectively held sets of meanings) that (1) engage other actors and define new relationships between them and (2) chart courses of action. The 'policy entrepreneur generates and attempts to propagate ideas that will define problems and solutions in ways that other actors find convincing and useful'. This definition is very close to the one provided by Kingdon (1984).

Kaunert (2007, 2009) has further extended this framework to constructivist insights of norm construction and norm entrepreneurship, widely discussed in the international relations literature (Finnemore 1996a, 1996b, Finnemore and Sikkink 1998). Why is this important? At the political bargaining stage (the politics stream), where decisions amongst different alternatives are taken, the EU is dominated by member states' preferences and interests, especially by the Council. In principle, this would indicate the benefits of a liberal intergovernmental analysis for the policy area. In this view, European integration can best be explained as a series of rational choices made by national leaders and dominated by national interests (Moravcsik 1998, 1999a, 1999b). Thus, EU integration occurs due to: (1) a change in interests within the member states or (2) the result of a grand political bargain. International institutions are merely there to bolster the credibility of interstate commitments (Moravcsik 1998, p. 18) by ensuring that member states keep their promises and thus dare to agree to a mutually favourable solution without the fear of 'free-riders'.

But where do member states' national interests and preferences come from? Moravcsik (1998) assumes national interests to be exogenous of the EU process. The interests of the member states are stable before they come to the bargaining table. However, it does not seem reasonable to assert that preferences are exogenous. In fact, it is important to note that Moravcsik has been criticised profoundly for his assumptions. Wincott (1995, p. 602) criticises the fact that Moravcsik chooses to isolate treaty reform from day-to-day policy-making. Treaty reform is constructed as an event rather than a process. The EU has created a system whereby member states continuously interact at different levels. Christiansen (2002, 2008) and Christiansen and Reh (2009) develop this point further – the bargaining process starts already at the policy-making stage. Thus, Moravcsik's claim that this would not change preferences over time appears doubtful. Even within the context of the international system with less social interaction amongst states, Katzenstein (1996) has demonstrated convincingly how norms and values shape national interests. Constructivist literature clearly showed how these norms change over time (Finnemore 1996a, 1996b, Finnemore and Sikkink 1998).

Yet, if national interests and preferences are shaped by different norms and values, as argued in this article, this implies that norms consequently influence the definition of political problems, the search for policy alternatives and finally the national preferences in the politics stream where decisions are taken. How can norms be constructed and how can they be observed? Firstly, actors provide reasons for action. The SPE constantly pushes for his reasons for action to become accepted as a norm, albeit in competition with other actors. This is the first stage of norm creation in the norm life cycle as described by Finnemore and Sikkink (1998), and is followed by the norm socialisation stage. Eventually, a norm becomes the dominant norm. An inclusion of the concept of norms is highly beneficial for the realities of EU policy-making. More often than not, the nature of the EU between a fully fledged state and an international organisation means that different norms are competing with one another, unlike an established domestic polity. National sovereignty is the prevailing and generally accepted norm within the international system. Yet, within the EU system this norm is constantly competing with the norm to pool national sovereignty at the EU level, and to drive forward the process of European integration. A successful SPE needs to push for an alignment of these norms, before any serious policy proposal be suggested.

Kaunert (2007, 2009) suggests the ways in which political entrepreneurs can achieve this:

(1) First mover advantage: SPEs need to come in faster with their proposals than their rivals.
(2) Persuasion strategy: as mentioned above, in order to achieve acceptance, other actors need to be convinced by the reasons for the action proposed.
(3) Alliances: it is vital for the SPE to form initial alliances with other powerful actors to create a bandwagon effect, whereby more actors will join the 'winning team'.

This article will move from the argument that 'institutions matter' (Elgström and Jönsson 2000, 2005, Tallberg 2002, 2003, 2006, 2008, Bailer 2004, Beach 2004, 2005, Lewis 2005, 2008). Specifically, it will apply the useful model elaborated by Kingdon (1984) as further developed by Kaunert (2007, 2009) and it also will take into account Lewis' (2005, 2008) insights on norms. In the following section, the role of the Commission in the adoption process of the LT is analysed in detail, taking Christiansen's (2002) point seriously – the bargaining process starts already at the policy-making stage in the AFSJ.

Evaluating the participation of the commission in the area of freedom, security and justice dimension of the Lisbon Treaty: to what extent an supranational policy entrepreneur?

This section examines whether the European Commission managed to play the significant role of an SPE. It analyses the role of the European Commission, acting to initiate and push for a process of normative change regarding national sovereignty in the AFSJ among EU decision-makers, as well as concrete institutional change, which is both part of its role as a SPE.

Methodologically, this has been based on the so-called 'triangulation of methods'. In practice, this means that empirical observations have been analysed from three different angles: (1) the academic literature on the AFSJ; (2) the most crucial policy documents; and (3) elite interviews with actors and decision-makers in the area. The initial findings of the documentary analysis were the starting points of the triangulation process. It was therefore of crucial importance to corroborate and substantiate the initial findings from the documentary analysis with evidence from in-depth semi-structured interviews with decision-makers, which were conducted over a six months period in 2004, the year the Constitutional Convention adopted its treaty draft, which ultimately became the basis for the CT and subsequently the LT. The interviewees can be subdivided as follows: (1) 28 officials and senior officials in the European Commission; (2) 44 JHA counsellors in 24 out of 27 Permanent Representations of the Member States and the candidate country Turkey; (3) nine officials from the Council Secretariat; (4) five members of the European Parliament (Committee on Civil Liberties, Justice and Home Affairs – LIBE); (5) 12 non-governmental organisation (NGO) representatives; (6) two officials from the intergovernmental organisations (IGOs), United Nations High Commissioner for Refugees (UNHCR) and international organisation for migration (IOM); and (7) two academic experts in the field.

Prior to the Convention: commission entrepreneurship by officials?

According to the late Sir Adrian Fortescue (1995), then the Director of the General Secretariat of the Commission and later the first Head of the JHA Directorate of the Commission, in the early days, the Commission was squeezed between the expectations by the European Parliament and the suspicions by the Council of Ministers. Member states tended to see the Commission as a competence-maximising institution that, in their view, lacked credible expertise in the area. The European Parliament tended to see the Commission's ambitions as too modest, and suspected it of pleasing member states too much. Consequently, the Commission needed to square this circle; not to be torn between these different expectations in the process of establishing its credibility. The key moment in the evolution of the EU's role in the area of Justice and Home Affairs, according to Fortescue (Interview COM25), was, when in 1985, instead of just talking about the internal market as a place in which goods and services circulated, the Commission was the first to start putting forward the phrase 'Europe without frontiers'. This can be demonstrated by examining Lord Cockfield's famous 1985 White Paper on completing the internal market.

Fortescue was subsequently appointed to form an initially small team of people into what came to be known as the Justice and Home Affairs Task Force. Due to limits imposed upon what it could do legally, in particular due to the fact that its usual right of initiative had to be shared with the member states and thus not guaranteed that it would receive attention, the Commission was forced to always table a better and more competitive proposal than any member state would and could. The interviews with permanent representations of 24 member states confirmed the fact that the Commission was able to do this during the Tampere programme (Interviews PR1–PR24), which was the time that the LT was shaped in its design in the Constitutional Convention. Indeed, there was a clear and widespread acknowledgement of the expertise that the Commission had acquired over the years.

According to Kingdon (1995, p. 181), a successful policy entrepreneur exhibits three fundamental characteristics: he/she must 'have some claim to a hearing', he/she must be well known for his/her political relations and/or negotiation ability and he/she must be very persistent in waiting for a policy window to open (Kingdon). This can be particularly attributed to Commissioner Vitorino (1999–2004 Commission). All permanent representations (Interviews PR1–PR24) rated the Commission unanimously very highly regarding its negotiations skills throughout the Tampere process (Interviews PR1–PR24 and NGO1–NGO11). Thus, there was a unanimous acceptance of the central role of the Commission in the future direction of the AFSJ (Interviews PR1–PR24), a vital element in its role as an SPE.

Furthermore, one of the most important ways to influence policy outcomes in the EU is the gradual building of alliances. The Commission succeeded very well on this criterion as well, though successively over the years. The European Commission first strong natural ally throughout the years in its efforts to supranationalise the AFSJ was the European Parliament (Interviews EP1–EP5) and its Committee on Citizens' Freedoms and Rights, Justice and Home Affairs (Commission des libertés et des droits des citoyens, de la justice et des affaires intérieures – LIBE). The alliance with the European Parliament was of particular importance regarding the LT, as a significant number of MEPs were also in the Convention that drafted the CT. The EP, as the only directly elected institution of the EU, was best placed to support changes to the treaties. It also helped that the Commissioner Vitorino (1999–2004) had previously been the Chairman of the LIBE Committee in the European Parliament (1994–99).

Furthermore, the Commission also worked very hard over the years to build up good relations with the plethora of NGOs in the field of AFSJ (Interviews NGO1–NGO11). There are instances where important actors of NGOs had even become important members of the services in the Commission (Interview COM16). Consequently, this led to a widespread support for a communitarisation of AFSJ matters by NGOs (Interviews NGO1–NGO11). In addition, NGOs provided it with invaluable supplementary input of information through informal information channels and job changes. Consequently, they represented an important ally for the Commission, and were thus invited to participate in the future of Europe debate for civil society in parallel with the Convention. This gave increased weight to the Commission's position in the Convention. In conclusion, the normative advancements to further the communitarisation of the AFSJ can be related to the strategy employed by the Commission throughout the 1990s, but in particular to its constructive role during the Tampere programme (for Tampere achievements, see Kaunert 2007, 2009).

During the Convention (2002–2003)

According to Kingdon (1984), a crisis or a prominent event can signal the emergence of a political problem. In response to this political problem, policy ideas sweep through policy communities through a constant process of discussions, speeches, hearings and bill introductions. Kingdon raises explicitly the importance of ideas for policy communities and implicitly the related importance of norms. The efforts made the Commission, as analysed in the previous section, to press for a normative change in attitude towards the supranationalisation of the AFSJ finally paid off during the Constitutional Convention, which subsequently laid the foundations for the LT (through the CT).

Why was the CT IGC prepared by a Convention for the first time in the history of the EU? Beach (2005, p. 178) suggests that this revolutionary procedural change had been pushed by the Commission, the European Parliament and federalist-oriented governments as a response to the 'crisis' in the negotiations of the Nice Treaty. The crisis impression was further confirmed by the first rejection of the treaty in Ireland, subsequently reversed in a second referendum, which had signalled that the 'old treaty-making' had become impossible with the enlargement of the EU. But what was the role of the European Commission during this Convention? The notion of the Commission playing an important role in the Convention has been popularly caricatured by journalists who tended to cite the supposedly failed 'Penelope' feasibility study led by Commission President Romano Prodi (BBC 2002). It is often portrayed as an attempt that antagonised member states rather than convinced them (Norman 2003, p. 162).

Yet, a close reading of both of these documents with a focus on the AFSJ reveals another interpretation – the Commission acted as a first mover to shape the debate on the future of the AFSJ. The main focus of the Commission's first contribution to the convention was the AFSJ. It clearly prioritised the AFSJ alongside the Charter of Fundamental Rights. It reasoned that further integration in the AFSJ was strongly desired by public opinion. Similarly, the 'Penelope' feasibility study of December 2002 can also be seen in this light. Thus, the aims and objectives in the Penelope study were very much in line with the conclusions of the working group on AFSJ in the Convention. While Beach (2005, p. 199) suggests that the Penelope study 'alienated even its allies', he concedes that the Commission was able to influence better when playing a low profile and realistic role. He suggests its successes included notably the Charter of Fundamental Rights.

Besides all the available policy documents, there is further significant evidence of the Commission's importance during the Convention: firstly, the choice of which Commissioner would represent the institution in the Convention was not accidental, but rather led by a clear choice of priorities. Antonio Vitorino was chosen due to his prior involvement in the Convention which led to the Charter of Fundamental Rights, but also due to his legal expertise, and his responsibility and longstanding expertise in the AFSJ (Interview COM10). Secondly, the Commissioner's attendance record was impeccable and unsurpassed, thus providing ample opportunity to push the Commission's viewpoint. The Working Group X on the AFSJ met nine times from September to December 2002 (CONV 256/02). From the minutes of these nine meetings, one can notice two people attending every meeting – the Chairman of the Working Group X, Mr John Bruton, who had to attend every meeting, and the Commissioner responsible for the AFSJ, Mr Antonio Vitorino, who also attended every meeting. From this, one can deduce that, at the very least, Vitorino acquired the best grasp of the ongoing negotiations. This provided significant opportunities to push the Commission's arguments, both during the official debate and more informally with the individual working group members.

Thirdly, the selection of experts was favourably inclined towards the Commission's arguments. As suggested by Kingdon (1984), in the problem stream where political problems are defined, one can empirically encounter a close-knit policy community in which a SPE can shape the way problems are defined. What shapes people's thoughts within policy communities? Commonly held sets of beliefs and norms certainly seem to influence people's ideas and behaviours. Participants interact with each other and are socialised according to the prevailing norms within this reference group. Norms may even facilitate who participates in this group. Furthermore, norms do not just guide the behaviour of people in this policy community, but are also shaped by the discussions and the social interaction within this group. In short, the presence of social norms appears to influence the behaviour of people in these policy communities. Amongst the participants of this policy community are Mr de Brouwer, who was responsible for asylum and migration in the Commission, and Mr de Kerchove from the Council Secretariat, responsible for criminal justice and well known amongst decision-makers for his positive views towards further integration (Interviews PR1–PR24), now the EU's counter-terrorism coordinator. Moreover, federalist-inclined academic scholars were also invited, such as Prof. Henri Labayle, who has previously made forceful legal arguments for a full communitarisation of the area. In essence, the sum of all these people represents a close-knit policy community favourably inclined towards further communitarisation of the AFSJ.

The intervention by Antonio Vitorino during the deliberation and his recommendations (Convention 2002b, WGX–WD14) were in line with previous documents and the advice given by his civil servants. The interventions advocated a full communitarisation of the AFSJ, including a common policy on asylum, a European immigration policy, a genuine area of justice both in civil and criminal law matters, enhanced police and judicial cooperation and full judicial oversight by the ECJ. The Commission also submitted a document (Convention 2002c, WGX–WD27) on the European public prosecutor. In his changes to the final working group report draft (Convention 2002d, WGX–WD30), Vitorino reiterated some of the Commission priorities, including the EU public prosecutor and the policy objectives of the AFSJ. The Franco-German intervention (Convention 2002e, WGX–WD32) by the Foreign Ministers Joseph Fischer and Dominique de Villepin resembled the prior contribution by the Commission.

But where in the debate do the final working group report and the final draft of the AFSJ article stand? Overall, the Commission had a significant impact first on the debate, second on the working group report and then on the final draft. The final outcome from the CT IGC (Conference of the Representatives of the Governments of the Member States 2004) was not significantly different from the Convention draft with regards to the AFSJ. The final Convention draft relied significantly on the report produced by the Working Group X on AFSJ (Convention 2002a, CONV 426/02). In turn, the working group report resembled the interventions of the European Commission. Thus, one can clearly trace the impact of the interventions made by the Commission.

Overall, Working Group X on the AFSJ proposed sweeping changes. It reinforced the drive for simplification of the treaties by proposing a common legal framework bringing all treaty provisions under a single title. It pushed for simplification of decision-making mechanisms, which meant a QMV in the Council in co-decision with the European Parliament. All major parts of the AFSJ were significantly strengthened. In addition, there was consensus that unanimity voting in the Council could not be sustained after enlargement. The working group report was divided over whether to create a European public prosecutor, but the final draft included the possibility of establishing one and hence fulfilled one of the most crucial aims of the Commission in the area (Interview COM10). Thus, in the light of the evidence presented, it can be suggested that the Commission with its representative, Antonio Vitorino, played a highly significant role during the Convention.

During the CT intergovernmental conference (2003–2004)

The actual IGC is the most difficult part to analyse for any researcher due to the lack of open source documents. In essence, this article relies on comparing the version of the draft before the IGC to the final version of the CT, which has been triangulated with interviews (in particular COM10), and some reporting in the media. IGCs are based upon Article 48 of the TEU (Beach 2005, 8). Governments of any member states may propose to the Council to amend existing treaties. They are convened either by agreement in the Council under Article 48 EU, or by a binding legal commitment included in the treaty. In the case of the CT, it was convened due to both the Laeken declaration and the commitment in the Nice Treaty. There are no formal provisions for how the agenda for an IGC should be prepared; here the agenda was already set by the Convention draft. Nonetheless, IGCs are formally outside of the institutional framework of the EU, thus effectively being an international/intergovernmental negotiation. While there are EU norms governing IGCs, all internal documents are under diplomatic secrecy.

When the IGC started in September 2003, convention member expressed the hope the conference would only rubber stamp the Conventional draft. Nonetheless, media commentators suggested 'the constitution to be in tatters' when the first summit in December 2003 under the Italian presidency failed due to the lack of compromise on voting weights (Economist 2003b). At that point in time, it was suggested that the UK had kept their so-called red lines, including their vetoes, amongst others, in judicial cooperation. This would seem to suggest that the UK had succeeded in redrafting parts of the articles on the AFSJ. A week prior to the summit, the Economist (Economist 2003a) also suggested that the UK had strong reservations about the Charter of Fundamental Rights, and that the UK, Ireland, Sweden and Denmark also opposed the European public prosecutor and further criminal law harmonisation. Apparently, these issues did not end the negotiations.

An interview with a senior Commission official present at the negotiations in the Convention and during the IGC (COM10) confirms that the UK delegation had been the biggest obstacle in finding a solution for the outstanding issues in the AFSJ. According to him, they supported the Convention proposals during the Convention. However, during the Italian presidency in late 2003, the UK delegation rediscovered their dislike of some of the advances in the AFSJ, in particular the European public prosecutor (to which they had acquiesced previously), the move to QMV in the Council in the area of criminal justice, and the legal inclusion of the Charter of Fundamental Rights. While the UK delegation succeeded in redrafting some of the aforementioned articles, this was not as comprehensive as newspapers suggested. In February 2004, the European constitution was 'back from the dead' (Economist 2004c), when the Irish presidency resurrected negotiations with a low-profile strategy. By March 2004, all 25 (then) member states had committed themselves to agreeing on a final text for the Constitution by their next summit on 17–18 June 2004 (Economist 2004d).

According to the senior Commission official (COM10), the UK delegation had again become the biggest obstacle just before the summit. Despite the fact that the media at the time claimed the UK was opposed to the European public prosecutor, the official insisted that the UK had already accepted its inclusion before the summit. Similarly, a solution for the legal inclusion of the Charter of Fundamental Rights had already been found as well – and the UK agreed to the compromise. The remaining sticking point was therefore the move to QMV in the area of criminal justice. The UK insisted on their principled opposition to it, while the Commission insisted that unanimity would be unacceptable. A large number of member states agreed with the Commission's arguments.

A compromise solution was found in the form of the aforementioned so-called 'emergency brake'. The UK wanted the latter to work in a way that would have meant that any member state could have blocked QMV by shifting the decision upwards to the European Council and its unanimity rule – on the legal grounds of a fundamental of national law being under threat. This would have effectively meant a continuation of unanimity in a different way. The Commission was fiercely opposed to that solution and the official predicted that the final solution would be different. The interviewee predicted – in an interview prior to the summit – that the eventual solution would also include an accelerator procedure. This would mean a member state could initially block QMV in the area of criminal justice. Yet, at the European Council, the decision would have to be sent back to the Council of Ministers within a tight deadline. The Commission was particularly insistent on this deadline. After that point, the accelerator would kick in – and the formerly blocking member state would be effectively excluded from the legislative procedure. Therefore, the fact that the prediction by the Commission official became a reality in June 2004 – only a month after the interview took place – is a highly significant and points to how closely involved Commissioner Vitorino was in the solution finding at the IGC, and how influential he was in pushing through his solutions. The EU summit of 18 June 2004 subsequently agreed on the final text of the CT. The articles on the AFSJ remained significantly intact compared to the Convention draft. From now on, the main foundation of the Lisbon AFSJ architecture did not to fundamentally change anymore.

During the reflection period (2005–2007)

During their respective referenda, on 29 May 2005 France voted No with 55 per cent, on 1 June 2005 the Netherlands voted No with 62 per cent, and, subsequently, the UK froze ratification of the Treaty on 6 June 2005. France and the Netherlands were perceived to be so central to the EU that the treaty had to be re-negotiated. The European Council summit of 17 and 18 June 2005, decided that a 'reflection period' lasting until 2007 was necessary. Despite this official reflection amongst member states in the hope for better domestic conditions for re-negotiation and ratification, a possible re-negotiation of the CT was also helped along by EU-level factors. Thus, in fact, it was possible to portray it as only a 'min-treaty', in Sarkozy's words, or as it was called until the signing, a 'Reform Treaty'. This argument relies on two developments in 2005. Firstly, the 'Hague programme' pre-empted the ratification of the CT to an extent. It urged the abolishing of the requirement of unanimous voting in the Council on all EU immigration and asylum law, except illegal immigration, alongside co-decision powers for the European Parliament. The actual change in the decision-making rules was subsequently made by a Council decision. Secondly, landmark decisions of the ECJ on 16 June 2005 and on 13 September 2005 created case law that solidified the CT advances in the area of criminal justice. Consequently, the treaty could be portrayed as less significant, and thereby ratifiable through parliament.

On 16 June and on 13 September 2005, the ECJ (2005a) issued two groundbreaking judgements, which changed the legal instruments available in the area of criminal justice significantly. The so-called 'Pupino case' (ECJ 2005a) considerably strengthened the legal instruments available in the field of police and judicial cooperation in criminal matters (de facto de-pillarisation) by introducing some form of direct effect, normally only found in first pillar instruments (Euroactiv 2005), and changed them into instruments that are very similar to those in the CT. The second landmark decision by the ECJ (2005b) granted the Commission the power to require criminal sanctions for environmental offences. Both judgements put together meant that third pillar legal instruments had become like first pillar instruments, and confirm the idea of a de facto de-pillarisation. While the changes in the AFSJ dimension had been very significant indeed, the policy entrepreneurship by the ECJ, acting on a request by the Commission, made it easier to present an abolition of the pillar structure as a modest endeavour. Thus, this increased the likelihood of the re-negotiation of the treaty to succeed at the end of the reflection period.

Renegotiation, the second IGC (2007) and ratification of the Lisbon Treaty (2009)

At the end of the reflection period, the LT was signed by the Heads of State or Governments in December 2007. A number of domestic factors made this signing more likely. Firstly, France elected Nicolas Sarkozy as President, who argued successfully for a smaller 'Reform Treaty' in the French presidential (May 2007) and parliamentary elections (June 2007). He suggested that he would choose to ratify this 'mini-treaty' by parliament. Ratification of an 'ordinary' treaty was perceived to be more easily achievable. This resulted in a strategy of active de-politicisation of negotiations by European elites towards a 'Reform Treaty' (Christiansen 2008, p. 42). Under the German Presidency of 2007, rapid progress was made to re-negotiate what was eventually to become the LT, which included all major AFSJ provision from the CT, and even went further slightly (including even the Prüm Convention acquis).

However, despite negotiation obstructions by the late Polish President Kaczynski, it was in fact (again) the UK delegation that had become the biggest obstacle just before the LT IGC summit. Within the UK domestic political debate, the extension of the community method to the AFSJ was widely under attack for infringing UK national sovereignty, despite the safeguards that were already in the CT (Donnelly 2008, p. 22). While the LT communitarised the AFSJ for most member states, the UK Government insisted on a generalised opt-in/opt-out from all newly communitarised parts of the AFSJ. On the back of this concession to the UK, Ireland also received the same protocol due to its 'common law' position. This new mechanism, at least for the UK and Ireland, meant that the LT was different to the CT. In the UK context, this helped to make the domestic argument against holding a referendum as a method for ratification, subsequently often used by PM Gordon Brown to ensure UK ratification.

Yet, the first Irish no-vote (53 per cent) in the referendum on the LT on 12 June 2008 made ratification uncertain. Given the fact that there was absolutely no appetite for re-negotiating the LT (again) amongst other EU governments, the Irish Government decided to enter into non-treaty negotiations, in which it secured a series of legal guarantees. At the EU summit on 18–19 June 2009, the Irish Taoiseach Brian Cowen received a declaration designed to reassure the Irish principal reservations derived from the first referendum (Hierlemann 2009). This resulted in an overwhelming success for the yes-campaign, as indicated at the beginning of this article. Of the Irish electorate, 67.1 per cent voted in favour of the LT, while 32.9 per cent voted against. Furthermore, eventually, all other obstacles were also successfully removed. Firstly, the German Constitutional Court accepted the LT as compatible with the German 'Basic Law', i.e. the German Constitution, despite severe Eurosceptic grumblings, which resulted in a new ratification law in Germany. German President Horst Köhler signed the LT at the end of September 2009, and the German ratification documents were deposited in time before the second Irish referendum. In addition, on 10 October 2009, the late Polish President Lech Kaczynski signed the Ratification Act of the LT (Zwolski 2009). This left the Czech Republic as the last country not to ratify the treaty under the strongly Eurosceptic President Klaus. With the Czech Constitutional Court finding three times in favour of the LT, Klaus finally accepted to sign the LT (after his demand of a future opt-out from the Charter of Fundamental Rights was accepted by a European Council summit in late autumn 2009). Thus, in the end, the LT entered into force on 1 December 2009.

Conclusions

In conclusion, this article demonstrated some very significant points. Most significantly, the LT will be a major advance for the AFSJ. Consequently, it may rightly be claimed that the EU's AFSJ has become one of the most important developments in the European integration process. The LT has the potential to push the AFSJ towards tremendous growth, and has provided the policy area with instruments that were unthinkable after the third pillar was created during the Maastricht Treaty negotiations. The LT has created an AFSJ which Delors would have wholeheartedly supported, and the UK delegation rejected during the Maastricht negotiations. Despite the central place that EU member states continue to have in the policy-making process, even after the entry into force of the LT with an enhanced role for the European Council, EU supranational actors, in particular the European Commission, have played a significant role in the adoption of the LT advances in the AFSJ.

This article suggested that the Commission, through alliances with other EU institutional actors, such as the European Parliament, and civil society groups, managed to incrementally contribute to a shift in political norms enabling decision-makers to consider the communitarisation of the AFSJ. This follows on the back of policy entrepreneurship by the Commission at the policy-making level in the AFSJ, as suggested in the academic literature; examples are the European Arrest Warrant (Kaunert 2007) or the Common European Asylum System (Kaunert 2009). Political norms shifted decisively from with the beginning of the Tampere programme from 1999 onwards (Kaunert 2005), and manifested themselves particularly during the negotiations of the CT, as well as the subsequent re-negotiation of the LT. The Commission has been a very active player – exerting the role of a SPE. This significantly contributed to member states preference building, even during the convention stage and the subsequent treaty negotiation stage, first for the CT and subsequently for the LT. This clearly adds to the growing body of literature that suggests that European institutions can be important players in Justice and Home Affairs areas (Kaunert 2007, 2009), as well as in other areas, such as telecommunications (Fuchs 1994, 1995), equal opportunities (Mazey 1995) and research (Peterson 1995).

The missing dimension: ratification as part of the process

However, it needs to be acknowledged that there are limitations to the arguments in the article. The ratification stage of the LT made it clear that scholars increasingly need to distinguish between treaty adoption and treaty ratification: during the ratification stage, member states are the only 'game in town'. The article showed clearly the importance of member states, and their respective national governments, during the treaty ratification stage. When the CT was rejected by France and the Netherlands, it was the UK government which effectively ended the ratification process. Furthermore, French President Sarkozy was needed in order to revive the CT in the form of a 'Reform Treaty', a term which he coined during his presidential election campaign. German Chancellor Merkel was needed as a broker for a new deal during the LT re-negotiations. Finally, the Irish electorate needed to vote twice before the LT could enter into force, which occurred not until Irish Taoiseach Cowen had secured non-treaty guarantees. Even the late Polish President Kaczynski and Czech President Klaus managed to delay the final ratification of the treaty. It was clear from the evidence presented in this article that the Commission was not an important player during the treaty ratification stage. This provides a clear limitation to the overall argument of the article: while it managed to play the role of an SEP during the treaty adoption stage, it became increasingly marginal during the ratification stage. But even at this most intergovernmental of decision-making moments in the EU, another EU institution managed to influence the agenda – the ECJ with its AFSJ verdicts discussed above. While not decisive for the eventual treaty outcome, it certainly facilitated the adoption of the LT. Thus, it remains clear that different analytical models apply for the different stages: SPE ship has shown its usefulness for the treaty adoption stage. However, for the treaty ratification stage, this article continues to recommend using analytical tools much closer to domestic politics. Despite the LT, this is not likely to change in the near future.

Notes on contributor

Dr Christian Kaunert is Lecturer in EU Politics & International Relations and Programme Leader of the Master (MA) in Terrorism and Security. He is the author of several articles on EU counter-terrorism and internal security, as well as a monograph entitled *European Internal Security? – Towards Supranational Governance* with Manchester University Press. He has been a Visiting Research Fellow at IBEI Barcelona, Spain, and from October 2010, a Marie Curie Research Fellow at the European University Institute in Florence, Italy.

References

Bailer, S., 2004. Bargaining success in the European Union. *European Union politics*, 5 (1), 99–123.

BBC News, 2002. *Prodi seeks strong powers for Brussels*. 5 December. Available from: http://news.bbc.co.uk/1/hi/world/europe/2545331.stm

Beach, D., 2004. The unseen hand in treaty reform negotiations: the role and impact of the Council Secretariat. *Journal of European public policy*, 11 (3), 408–439.

Beach, D., 2005. *The dynamics of European integration – why and when EU institutions matter*. London: Palgrave Macmillan.

Carrera, S. and Geyer, F., 2008. The reform treaty and justice and home affairs: implications for the common area of freedom, security and justice. *In*: E. Guild and F. Geyer, eds.

Security versus justice? Police and judicial cooperation in the European Union. Aldershot: Ashgate.

Christiansen, T., 2002. The role of supranational actors in EU treaty reform. *Journal of European public policy*, 9 (1), 33–53.

Christiansen, T., 2008. The EU treaty reform since 2000: the highs and lows of constitutionalising the European Union. *EIPAscope*, (1).

Christiansen, T. and Reh, C., 2009. *Constitutionalizing the European Union*. London: Palgrave MacMillan.

Conference of the Representatives of the Governments of the Member States, 2004. *Treaty establishing a constitution for Europe*. Brussels: Convention Praesidium, CIG 87/04.

Convention, 2002a. *Final report of the Working Group X 'Freedom, Security And Justice'*. Brussels: Convention Praesidium, CONV426/02, 2 December 2002.

Convention, 2002b. *Paper by Mr Antonio Vitorino*. Working Group X, Document 14, WGX–WD14, 15 November 2002.

Convention, 2002c. *A European Public Prosecutor*. Working Group X, Document 27, WGX–WD27, 25 November 2002.

Convention, 2002d. *Changes To The Draft Final Report By Mr Antonio Vitorino*. Working Group X, Document 30, 26 November 2002, WGX–WD30.

Convention, 2002e. *Franco-German Proposals By Mr Fischer And Mr De Villepin*. Working Group X, Document 32, 27 November 2002, WGX–WD32.

Donnelly, B., 2008. Justice and home affairs in the Lisbon Treaty: a constitutionalising clarification? *EIPAscope*, (1).

Economist, 2003a. *Might it all tumble down*. 11 December 2003. Available from: www.economist.com/PrinterFriendly.cfm?Story_ID = 2291407

Economist, 2003b. *A constitution in tatters*. 16 December 2003. Available from: www.economist.com/agenda/PrinterFriendly.cfm?Story_ID = 2295754

Economist, 2004c. *Back from the dead*. 5 February 2004. Available from: www.economist.com/PrinterFriendly.cfm?Story_ID = 2410025

Economist, 2004d. Revived to die another day? 26 March 2004. Available from: www.economist.com/agenda/PrinterFriendly.cfm?Story_ID = 2550082

Elgström, O. and Jönsson, C., 2000. Negotiation in the European Union: bargaining or problem-solving? *Journal of European public policy*, 7 (5), 684–704.

Elgström, O. and Jönsson, C., eds., 2005. *European Union negotiations: processes, networks, and institutions*. London: Routledge.

Euractiv, 2009. *Resounding Irish "Yes" to EU's Lisbon Treaty*. 3 September 2009. Available from: www.euractiv.com/en/future-eu/resounding-irish-eu-lisbon-treaty/article-186051

Euroactiv, 2005. *EU law supremacy even in criminal matters*. 18 June 2005. Available from: www.euractiv.com/Article?tcmuri = tcm:29-141124-16&type = News

European Court of Justice (ECJ), 2005a. *Judgment of the court of justice in case C-105/03*. Press Release No. 59/05. Luxembourg: European Court of Justice.

European Court of Justice (ECJ), 2005b. *Judgment of the court of justice in case C-176/03*. Press Release No. 75/05. Luxembourg: European Court of Justice.

Finnemore, M., 1996a. *National interest in international society*. Ithaca, NY: Cornell University Press.

Finnemore, M., 1996b. Norms, culture and world politics: insights from sociology's institutionalism. *International Organization*, 50 (2), 325–348.

Finnemore, M. and Sikkink, K., 1998. International norm dynamics and political change. *International organization*, 52 (4), 887–917.

Fortescue, A., 1995. First experiences with the implementation of the third pillar provisions. *In*: R. Bieber and J. Monar, eds. *Justice and home affairs in the European Union: the development of the third pillar*. Brussels: Interuniversity Press.

Fuchs, G., 1994. Policy-making in a system of multi-level governance – the commission of the European community and the restructuring of the telecommunications sector. *Journal of European public policy*, 1 (2), 176–194.

Fuchs, G., 1995. The European commission as corporate actor? European telecommunications policy after Maastricht. *In*: C. Rhodes and S. Mazey, eds. *The state of the European Union. Vol. 3: building a European polity*. Harlow: Longman.

Haas, E., 1958. *The uniting of Europe: political, social, and economic forces 1950–57*. Stanford: Stanford University Press.

Haas, E., 1964. *Beyond the nation state: functionalism and international organization*. Stanford: Stanford University Press.

Haas, E., 1967. The uniting of Europe and the uniting of Latin America. *Journal of Common Market Studies*, 5, 315–344.

Hierlemann, D., 2009. *Ireland's second attempt*. Spotlight Europe, No. 2009/09. Germany: Bertelsmann Stiftung.

Hix, S., 1994. The study of the European community: the challenge to comparative politics. *West European politics*, 17 (1), 1–30.

Hix, S., 1998. The study of the European Union II the "New Governance" agenda and its rival. *Journal of European public policy*, 5 (2), 38–65.

Hix, S., 1999. *The political system of the European Union*. London: Macmillan.

Katzenstein, P., 1996. *The culture of national security: norms and identity in world politics*. New York: Columbia University Press.

Kaunert, C., 2005. The area of freedom, security and justice: the construction of a 'European Public Order'. *European security*, 14 (40), 459–483.

Kaunert, C., 2007. 'Without the Power of Purse or Sword': The European arrest warrant and the role of the commission. *Journal of European integration*, 29 (4), 387–404.

Kaunert, C., 2009. Liberty versus security? EU asylum policy and the European commission. *Journal of contemporary European research*, 5 (2), 148–170.

Kingdon, J.W., 1984. *Agenda, alternatives, and public policies*. Boston: Little, Brown.

Kingdon, J.W., 1995. *Agenda, alternatives, and public policies*. New York: Longman.

Lewis, J., 2005. The Janus face of Brussels: socialization and everyday decision making in the European Union. *International organization*, 59 (4), 937–971.

Lewis, J., 2008. Strategic bargaining, norms and deliberation. *In*: D. Naurin and H. Wallace, eds. *Unveiling the council of the European Union: games governments play in Brussels*. Basingstoke: Palgrave Macmillan.

Lindberg, L., 1963. *The political dynamics of European economic integration*. Stanford: Stanford University Press.

Lindberg, L.N. and Scheingold, S.A., 1970. *Europe's would-be polity. Patterns of change in the European community*. Englewood Cliffs: Prentice-Hall.

Lindberg, L.N. and Scheingold S.A. eds., 1971. *Regional integration. Theory and research*. Cambridge, MA: Harvard University Press.

Mazey, S., 1995. The development of EU equality policies: bureaucratic expansion on behalf of women? *Public administration*, 73 (4), 591–609.

Monar, J., 2005. A new area of freedom, security and justice for the enlarged EU? The results of the European convention. *In*: K. Henderson, ed. *The area of freedom, security and justice in the enlarged Europe*. Basingstoke: Palgrave Macmillan.

Moravcsik, A., 1998. *The choice for Europe. Social purpose & state power from Messina to Maastricht*. Ithaca and New York: Cornell University Press.

Moravcsik, A., 1999a. A new statecraft? Supranational entrepreneurs and international cooperation. *International organization*, 53 (2), 267–306.

Moravcsik, A., 1999b. Theory and method in the study of international negotiation: a rejoinder to oran young. *International organization*, 53 (4), 811–814.

Norman, P., 2003. *The accidental constitution*. Brussels: EuroComment.

Peterson, J., 1995. Playing the transparency game: consultation and policy-making in the European commission. *Public administration*, 73 (3), 474–492.

Pollack, M.A., 1997. Delegation, agency and agenda setting in the European community. *International organization*, 51 (1), 99–134.

Pollack, M.A., 2003. *The engines of European integration*. Clarendon: Oxford University Press.

Sandholtz, W., 1993. Institutions and collective action: the new telecommunications in Western Europe. *World politics*, 45 (2), 242–270.

Sandholtz, W. and Zysman, J., 1989. 1992: Recasting the European bargain. *World politics*, 42 (1), 95–128.

Stone Sweet, A. and Sandholtz, W., 1997. European integration and supranational governance. *Journal of European public policy*, 4 (3), 297–317.

Stone Sweet, A., Sandholtz, W., and Fligstein, N., 2001. *The institutionalization of Europe.* Oxford: Oxford University Press.

Tallberg, J., 2002. Delegation to supranational institutions: why, how, and with what consequences? *West European politics*, 25 (1), 23–46.

Tallberg, J., 2003. *European governance and supranational institutions.* London: Routledge.

Tallberg, J., 2006. *Leadership and negotiation in the European Union.* Cambridge: Cambridge University Press.

Tallberg, J., 2008. Bargaining power in the European council. *Journal of common market studies*, 46 (3), 685–708.

Wincott, D., 1995. Institutional interaction and European integration: towards an everyday critique of liberal intergovernmentalism. *Journal of common market studies*, 33 (4), 597–609.

Zwolski, K., 2009. Euthanasia, gay marriages and sovereignty: polish ratification of the Lisbon Treaty. *Journal of contemporary European research*, 5 (3), 82–96.

Interviews

(1) The European Commission: 25 interviews in 2004 (COM1–COM25).
(2) The European Council Secretariat: nine interviews in 2004 (CON1–CON9).
(3) The European Parliament: five interviews in 2004 (EP1–EP5).
(4) The Permanent Representations of the Member States and the Missions to the EU of Candidate Countries: 26 interviews in 2004 (PR1–PR26).
(5) NGOs in Brussels: 11 interviews in 2004 (NGO1–NGO11).

Point of no return? The European Parliament after Lisbon and Stockholm

Ariadna Ripoll Servent

Sussex European Institute, University of Sussex, Sussex, UK

The entry into force of the Treaty of Lisbon has raised new expectations in the area of freedom, security and justice (AFSJ). The extension of co-decision increases the capacity of the European Parliament (EP) to have an influence on decision-making. This article engages with securitisation theories in order to analyse the evolution of the AFSJ as well as the role of its main actors in the securitisation process. It evaluates the past role of the EP as well as the recent changes introduced by the extension of co-decision in order to establish whether it will become a new securitising actor or will have the potential for de-securitisation of the agenda. The macro-institutional changes in the Treaty of Lisbon indicate that the EP will have opportunities to de-securitise, although the emphasis on EU citizens' rights introduced in the Stockholm programme offers it a chance to appeal to domestic audiences at the expense of more diffuse issues such as immigration and asylum.

A date to remember for the area of freedom, security and justice (AFSJ) will be 1 December 2009. With the entry into force of the Treaty of Lisbon and the Stockholm programme, this day signals the start of a new institutional and policy framework. Although the repercussions will affect the EU as a whole, these instruments will have a particular impact on the European Parliament (EP). The EP has generally been restricted to the sidelines on issues related to security, but has steadily increased its powers in each successive treaty reform. With the Treaty of Lisbon, the EP's role in the AFSJ has been expanded significantly, including it almost fully into decision-making and therefore increasing its legislative influence. The institutional framework established by the Treaty is accompanied by a revamped policy agenda set by the 5-year Stockholm programme.

These substantial changes raise new expectations in relation to the direction and purpose of the AFSJ. The new Treaty accords a more prominent place to this policy area by placing it second in its aims[1] – even before the establishment of an internal market. It also facilitates and streamlines decision-making by formally removing the three-pillared structure. In consequence, the ordinary legislative procedure (i.e. co-decision with the EP and qualified majority voting (QMV) in the Council of the EU (Council)) is extended to areas formerly ruled under unanimity in the Council and a mere role of consultation for the EP. In consequence, the EP will now have a chance to intervene in particularly sensitive areas such as counter-terrorism and police and judicial cooperation in criminal matters.

On the other hand, the Stockholm programme (Council of the European Union 2010b) is a multi-annual working programme setting the priorities for the AFSJ over the next 5 years. A follow-up to the Tampere and the Hague programme, it sets out the policy priorities of the EU, both in terms of general principles and specific operational instruments. In this sense, the Stockholm programme complements and develops the policy issues already introduced in the Treaty of Lisbon. The programme, agreed by the European Council, sets the policy-agenda for the period 2010–2014, leaving little leeway to the Commission or the other EU institutions to propose instruments not foreseen in the programme. It is thus an essential instrument to define the goals of the AFSJ and specify the mechanisms necessary to achieve these goals.

The enhanced role of the EP opens new questions in the debates surrounding the AFSJ. The area, characterised by its emphasis on security at the expense of freedom and justice (Mitsilegas *et al.* 2003), has been dominated for a long time by inter-governmental dynamics. National security actors have been mostly responsible for formulating and defining European security during the last decades, and this has sidelined supranational institutions – especially the EP and the European Court of Justice (ECJ). In this particular framework, the EP has developed a reputation for engaging in a strategy of contestation that questions the given balance between security and liberty.

In view of this long-term strategy, consecutive institutional changes enhancing the role of the parliament in the AFSJ have raised new expectations for the future of the policy area. First in 2005, when co-decision was extended to most first-pillar issues,[2] and most recently with the entry into force of the Treaty of Lisbon, the enhanced role of the EP has been perceived as a chance to open up the political debates (Donnelly 2008, p. 21) and find a more balanced approach to security and liberty (House of Lords, European Union Committee 2008, pp. 114–117).

In order to analyse the potential role of the EP in redefining European security and opening up the debate surrounding the necessity and proportionality of specific measures, the study engages with recent reflections and reconceptualisations of securitisation (and de-securitisation) theories derived from the Copenhagen school. The first section reviews the evolution of the AFSJ from the perspective of securitisation, discussing the limitations of its classical understanding in the context of EU governance. Since the purpose of the article is to analyse the role of the EP in processes of securitisation and de-securitisation, the second section focuses on securitising actors in the AFSJ, both during the intergovernmental period and since the extension of co-decision to most first-pillar issues in 2005. Finally, the last part engages with both primary and secondary sources as well as information extracted from interviews carried out during 2009 and 2010, in order to analyse the current developments in the light of securitisation theory.

Securitisation and the area of freedom, security and justice

Securitisation theory in EU studies: beyond the Copenhagen school

The introduction of securitisation in the area of security studies amounted to a minor revolution during the 1990s. Breaking with the traditional and rather narrow conceptualisations of security during the cold war, the concept of securitisation enlarged the field of study and broke with the neo-realist mainstream. As formulated by the Copenhagen school, securitisation considers that 'labelling something as a security issue imbues it with a sense of importance and urgency that legitimises the use of special measures outside of the usual political process to deal with it' (Smith 1999, p. 85). Securitisation is thus 'the move that takes politics beyond the established rules of the game and frames the issue either as a special kind of politics or as above politics' (Buzan *et al.* 1998, p. 23).

In order to become securitised, an issue has to first enter the realm of politics, i.e. become an object of policy-making or policy-speaking and then be addressed inside the public debate as an issue linked to security. During this two-step process, the issue grows to be constructed as a threat to a (equally constructed) referent object (e.g. state, identity, values, etc.) (Buzan *et al.* 1998, p. 23). Consequently, de-securitisation is understood as 'the shifting of issues out of emergency mode and into the normal bargaining process of the political sphere' (Buzan *et al.* 1998, p. 4). In the case of the EU, de-securitising an issue would imply discussing the necessity and proportionality of specific measures as well as contesting the security rationale underpinning the AFSJ.

The Copenhagen school emphasises three elements: the speech act (understood as a performative *moment*); the securitising actors; and the audience. However, these notions have revealed themselves to be rather narrow, especially when they are applied to EU policies and policy-making (Stritzel 2007, Balzacq 2008, McDonald 2008, Baker-Beall 2009). Given the specific governance system of the EU and its relationship with national arenas, the concept of securitisation needs to be redefined and expanded in the direction taken by Stritzel (2007), namely towards a sequential practice embedded in a historic, political and social context. An analysis of the AFSJ from a long-term and contextualised understanding of securitisation is more adequate to appreciate its dynamics and evaluate the current state of play.

Context, practices and audiences of securitisation in the area of freedom, security and justice

In order to understand the practices of securitisation in the EU, it is essential to go beyond the *speech act* as a moment of uttering security and understand it as a process of long-term institutionalisation (Bigo 1998, Huysmans 2006, McDonald 2008). EU security discourses amalgamate and build on different dynamics that give a specific sense and content to the AFSJ. From the TREVI groups – organised as a form of inter-governmental cooperation, mostly focused on organised crime and internal terrorism – to the Schengen agreement, the construction of an internal space of security and freedom of movement has been built around the idea of *compensatory measures*, i.e. internal instruments that compensate for the removal of internal borders (Geddes 2000, Melis 2001, Monar 2001, Huysmans 2006). In this sense, external borders have become the cornerstone of internal security policies in the EU, thereby linking internal security to migrants and foreigners as a whole.

The linkage between migration and security was enhanced during the 1990s by conflating asylum and economic migration under the same umbrella and stressing their weight on domestic societies and economies. From the 1990s, member states have hardened both immigration and asylum discourses and practices, a tendency translated at EU level with the construction of common policies (Geddes 2000). The terrorist attacks of 11 September 2001 created a new impetus for security discourses, transforming terrorism into a new *master signifier*, a legitimising tool that is embedded in a process of *macro-securitisation* developed at the system level (Buzan and Wæver 2009, p. 267). Along the same lines, Baker-Beall (2009) has shown how EU counter-terrorism measures link terrorism to migration through narratives of *otherness* and risk prevention.

However, in order to understand the process of securitisation at EU level, it is important to go beyond discourses and include institutional practices (Bigo 1998) and tools (Balzacq 2008). Given the nature of EU governance, the capacity of the European Union to produce positive legislation is limited (Lavenex and Wagner 2007). In consequence, most actions undertaken in the AFSJ are of a regulatory nature, anchored in legal definitions of security and threats. Neal (2009, p. 337) appropriately questions 'whether any of the EU institutions have the constitutional, institutional, political or legal capacity to "use extraordinary means" or "violate rules that otherwise would bind"'. Instead, EU practices and tools have developed a *governmentality of unease* that by using technical controls such as databases and biometrics has developed a *security continuum* that reinforces the link between migrants and security (Bigo 1998, 2000).

In this sense, Balzacq (2008) has identified specific tools such as databases – for instance the Schengen Information System (SIS) or the Visa Information System (VIS) – as (unexpected) sources of securitisation due to their potential to profile and control movement for counter-terrorism purposes. The result is that practices of securitisation have shaped the AFSJ by emphasising control and profiling techniques around the border, preventing entrance – mostly by using visa policies (Melis 2001, p. 133, Guild and Bigo 2003) – and facilitating removal from the territory, as exemplified by the recent initiatives on *returns* (European Parliament & Council of the European Union 2008) and *readmission* (Bouteillet-Paquet 2003).

Finally, the question of audiences has also been put to the front, due to the difficulty in identifying a European public (Balzacq 2005). Neal (2009) has underlined the differences between national dynamics of securitisation, where speech acts uttered by securitising actors – especially political leaders – are easy to broadcast through national media, and the diffuse linkage between EU actors and audiences that remain domestic and disconnected from EU messages. However, audiences can be understood as a social context with which discourses need to resonate in order to be effective. For instance, Buzan and Wæver (2009, p. 274) indicate how the US *Global war on terror* is becoming less effective as a legitimising tool, since its message is losing resonance with the US audience, especially when it involves infringements of domestic civil liberties. As will be shown in the following sections, a similar development is taking place in the EU, where infringements on data protection are becoming less tolerated by domestic audiences, especially when one compares it to the reactions offered when third-country nationals' rights are reduced.

In spite of these caveats, a politically, historically and socially contextualised theory of securitisation accords better chances to identify processes of securitisation in the AFSJ that are not limited to discourses but encompass practices and tools.

Securitising actors in the area of freedom, security and justice before Lisbon

The inter-governmental period

As in any process of securitisation, not everybody is in the necessary position to transform an issue into a security element. To be successful, the securitising actor has to possess a *security capital* that legitimates the discourse. This capital gives the necessary authority to add a performative element to the speech act or institutional practice. In the EU, securitising actors are diverse but have been limited for a long time to the inter-governmental side of EU governance. National representatives in the Council as well as security agencies understood in its largest conception – from national police, army or intelligence services to EU-wide networks gathered in agencies such as Frontex or Europol – have been at the core of European security discourses and have constructed different sources of legitimacy for the AFSJ (Lavenex and Wagner 2007). As perceived holders of security knowledge, they have a wider legitimacy and capacity to change neutral or politicised issues into security issues. It is, however, important to underline that this capacity to create security is not stable but contingent on dynamics of competition, domination and change among securitising actors (Bigo 2000).

In the case of national representatives, cooperation at a higher level has developed an 'autonomy-seeking behaviour' among security actors (Lavenex 2006, p. 332). By pushing security issues up to the European level, national actors have constructed a new field where they share a set of definitions, semantics, technology, etc. that is independent from national networks, yet not completely disconnected from them (Bigo 2000, p. 185, Huysmans 2006, pp. 91–95). They have also used Europe to *venue-shop*, in order to bypass national constituencies, parliaments or political debates (Guiraudon 2000). In consequence, security actors and politicians have had a complete freedom to develop the policies and definitions that suited them best, often playing with ideas that could not have been used at home. Besides, they have been able to shape the AFSJ at will, since the intergovernmental nature of this area has left the EP, the ECJ – and for a long time the Commission – sidelined.

Securitising the European Parliament under co-decision?

The exclusion of the EP and the ECJ has been related to the facility with which the AFSJ has been securitised. Their absence is perceived as a missed opportunity to create more open debates that could have attempted to de-securitise the AFSJ. It is also assumed that unanimity in the Council has also pre-empted positive integration and enhanced minimum standards, characteristic of the AFSJ (Lavenex and Wagner 2007). In consequence, the end in 2005 of the 5-year transitional period instituted by the Treaty of Amsterdam was seen as a turning point for the AFSJ.

In practice, the change to co-decision meant that the EP would have the possibility to co-legislate with the Council, a traditional arena for securitising actors. The full inclusion of the EP in decision-making raised high expectations. The EP was seen as a venue for de-securitisation: on the one hand, it was expected that it would open debates, narrow the democratic gap and make this area more responsive to citizens' needs (Maurer 2001, Carrera and Geyer 2007). On the other hand, it was expected that the long-standing pro-civil liberties orientations of the EP would tip the balance towards a more rights-based approach (Grabbe 2002, Guild and Carrera 2005). The extension of co-decision has not fulfilled these expectations. However, if one examines the functioning of co-decision and its norms of behaviour, the lack of success at de-securitising is not surprising. Under co-decision, the EP has essentially faced a point of no return whereby it has had to choose between de-securitisation and inclusiveness.

During the inter-governmental period, the EP remained an outsider since consultation was the main decision-making procedure in the AFSJ. Under consultation, the Commission had the power to initiate legislation – although in this area it was often shared with member states – and the Council was the sole legislator. In consequence, the EP had only the right to submit an opinion that was often ignored or only partially taken into account by the Commission or the Council (Kostakopoulou 2000, p. 498, Peers 2006, p. 26). Over the years, the role of outsider made it easier for the EP to develop a taste for confrontation because opposing the Council bore no political consequences.

Co-decision[3] incorporated an EP with a long-term engagement for de-securitisation but also a low security capital in the eyes of the Council and other security actors. Co-decision also demanded consensual behaviour from the EP which was necessary for agreement between institutions, but in particular between the Council and EP (Shackleton 2000). As a consequence, it faced the choice of either pursuing a strategy of de-securitisation that would have been blocked by the Council or engaging in consensual behaviour with the Council in order to become a legitimised actor in the field of internal security. Due to its past behaviour, the EP was subjected to increasing pressure from the Council and external observers demanding a change in its behaviour so that it started acting *responsibly*, i.e. that, as co-legislator, it assumed the political consequences of EU decisions and acknowledged its participation in them (Alvaro, Busuttil, Hennis-Plasschaert, Weber, MEPs, interviews 2009, 2010).

The need to find agreements that could be accepted by all the parties involved (EP political groups, Commission and Council) made it necessary to dilute radical proposals. It became very difficult for the EP to change the content of policies diametrically, i.e. to engage in processes of de-securitisation. Recent examples such as the *Data Retention* directive or the *Returns* directive show how the change to co-decision has transformed de-securitisation into a synonym for *irresponsibility* in the EP (Ripoll Servent 2009).

As an examination of the Treaty of Lisbon and the Stockholm programme will show, the incapacity to de-securitise is especially prominent in those issues where consensus in the EP is weaker and where the audiences are more diffuse. In broader areas such as migration and border issues it is more difficult to target specific audiences since they do not create rights for EU citizens and therefore are less likely to have an electoral impact. On the other hand, data protection, which does provide rights for EU citizens, enjoys a wider consensus and draws the attention of domestic audiences. As it will be shown, this distinction between those issues creating rights for citizens and those having broader audiences is crucial to understand where the AFSJ is going and where are the prospects for de-securitisation.

Streamlining the area of freedom, security and justice: after the Treaty of Lisbon and into the Stockholm programme

In order to evaluate the performance of the EP under the Treaty of Lisbon and the new Stockholm programme, it is necessary to examine the content of both texts and identify those instruments that might bring the EP closer to the securitising mainstream and those that might offer some chances of de-securitisation. The Treaty of Lisbon and the Stockholm programme offer a division of labour in defining practices and audiences. While the former identifies new fields of practice and macro-institutional dynamics that might present new opportunities and challenges for the EP, the Stockholm programme develops the future policy framework by enhancing the identification of target audiences.

Practices and macro-institutional challenges under the Treaty of Lisbon

After a difficult inception and ratification process, the Treaty of Lisbon saw the light on 1 December 2009. The new Treaty introduces considerable modifications to the AFSJ. In terms of substance, the Treaty does not introduce many new competences but it does widen the scope of existing competences, such as asylum (art. 78 TFEU[4]), and it streamlines some other policy issues such as data protection, previously divided between the first and the third pillar (art. 16 TFEU[5]). In macro-institutional terms, the Treaty introduces some major changes, especially in relation to the governance structure of the AFSJ. First and foremost, Lisbon formally eliminates the pillar structure thus extending the community method to most issues included in the old third pillar (police and judicial cooperation in criminal matters). Most AFSJ issues are now dealt with under the ordinary legislative procedure, namely co-decision with the EP and QMV in the Council.

Although policy-making will certainly become simpler, more transparent, easier to understand and will be subjected to a higher degree of protection due to the extended role of the ECJ,[6] the dynamics of intergovernmentalism could still affect the AFSJ. On the one hand, some matters remain outside the community method. For instance, family law is still ruled by consultation with the EP and unanimity in the Council, while other issues such as maintenance of law and order, internal security cooperation and coordination among national security authorities, passports and other identification documents continue to have an intergovernmental character or are kept outside the EU framework.

On the other hand, the Treaty foresees the possibility for a group of member states to initiate legislation in certain matters. Article 76 TFEU opens the possibility for a quarter of member states to propose legislation in judicial cooperation in criminal matters, police cooperation and administrative cooperation, with the Commission having only the right to provide an opinion. This new provision has already created some inter-institutional tensions and uncertainties, since two proposals on the *right to interpretation and to translation in criminal proceedings* have been submitted to the EP for consideration, one coming from 13 member states and a later version coming from the Commission (Council of the European Union 2010a, European Commission 2010).

These exemptions from the rule – together with other AFSJ particularities, such as the British, Irish and Danish opt-outs – maintain an element of exceptionality in the area and a potential to retain an intergovernmental flavour that can help maintain the *security capital* of member states as well as their chances of venue-shopping. Given the continuity of some core elements of intergovernmentalism, what are the chances offered by the Treaty to the EP in terms of de-securitisation?

The main opportunity opened up to the EP is the possibility to streamline decision-making in the AFSJ, leaving co-decision as the main procedure. This means that the EP will have more chances to intervene in matters intimately linked to national security, such as terrorism and police cooperation. However, the experience of co-decision both in the AFSJ and other policy areas should serve as a note of caution. The extension of co-decision does not always offer more open debates. The norm of consensus leads to early agreements and informal practices which are not always a synonym for more transparency or better chances for smaller groups or individual Members of the European Parliament (MEPs) to influence policy outcomes (Neuhold 2001). Therefore, although the extension of co-decision benefits the EP as a whole, especially by tipping the inter-institutional balance towards an EP-Council bilateral relationship, it has to be taken with caution when examining the extent of transparency and openness offered internally to its members.

This has immediate consequences for de-securitisation. Fewer chances to openly debate issues and include diverging voices mean that the capacity of the EP to actively engage in de-securitisation is quite limited, especially if the larger political groups engage in a dialogue with the Council in order to find solutions regarded as *responsible* at the inter-institutional level. This is indeed the strategy of the European People's Party (EPP), the centre-right group in the EP, now the largest group in the chamber and therefore potentially the biggest obstacle to de-securitisation. However, co-decision has also affected the behaviour of smaller groups. It is especially important to look at the behaviour of the liberal group Alliance of Liberals and Democrats for Europe (ALDE): traditionally an active de-securitising actor, the pressure of co-decision is now forcing it to find a new policy line that combines its long-term tradition with a more pragmatic approach towards coalition-building that will allow its members to participate fully in negotiations (MEP assistant, interview 2009).

However, even if co-decision becomes the normal legislative procedure and is accepted internally and inter-institutionally as the default rule of the game, one should not overrule the possibility that the EP finds other opportunities to engage in contestations of the predominant discourse. In the light of its history (Priestley 2008), it is more than probable that the EP will use any new provision introduced by the Treaty of Lisbon that may help it broaden its prerogatives. These provisions could be used to limit any attempt to broaden the process of securitisation.

The first option, consultation, is the most obvious contestant in the near future. Given that the EP has used this procedure to contest the understanding of security offered by the Council in those issues still ruled under the consultation procedure, it might try to maintain this long-term behaviour and present its own alternative understandings of security. However, since they will probably be marginal issues, a confrontational behaviour might be viewed as less adequate if the norm of consensus grows and becomes accepted as the appropriate inter-institutional behaviour.

A second option might see the EP use the new provisions that give national parliaments an oversight over subsidiarity principles. In the AFSJ, it is easier for national parliaments to stop proposals on the ground of a violation of subsidiarity. Article 7 of the *Protocol on the application of the principles of subsidiarity and proportionality* attached to the Treaty specifies that, in this area, only a quarter of national parliaments are needed to force the Commission to reconsider the proposal and issue a new text. For any other issue, the number of national parliaments necessary to stop an act raises to one third. Therefore, the lower number of negative opinions needed to stop a proposal might make it easier for the EP or some of its political groups to mobilise national parliamentarians in order to oppose a proposal, especially in a very sensitive area at the domestic level.

However, the intervention of national parliaments has not raised a lot of enthusiasm in Brussels. Some EU officials (interviews, 2010) have expressed doubts, since they consider that national parliaments generally lack expertise and they question their capacity to coordinate and react in the short time foreseen by the Treaty. Raunio (2009) also underlines some difficulties in creating links between MEPs and national MPs, for instance problems of synchronising their respective calendars or the priority given to party contacts and national ministries over EP sources when requiring information. He also points to other difficulties in activating the early warning system, such as the implausibility that a majority of MPs will oppose their government if they belong to the same party. Finally, he also underlines that in practice the subsidiarity principle is rarely violated. All these concerns make it difficult to envisage how the EP could use this instrument in its favour in order to broaden the debate and engage domestic audiences. The possibility is, however, always there and the EP is well-known for using its prerogatives to their greatest extent.

Finally a more promising instrument that the EP can develop to engage in an in-depth debate is the consent procedure, especially in the development of external policies. This procedure basically copies the existing assent procedure used in some international agreements and in decisions to enlarge the EU, but extends it to most international agreements affecting EU competences. The increased interest on the external dimension of the AFSJ can already be seen in the EP's resolution of 25 November 2009. The document underlines the low level of EP involvement in international negotiations – where it has only a right of consent – and the necessity to integrate better the internal and external EU policies affecting the AFSJ (European Parliament 2009b, points 12, 139).

The possibility of using the consent procedure to expand the security debate is not just a long-term option but a process that has already started. On 11 February 2010, the EP plenary decided to withdraw its support for an EU–US interim agreement on bank data transfers (the so-called SWIFT agreement, officially known as *Terrorist Finance Tracking Program* (TFTP) agreement). The refusal to support the agreement negotiated by the Council and the Commission was a warning sign from the EP, which asked to be better informed and involved in a negotiation requiring its final consent (European Parliament 2010). Although the negative vote in the EP was first and foremost a reaction to the long-term treatment that the EP had received from the Council on third-pillar matters, it has also rendered the debate on data protection more open and public.

Some MEPs – especially those working in the committee on civil liberties and justice and home affairs (LIBE) – raised concerns about the content, considering that the data protection standards were not high enough (Hennis-Plasschaert, Albrecht, Busuttil, MEPs, interviews 2010). Independently from the eventual result, the EP has set a new path for the consent procedure, since by voting 'no' it has effectively shaped the procedure, forcing Council and Commission to involve the EP in international negotiations. However, both institutions resist this attempt of the EP to be involved in negotiations and are trying to limit its role by interpreting the Treaty restrictively, namely by keeping the EP informed at all stages but not letting it participate in negotiations with third partners (European Commission, Official A, Council of the European Union, Official D, interviews 2010). The significant number of consent procedures still pending, such as the new Passenger Name Records agreements, might give a better idea of what form the procedure will take. The next consent procedures might also give us a better idea of the extent to which the EP is allowed to participate in negotiations, for instance by shaping the Commission mandates or forming part of the negotiating team.

Stockholm: targeting audiences and opening venues for de-securitisation

The entrance into force of the Treaty has coincided with the renewal of the 5-year working programme. As mentioned previously, the Stockholm programme is a crucial instrument to define the long-term agenda for the AFSJ. In this sense, it restricts the capacity of action of all EU institutions, including the EP which has to react to the objectives set by the working programme. Yet, although being bound by the contents of the programme, the EP was alien to the difficult negotiations that took place mostly under the Swedish presidency.

It is certainly difficult to assess the actual influence that the EP had on the different drafts, especially through informal channels. However, a comparison between the final version of the programme and the version proposed by the European Council days before the EP issued its resolution (European Parliament 2009b) shows few substantial changes that may be a response to an EP proposal. Moreover, some MEPs have expressed their 'regret that the Council is not taking on the EP recommendations and it is blindly continuing down the path already charted, ignoring the proposals of the Parliament to the Programme' (Sophie In't Veld in ALDE Group 2009), which seems to confirm the absence of the EP during negotiations. Whether this absence was forced upon them or chosen is a matter for discussion. A diplomatic source (interview, 2010) has noted that the EP itself was not especially interested or active during the negotiations, probably because its members knew that they would not have much influence on the final result.

In terms of substance, the new Stockholm programme, and the reaction offered by the EP to it, present an interesting development and the start of new dynamics both for EU security as a whole and for the EP's role in particular. In general terms, during the last 5 years European security has evolved towards a better balance between security and liberty in the AFSJ. This does not mean, however, that the main rationale of this policy-area has significantly changed. Security remains the main focus of interest and although the Stockholm programme seems to offer a more balanced approach, past experience raises a note of caution and requires one to wait until specific policies are implemented. The last Commission scoreboard evaluating the implementation of the Hague programme for 2008 identified citizenship rights, mutual recognition in criminal matters and police cooperation and regular immigration as the weakest links of the programme and where progress had been less substantial (European Commission 2009).

Regular immigration and integration measures are indeed a good example of this lack of balance between security and liberty. In contrast to irregular immigration, where several legislative measures have been decided in the past years, regular immigration and especially integration of third-country nationals have been developed mostly via a quasi-OMC (Open Method of Coordination), which tends to regulate only minimum standards and leaves a wide room of manoeuvre for member states (Guild *et al.* 2009). Certainly, some of these shortcomings have been attributed to the existence of unanimity in the Council, but even under QMV one still needs a substantial group of member states that want a specific piece of legislation and are ready to put liberty in front of security in order to de-securitise the AFSJ. Even if the EP achieves an internal majority wishing to introduce such changes, it will still need some core member states to support its views and to mobilise the rest of the Council. In consequence, if member states are reluctant to agree on specific matters such as integration of third-country nationals, then the Stockholm programme might suffer the same fate as its predecessors.

However, the Stockholm programme does open new doors to the EP, since its policy orientations might be used by political groups to target different audiences. The working programme introduces a key differentiation in the beneficiaries of rights, with an emphasis on EU citizens' rights that is new to the debate dealing with the adequate balance between security and liberty. Previously, this debate did not specify for whom there should be more liberty, while now the stress is on the need to 'strike a better balance between security *of citizens* (...) and the protection of their individual rights; provide *citizens* with fair access to justice; and settle the practical problems which *citizens* face in the European Union in matters subject to different legal orders' (EP President Jerzy Buzek in European Parliament 2009a, emphasis added). Similarly, the EP has underlined that '*EU citizens*' rights and rights of protection, especially data protection, must be preserved'(European Parliament 2009b, point I, emphasis added). Some MEPs have even signalled that the new prerogatives given by the Treaty of Lisbon on fundamental rights seem to be confined to EU citizens' rights and do not to extend to third-country nationals (Flautre 2009, p. 2).

It is, however, not difficult to understand why MEPs might have an interest in stressing the benefits EU rights provide to citizens. Issues such as data protection or procedural rights, privileged by MEPs, provide more rights essentially to EU citizens. Therefore, it is not surprising that the EP has made such issues its battleground for de-securitisation (especially data protection, on which it had more chances to legislate during the last 5 years). The SWIFT agreement, mentioned above, is a perfect example of such rewarding victories. With a negative vote on the agreement, the EP has been able to secure a victory in future consent procedures while at the same time portraying itself as the protector of EU citizens' data (European Union, Official D, interview 2010). In consequence, EP political groups have rallied around data protection issues because they offer a clear chance to fight for EU citizens concerns and thus appeal to domestic audiences. MEPs depend after all on re-election; therefore, putting an emphasis on EU citizens' rights is politically more rewarding than being very liberal on migration matters, a hot topic in most national arenas and one with very diffuse audiences.

As a result, data protection and citizens' rights such as legal procedures might emerge as the most consistent inter-institutional battles, with the EP claiming a more balanced approach and a reconsideration of such topics as a security matter. The same though is not to be expected for those issues that do not openly accord more rights to EU citizens. Issues such as migration, borders or terrorism, among others – where both threats and audiences are very diffuse – will open new areas of conflict inside the EP and offer chances to bring the EP into the securitising mainstream. Past examples, such as the *Returns* or the *Sanctions* (European Parliament & Council of the European Union 2008, 2009) directives, follow this pattern already: both directives show a more sympathetic approach to security, closer to the Council's views, especially compared to other data protection proposals.

This evolution pleases the members of the EPP group in particular, who see it as a step towards a more *realistic* form of policy-making (Speiser, EPP-ED political advisor; Weber, Busuttil, MEPs, interviews 2009, 2010). For instance, Simon Busuttil, EPP Co-ordinator in the LIBE committee, has emphasised the preference of his political group for a more cautious approach to the AFSJ given that 'a rights-based approach for a common policy [is] fine as long as it remain[s] a *realistic* policy that [takes] into account the concerns of both immigrants as well as countries that are shouldering a disproportionate influx' (Simon Busuttil in Mizzi 2010, emphasis added).

The latter point is also revealing. It seems indeed that some MEPs have been more successful at emphasising the need for burden-sharing (understood as solidarity between member states), especially in issues related to irregular immigration and asylum, than on de-securitising them. The Stockholm programme approaches migration and border issues mainly as a question of solidarity and partnership stating that 'the development of a forward-looking and comprehensive European migration policy, based on solidarity and responsibility, remains a key policy objective for the European Union' (Council of the European Union 2010b, par. 5). The idea of solidarity and responsibility is understood as 'a comprehensive and sustainable European migration and asylum policy framework, which in a spirit of solidarity can adequately and proactively manage fluctuations in migration flows and address situations such as the present one at the Southern external borders' (Council of the European Union 2010b, par. 59).

However, the understanding of security that prevails in the area of irregular immigration has not changed, since the document also mentions that 'it is necessary to prevent, control and combat illegal migration as the EU faces an increasing pressure from illegal migration flows and particularly the Member States at its external borders, including at its Southern borders' (Council of the European Union 2010b, par. 5). The same point has been stressed also by MEPs in their resolution by vigorously demanding that 'the principle of solidarity between Member States, and between Member States and the Union, takes on particular significance in the AFSJ and must be converted into active, compulsory solidarity particularly as regards border control, immigration, civil protection and the solidarity clause' (European

Parliament 2009b, point 6), although the document also corroborate the principles of return and circular migration developed during the last few years.

Therefore, the Stockholm programme and the response to it by the EP show that there is an increasing division between beneficiaries of rights. In consequence, MEPs seem ready to engage in de-securitising – or at least seeking a better balance between security and liberty – those cases where audiences are more aware of the implications and can reward their efforts, while keeping a lower profile in more diffuse issues such as migration or borders. In the latter, pragmatism and burden-sharing seem to be forefront in the agenda; substituting the older claims for higher human rights standards in issues such as asylum or immigration.

Conclusion

Simon Busuttil expressed in a recent occasion that his group 'wants a citizen's [*sic*] Europe and a *safer* Europe, with the *emphasis on the second element*' and that he 'regretted that in the draft resolution, "the axis on *security* seems to have been *watered down*"' (Simon Busuttil in Euractiv 2009, emphasis added). Such a statement is in itself a reflection of the transformation undergone by the EP during the last 5 years. Under the old governance system, the EP – for the most part excluded from inter-institutional negotiations – was able to engage in processes of de-securitisation, contesting the definition of European security as well as the necessity and proportionality of the measures proposed.

Five years after the introduction of co-decision, the EP is not the same institution that entered with cautious steps the co-decision game. It has become a more *responsible* actor, accepting thus its share in the construction of an EU area of internal security. As a consequence, its chances to de-securitise the AFSJ have diminished notably. Although the EP has been successful in tempering the language and contents of legislation, all the agreements reached under co-decision maintain a predominant security rationale. The EP might have been able to slightly tip the balance between security and liberty but it has not been successful in bringing issues such as asylum, immigration or even data protection out of the security sphere.

Indeed, the culture of consensus prevailing in co-decision has actually helped to bring the EP closer to the mainstream and turned it into a *responsible* partner for the Council, traditionally the main arena for securitisation among EU institutions. Certainly, the move towards the mainstream is not equally accepted by all political groups in the EP. While left-wing political groups show more reticence, the larger groups seem readier to accept the move towards the mainstream. As Busuttil's words show, the centre-right has become bolder in its policy stances, taking advantage of its central position as the largest group in the chamber. However, co-decision has also affected the behaviour of other groups: for instance, the liberal group (ALDE) is now trying to find a new policy line that combines its long-term tradition of pro-liberties beliefs with a more pragmatic approach towards coalition-building that will allow its members to participate fully in negotiations.

In the light of the new Treaty and the Stockholm programme, the position of the EP is deemed to evolve again. Co-decision will now become the normal decision-making procedure, forcing those that still hang on the long-term culture of de-securitisation developed under the consultation procedure to either find new strategies or be sidelined. Even the new macro-institutional changes introduced by the Treaty of Lisbon leave little leeway to engage in such strategies of de-securitisation. With the consultation procedure left to residual issues and an improbable use of national parliaments to support a broader political debate, the only possibility rests in the enlarged consent procedure. The negative vote on a bank-data sharing agreement with the USA (SWIFT) seems to indicate that the right of the EP to give its consent on international agreements might be the new weapon used to de-securitise. By publicising the political debates and questioning the content of such agreements, especially when they are related to data protection, the EP can successfully question the understanding of security behind the agreements and the necessity to link data protection with counter-terrorism.

Indeed, issues such as data protection or procedural rights seem to be the future potential area of de-securitisation. The Stockholm programme seems to emphasise the rift between audiences. With a growing contestation regarding the appropriate-ness and necessity of data protection and procedural rights infringements for the purposes of fighting terrorism, the EP might capitalise on such issues in order to engage in big inter-institutional battles. Other subject matters that do not accord direct rights to citizens and thus appeal to more diffuse audiences will probably become a new field of ideological confrontation and thus more difficult to de-securitise. There, the relative weight of political groups and the capacity of key players to convince a majority of MEPs as well as the Council might provide a chance to at least temper the extent of securitisation; however, it is difficult to imagine that in such sensitive areas a complete U-turn towards a rights-based approach will soon see the light.

Acknowledgements

An earlier version of this article was presented at the conference on 'European Internal Security Policies – After the Stockholm Programme: An area of freedom, security and justice in the European Union?' in Salford. I wish to thank all participants for their input and especially the editors of this special issue, Christian Kaunert and Sarah Léonard. I would also like to thank Jörg Monar and Paul Taggart for their support and comments, as well as Alex Mackenzie and Dan Keith for their feedback and linguistic help.

Notes

1. Article 3(2) TEU: The Union shall offer its citizens an area of freedom, security and justice without internal frontiers, in which the free movement of persons is ensured in conjunction with appropriate measures with respect to external border controls, asylum, immigration and the prevention and combating of crime.
2. Family law and legal migration, together with third pillar matters (police and judicial cooperation in criminal matters) continued to function under consultation and unanimity in the Council.
3. Since the expansion of co-decision took place in 2005, i.e. during the same parliamentary term (2004–2009), it can be assumed that the positions of MEPs did not shift fundamentally and that external factors such as enlargement might have had only a minor effect (for instance, only four new MEPs joined the LIBE committee after the 2007 enlargement).
4. Article 78 establishes the necessity to create a common asylum policy, requiring uniform standards instead of the previous minimum standards.

5. Article 16 TFEU states the right to the protection of personal data processed by EU bodies or member states when carrying out activities related to EU law and provides for EU competences on freedom of personal data.
6. Note that all instruments agreed before the entrance into force of the Treaty of Lisbon will be subjected to a 5-year transitional period that will prevent the ECJ from examining them.

Notes on contributor

Ariadna Ripoll Servent is a DPhil candidate at the Sussex European Institute, University of Sussex, UK.

References

ALDE Group, 2009. *Liberals and democrats push for balance between security and fundamental rights*. Available from: http://www.alde.eu/en/details/news/liberalsand-democrats-push-for-balance-between-security-and-fundamental-rights-4/ [Accessed 27 January 2010].

Baker-Beall, C., 2009. The discursive construction of EU counter-terrorism policy: writing the 'migrant other', securitisation and control. *Journal of contemporary European research*, 5 (2), 188–206.

Balzacq, T., 2005. The three faces of securitization: political agency, audience and context. *European journal of international relations*, 11 (2), 171–201.

Balzacq, T., 2008. The policy tools of securitization: information exchange, EU foreign and interior policies. *Journal of common market studies*, 46 (1), 75–100.

Bigo, D., 1998. Sécurité et immigration: vers une gouvernementalité par l'inquiétude? *Cultures & conflits*, 31–32, 13–38.

Bigo, D., 2000. When two becomes one: internal and external securitisations in Europe. *In*: M. Kelstrup and M.C. Williams, eds. *International relations theory and the politics of European integration: power, security and community.* London: Routledge, 171–204.

Bouteillet-Paquet, D., 2003. Passing the buck: a critical analysis of the readmission policy implemented by the European Union and its member states. *European journal of migration and law*, 5, 359–377.

Buzan, B. and Wæver, O., 2009. Macrosecuritisation and security constellations: reconsidering scale in securitisation theory. *Review of international studies*, 35 (2), 253–276.

Buzan, B., *et al.*, 1998. *Security: a new framework for analysis.* Boulder: Lynne Rienner.

Carrera, S. and Geyer, F., 2007. The reform treaty and justice and home affairs-implications for the common area of freedom, security and justice. *CEPS policy brief*, 141. Available from: http://www.ceps.eu/book/reform-treaty-justice-and-home-affairs-implications-comm on-area-freedom-security-and-justice [Accessed 11 August 2009].

Council of the European Union, 2010a. Initiative for a directive of the European parliament and of the council on the rights to interpretation and to translation in criminal proceedings, 2010/0801/COD. Brussels.

Council of the European Union, 2010b. The Stockholm programme – an open and secure Europe serving and protecting the citizens, 5731/10. Brussels.

Donnelly, B., 2008. Justice and home affairs in the Lisbon Treaty: a constitutionalising clarification? *Eipascope*, 1. Available from: http://aei.pitt.edu/11043/01/20080509184107_SCOPE2008-1-4_BrendanDonnelly.pdf [Accessed 18 March 2010].

Euractiv, 2009. Parliament split on 'progressive' Swedish immigration programme. *Euractiv.* Available from: http://www.euractiv.com/en/socialeurope/parliament-split-progressive-swed ish-immigration-programme/article-186266 [Accessed 18 March 2010].

European Commission, 2009. Communication from the Commission to the Council, the European Parliament, the European Economic and Social Committee and the Committee of the regions. Justice, freedom and security in Europe since 2005: an evaluation of the Hague programme and action plan, COM(2009) 263 final. Brussels.

European Commission, 2010. Proposal for a directive of the European Parliament and of the Council on the right to interpretation and translation in criminal proceedings, COM(2010) 82 final. Brussels.

European Parliament, 2009a. *MEPs and national MPs debate Stockholm programme.* Available from: http://www.europarl.europa.eu/news/expert/infopress_page/008-64530-320-11-47-901-20091116IPR64527-16-11-2009-2009-false/default_en.htm [Accessed 18 March 2010].

European Parliament, 2009b. Resolution of 25 November 2009 on the communication from the commission to the European Parliament and the council – an area of freedom, security and justice serving the citizen – Stockholm programme, P7_TA-PROV(2009)0090. Brussels.

European Parliament, 2010. Recommendation on the proposal for a Council decision on the conclusion of the agreement between the European Union and the United States of America on the processing and transfer of financial messaging data from the European Union to the United States for purposes of the Terrorist Finance Tracking Program, A7-0013/2010. Brussels.

European Parliament & Council of the European Union, 2008. Directive of 16 December 2008 on common standards and procedures in Member States for returning illegally staying third-country nationals, 2008/115/EC, Official journal, L348/98. Brussels.

European Parliament & Council of the European Union, 2009. Directive of 18 June 2009 providing for minimum standards on sanctions and measures against employers of illegally staying third-country nationals, 2009/52/EC, Official journal, L 168/24. Brussels.

Flautre, H., 2009. *Programme de Stockholm: analyses et perspectives.* Available from: http://europeecologie.eu/IMG/article_PDF/article_a635.pdf [Accessed 18 March 2010].

Geddes, A., 2000. *Immigration and European integration: towards fortress Europe.* Manchester: Manchester University Press.

Grabbe, H., 2002. Justice and home affairs: faster decisions, secure rights. *CER policy brief.* Available from: http://www.cer.org.uk/pdf/policybrief_jha.pdf [Accessed 19 February 2009].

Guild, E. and Bigo, D., 2003. Le visa: instrument de la mise à distance des étrangers. *Cultures & conflits*, 49, 82–95.

Guild, E. and Carrera, S., 2005. No constitutional treaty? Implications for the area of freedom, security and justice. *CEPS working document*, (231). Available from: http://www.ceps.eu/book/no-constitutional-treaty-implications-area-freedom-security-and-justice [Accessed 18 March 2010].

Guild, E., *et al.*, 2009. Challenges and prospects for the EU's area of freedom, security and justice: recommendations to the European Commission for the Stockholm programme. *CEPS working documents*, (313). Available from: http://new.ceps.eu/ceps/download/1652http://new.ceps.eu/ceps/download/1652 [Accessed 18 March 2010].

Guiraudon, V., 2000. European integration and migration policy: vertical policy-making as venue shopping. *Journal of common market studies*, 38 (2), 251–271.

House of Lords, European Union Committee, 2008. *The Treaty of Lisbon: an impact assessment, 10th report of session 2007–08, HL Paper 62-I.* London: House of Lords.

Huysmans, J., 2006. *The politics of insecurity: fear, migration and asylum in the EU.* London: Routledge.

Kostakopoulou, T., 2000. The 'Protective Union'; Change and continuity in migration law and policy in post-Amsterdam Europe. *Journal of common market studies*, 38 (3), 497–518.

Lavenex, S., 2006. Shifting up and out: the foreign policy of European immigration control. *West European politics*, 29 (2), 329–350.

Lavenex, S. and Wagner, W., 2007. Which European public order? Sources of imbalance in the European area of freedom, security and justice. *European security*, 16 (3), 225–243.

Maurer, A., 2001. Democratic governance in the European Union: the institutional terrain after Amsterdam. *In*: J. Monar and W. Wessels, eds. *The European Union after the Treaty of Amsterdam*. London: Continuum, 96–124.

McDonald, M., 2008. Securitization and the construction of security. *European journal of international relations*, 14 (4), 563–587.

Melis, B., 2001. *Negotiating Europe's immigration frontiers.* The Hague: Kluwer Law International.

Mitsilegas, V., *et al.*, 2003. *The European Union and internal security: guardian of the people?* Houndmills: Palgrave Macmillan.

Mizzi, K., 2010. *MEP addresses CEPS on Stockholm programme.* Available from: http://www.simonbusuttil.eu/default.asp?module = news&ID = 10957 [Accessed 27 January 2010].

Monar, J., 2001. The dynamics of justice and home affairs: laboratories, driving factors and costs. *Journal of common market studies*, 39 (4), 747–764.

Neal, A.W., 2009. Securitization and risk at the EU border: the origins of FRONTEX. *Journal of common market studies*, 47 (2), 333–356.

Neuhold, C., 2001. The 'legislative backbone' keeping the institution upright? The role of European Parliament committees in the EU policy-making process. *European integration online papers (EIoP)*, 5 (10). Available from: http://papers.ssrn.com/sol3/papers.cfm?abstract_id=302785 [Accessed 19 February 2009].

Peers, S., 2006. *EU justice and home affairs law.* 2nd ed. Oxford: Oxford University Press.

Priestley, J., 2008. *Six battles that shaped Europe's Parliament.* London: John Harper.

Raunio, T., 2009. National parliaments and European integration: what we know and agenda for future research. *The journal of legislative studies*, 15 (4), 317–334.

Ripoll Servent, A., 2009. Setting priorities: functional and substantive dimensions of irregular immigration and data protection under co-decision. *Journal of contemporary European research*, 5 (2), 225–242.

Shackleton, M., 2000. The politics of codecision. *Journal of common market studies*, 38 (2), 325–342.

Smith, S., 1999. The increasing insecurity of security studies: conceptualizing security in the last twenty years. *Contemporary security policy*, 20 (3), 72–101.

Stritzel, H., 2007. Towards a theory of securitization: Copenhagen and beyond. *European journal of international relations*, 13 (3), 357–383.

Refugee protection as a collective action problem: is the EU shirking its responsibilities?

Eiko Thielemann[a] and Nadine El-Enany[b]

[a]London School of Economics and Political Science, London, UK; [b]Brunel University, Middlesex, UK

Refugee protection efforts have been shown to suffer from substantial collective action problems due to the capacity of restrictive policy measures adopted by one region as a means of shifting refugee responsibilities to other regions. Such responsibility-shifting dynamics have been identified between north and south as well as within these regions. European Union (EU) cooperation on asylum and refugee policies has been criticised for facilitating the adoption of restrictive policy measures and the creation of a 'Fortress Europe'. Fears about the hollowing out of refugee standards have been coupled with concerns about the EU's free-riding on the refugee protection efforts of countries outside the EU. This paper shows that overcoming collective action problems between the Member States has indeed been a key motivation for EU cooperation in this area. However, a comparative analysis of EU asylum laws and refugee protection efforts with those of similar developed countries outside the EU leads to the rejection of some of the assumptions and implications of the 'Fortress Europe' thesis. While there is evidence of north/south burden-shirking and substantial room for improvement in the EU's asylum and refugee regimes, comparative legal research and the analysis of available UNHCR data on other OECD countries suggests that there is no evidence to support the claim that European cooperation has led to uniquely restrictive refugee policies and protection outcomes.

Introduction

Refugee protection entails a number of collective action problems (Suhrke 1998, Betts 2003, Thielemann 2003, Thielemann and Dewan 2006, Roper and Barria 2010). The basic challenge of the international refugee regime is that the responsibilities of states under the 1951 United Nations Convention Relating to the Status of Refugees and its 1967 Protocol (the Refugee Convention) are limited to those asylum seekers that arrive on their territory. Only once the asylum seeker has reached the territory of a signatory state is that state required to engage in an often time-consuming and costly process of determining whether or not she deserves protection and therefore access to a series of rights, including residence, in that state. States face no similar obligations for forced migrants and refugees outside their territory. This provides states with an incentive to discourage or prevent asylum seekers from seeking protection on their territories, or to encourage them indirectly to seek protection elsewhere.

The Stockholm programme highlights the increasingly influential role that the European Union (EU) plays in the management of asylum seekers and refugees in Europe. Asylum has long been considered a potential threat to internal security by European policy-makers. Such treatment of a traditionally humanitarian policy area has led to allegations of the building of a 'Fortress Europe'. It is a widely held view that EU cooperation on asylum policy has facilitated the introduction of restrictive asylum policies in Europe, making it increasingly difficult for asylum seekers to reach European territory and benefit from effective protection. This has been termed by some as the 'Fortress Europe' thesis (Geddes 2000, Luedtke 2009). According to this thesis, Member State cooperation on asylum and refugee matters has fostered restrictiveness through processes of 'venue shopping' (Guiraudon 2000), 'securitisation' (Huysmans 2000) and the legitimisation of 'lowest common denominator standards' (Lavenex 2001). This increase in restrictions is said to have limited the ability of asylum seekers to seek and find protection in Europe. This means that forced migrants who seek protection in the north have to turn to other developed countries outside the EU, effectively allowing the EU to free-ride on the protection efforts of other states.

This paper shows that the desire to overcome such collective action problems and free-riding incentives between the Member States has indeed been a key motivation for EU cooperation in this area. However, a comparative analysis of EU asylum laws and refugee protection efforts with those of similar developed countries outside the EU leads one to reject the key assumptions and implications of the 'Fortress Europe' thesis. While there is indeed evidence of north/south burden-shirking and while there remains substantial room for improvement in the EU's asylum and refugee regimes, comparative legal research and the analysis of available UNHCR data on other OECD countries, such as the US, Canada or Australia, suggest that there is no evidence to support the claim that European cooperation has led to particularly restrictive refugee policies and protection outcomes in the EU.

We will first set out the conceptual arguments derived from the literature on collective action before providing an analytical overview of EU asylum and refugee policies. This is followed by a comparative analysis of EU legal standards with those in other OECD countries. Finally, we will scrutinise the available UNHCR data on asylum and refugee protection trends.

Refugee protection as a collective action problem: motivation for and consequences of EU cooperation

The collective action challenges of refugee protection facing policy-makers stem from the requirement in the Refugee Convention for states to assess whether a claimant is a refugee only once she has reached its territory. The procedure for doing so is often lengthy and states incur costs both at this initial application stage and once refugee status is granted, with both triggering entitlements for the individual migrant. States face no similar obligations to forced migrants and refugees outside their territory. This provides states with an incentive to use restrictive policies in an attempt to limit the number of asylum seekers that are able to access their territories and indirectly to encourage them to seek protection in another country or region.

Several scholars (Suhrke 1998, Betts 2003, Thielemann 2003, Thielemann and Dewan 2006, Roper and Barria 2010) have claimed that refugee protection has some important 'public good' characteristics. Suhrke (1998) argues that all states benefit from some countries providing refuge to displaced persons. In her view, increased security is the principal (non-excludable and non-rival) benefit as the accommodation of displaced persons may reduce the risk of their causing the conflict from which they are fleeing to spread or simply limit the disruptions caused by large-scale movements of asylum seekers across borders. As with the provision of other international public goods, such as collective defence or peace-keeping (Olson and Zeckhauser 1966, Oneal 1990, Shimizu and Sandler 2002), one might therefore expect substantial free-riding opportunities with regard to refugee protection. When introducing restrictive asylum and refugee policies, states will anticipate at least some of the protection needs to be picked up by others with them reaping parts of the benefits of such protection.

And indeed, given the substantial degree of disparities in international responsibilities outlined above, it is therefore no surprise that there have been protests and accusation of free-riding from the main receiving countries of asylum seekers as well as threats by some states to withdraw from the Geneva Convention for the Protection of Refugees. This also begs the question of why countries, in particular EU Member States, have begun to formulate common asylum and refugee policies, including refugee burden-sharing measures. For Shuck (1997, 249) the answer is hardly obvious as he writes:

> Under the existing regime, after all, states that are not states of origin or of first asylum are entirely free to join in, or refrain from, refugee protection efforts, as their interests dictate. Why then would they choose to surrender that freedom of action and accept a responsibility-sharing obligation that is likely to be costly, risk domestic political tensions, and probably ratchet upwards over time.

In the EU context, one can point to at least three possible motivations for Member States cooperation in this area: (1) promoting European integration; (2) enabling more effective protection; and (3) exploiting free-riding opportunities.

First, in the EU context, references to European solidarity and fairness as a driving force for common action should probably neither be taken at face value nor should they be dismissed outright. In a recent Commission statement, one finds the following: 'A better balance between the efforts made by the Member States in the reception of refugees and displaced persons will be achieved by means of the principle of solidarity'.[1] Another example is the EU's Temporary Protection Directive which devotes an entire chapter to the issue of Community solidarity, outlining in detail how 'soft' solidarity mechanisms are to achieve an equitable distribution in the case of a 'mass influx'.[2] While it is easy to dismiss these pledges as non-binding and therefore inconsequential, there can be little doubt that since the start of the integration process, some of the EU's most prominent political leaders have viewed expressions of Member State solidarity as an important test for the EU as an emerging political community (Thielemann 2003). Moreover, there might also be an insurance element to the idea of European solidarity in this area. A suitable responsibility-sharing regime can provide a degree of mutual insurance against the occurrence of a particular external shock that might put pressures on certain countries. Responsibility-sharing schemes allow states to set off today's contributions against the expected reduced costs in a future crisis. On the basis of an insurance rationale, it might make sense for states to accept losses in the short term in order to insure themselves against the possibility of being faced with even higher costs at some point in the future. Shuck (1997, p. 249) suggests that states

> might be attracted to burden-sharing for the same reason that many individuals are attracted to catastrophic health insurance: States may rationally prefer to incur a small and predictable protection responsibility now in order to avoid bearing large, sudden, unpredictable, unwanted, and unstoppable refugee inflows in the future.

> [...] As the world grows smaller and more interconnected, and as an increasing number of refugees can more easily reach more places and claim protection there, such 'refugee crisis insurance' might well be a 'good buy' – perhaps even for relatively insular states.

From a cost–benefit perspective, however, such a scheme can only be expected to include those who have a similar perception of risks that are worth sharing and will only be agreed upon when contributions reflect the differences in the relative risk perception of each participant. Common asylum policy and EU burden-sharing initiatives might of course also be motivated by a perceived threat to other 'higher order' objectives such as their interest averting potential threats to the Single Market. In the absence of a common European approach on refugee responsibility-sharing, migration pressures from third countries might pose a serious threat to the Single Market, in particular the achievement of the principle of free movement. In other words, a failure to agree on a common approach would lead to increased pressure for a reestablishment of border controls in the Schengen area, thus threatening the operation of the Single Market.

Second, Member States' long-standing commitments to refugee protection might enable effective protection in the context of significant collective action challenges and thus can be regarded as another possible motivation for common action. There are strong incentives for Member States to unilaterally restrict their asylum policies in an attempt to limit their responsibilities for asylum seekers and refugees. As such, uncoordinated action risks leading to a competitive 'race to the bottom' in protection standards among Member States since no country wants to be perceived as a 'soft touch' and be faced with disproportionate costs. Ultimately, such a 'race to the bottom' could lead to states adopting deterrence measures that could be considered as breaches of their obligations under international law. Arguably, responsibility-sharing initiatives can help to break this cycle of 'tit for tat' increases in deterrence measures and ensure that states adhere to their obligations under international law. The adoption of certain restrictive measures at the EU level would not necessarily contradict that rationale. Initiatives such as the Dublin Convention were introduced to prevent possible abuses of the asylum system such as the possibility of 'asylum shopping', i.e. the submission of multiple asylum applications across the EU. By preventing abuses of the European asylum system, its credibility and the public's support for the system might be maintained.

Collective free-riding incentives could be regarded as a third motivation for common EU asylum and refugee policies. Using restrictive measures to escape responsibilities and shift burdens onto other states is a dynamic that can work not only within the EU context, but also at a wider regional and global level. The EU has been accused by other states of using common external border controls and other restrictive measures to collectively shift responsibilities for asylum seekers and refugees. In particular, the EU's use of so called 'safe country' provisions have been widely criticised (Lavenex 1999, Byrne *et al.* 2002, Costello 2005). Such measures enable states to prevent asylum-seekers' access to their territory where the authorities can prove that the claimant has originated from, or passed through in transit, a safe country where either no persecution is deemed to exist or where the asylum seekers could have sought protection status. Particular countries in Eastern Europe and North Africa have consequently complained that such EU policies have effectively turned them into 'buffer zones', protecting the EU from asylum seekers that might otherwise reach Member State territory.

Bearing in mind that it is this alleged EU burden-shirking logic that is ultimately at the heart of the 'Fortress Europe' critique, it is this third alleged motivation that this paper takes as its focus. In what follows, we seek to assess to what extent such allegations of collective EU burden-shirking efforts are supported empirically. Before doing so, we will briefly summarise the EU's key legislative initiatives in this area.

The evolution of EU refugee policy

The EU has worked towards the convergence of Member States' laws on forced migration since the mid-1980s. What began as a set of non-binding intergovern-mental initiatives has since been followed by developments in EU law. Most noteworthy here are several directives that have aimed to level the asylum playing field and to lay the foundations for a Common European Asylum System (CEAS).[3] The objectives of the CEAS, to establish a common asylum procedure and a uniform protection status applicable throughout the EU, were first defined in the Tampere programme of 1999. They were then elaborated in the Hague programme of 2004 and most recently in the Stockholm programme of December 2009. In its 2007 Green Paper on the future of the CEAS, the Commission stated its 'ultimate objective' as being to create a 'level playing field, a system which guarantees to persons genuinely in need of protection access to a high level of protection under equivalent conditions in all Member States while at the same time dealing fairly and efficiently with those found not to be in need of protection' (Green Paper on the future CEAS, Brussels, 6 June 2007, COM(2007) 301 final, 2). The first stage of the establishment of the CEAS was thus designed to achieve a set of minimum standards on specific areas of asylum policy applicable in the legal systems of all Member States. Four important legislative instruments that have been adopted comprise Directive 2003/9 laying down minimum standards for the *reception* of asylum seekers (OJ L 31, 6 February 2003, p. 18), Directive 2004/83 on minimum standards for the *qualification* of persons as refugees or those in need of subsidiary protection (Council Directive 2004/83/EC of 29 April 2004 on minimum standards for the qualification and status of third country nationals or stateless persons as refugees or as persons who otherwise need international protection and the content of the protection granted (OJ L 304, 30 September 2004, p. 12), Directive 2005/85 on minimum standards on *procedures* in Member States for granting and withdrawing refugee status (O J L 326, 13 December 2005, p. 13) and finally the Directive on common standards and procedures in Member States for returning illegally staying third country nationals (OJ L 348, 24 December 2008, p. 98).

However, it is the highly problematic Dublin Convention that is central to the EU's asylum *acquis*. It provides the rules that determine the responsible Member State for dealing with a particular asylum claim. In essence, the rule states that asylum seekers who move to another Member State as a secondary movement can be sent back to the 'state of first entry'. Its principal aim is to 'establish which Member State is responsible for the examination of an asylum application lodged on EU territory [...] and to prevent secondary movements between Member States' (Commission of the European Communities 2007). The Dublin Convention remains highly controversial as it allows for the return of asylum seekers to Member States where adaptation to common EU standards remains unsatisfactory.

The Commission's 2007 Green Paper describes the underlying logic of EU policy harmonisation as a burden-sharing instrument as follows: 'Further approximation of national asylum procedures, legal standards and reception conditions, as envisaged in creating a Common European Asylum System, is bound to reduce those secondary movements of asylum seekers which are mainly due to the diversity of applicable rules, and could thus result in a more fair [*sic*] overall distribution of asylum applications between Member States' (Commission of the European Communities 2007).

The Stockholm programme has promised a common area of protection and solidarity, stating that the achievement of a CEAS is to remain high on the agenda. The commitments made in the programme have confirmed that the role of the EU in the formulation and application of asylum policy is to continue. The importance of the link between asylum and internal security that has long been the underlying premise of European policy in the field has been reiterated once more. While the CEAS remains high on the Stockholm agenda, in the same breath we find mention of the need for procedures which will be effective in preventing abuse and safeguarding security. Also a priority is effective solidarity between the Member States in tackling asylum and migration pressures. The programme promises joint processing of asylum applications as well as further development of mechanisms for voluntary and coordinated responsibility sharing between Member States. The European Asylum Support Office is to be given a central role in coordinating capacity-building measures. In late 2008 and early 2009, the Commission presented a number of legislative proposals for new versions of the asylum directives. The aim of the proposals is to begin the second phase of EU asylum policy harmonisation across Member States.

The evolution of refugee standards within the EU

In this section of the paper, we demonstrate firstly that EU Member States have seen improved refugee protection standards as a result of harmonisation of asylum policy at the EU level. We then show that EU asylum policy is not more restrictive than that of non-EU countries of equivalent wealth and development to EU Member States, focusing in particular on procedures and return policy. In this respect, we explore some aspects of Norwegian, Australian, Canadian and US asylum policy. We also assess the European Commission's recent proposals for a new round of asylum directives, arguing that they are indicative of further liberalisation of EU and Member State asylum regimes, partly as a result of changes in the governance of the CEAS that were recently consolidated with the adoption of the Lisbon Treaty.

Thielemann and El-Enany (2009) have argued that EU cooperation has had some significant rights-enhancing effects on protection standards within the EU. They have shown theoretically and empirically how European cooperation and the development of a common asylum law on the basis of EU minimum standards in this area has curtailed regulatory competition and in doing so has largely halted the race to the bottom in protection standards in the EU. Rather than leading to policy harmonisation at the 'lowest common denominator', EU asylum laws have frequently led to an upgrading of domestic asylum laws in several Member States, strengthening protection standards for several groups of forced migrants, even in the case of EU laws that have been widely criticised for their restrictive character. While many aspects of EU asylum law reflect restrictive trends similar to those in other parts of the world, some EU provisions have clearly had a positive impact not only on countries in Central and Eastern Europe, but also in some of the older Member States. In assessing the impact of EU refugee policy on protection standards in Member States, it is possible to identify various areas for analysis including procedures, qualification, reception and return. Here we have chosen to focus on the Procedures Directive and the Return Directive, primarily because these are the two policy areas that have been most contested.

Procedures

The Procedures Directive was formally adopted on 1 December 2005. The key elements that fall under the topic of asylum procedures include the question of access to procedures, procedural guarantees such as the opportunity to communicate with the relevant authorities, access to an appeal process as well as the procedure for the withdrawal of refugee status. The Directive faced calls for withdrawal (ECRE 2004) as well as general criticism from the UN High Commissioner for Refugees (UNHCR 2004) and from within the EU institutions (European Parliament 2004). However, the Directive can be seen to have improved standards of protection for individuals accessing EU territory in some Member States. The 'safe third country' provisions in the Directive can also be seen as having undergone rights enhancement during the negotiations on the Directive. As Ackers (2005, p. 30) reports, 'There were drafting sessions which resulted in considerably improving the text on rules with respect to the individual consideration in safe third country cases'. The Commission has stated that the first instance procedures are fully in accordance with the essential rights provided for in Section 192 of the UNHCR Handbook on procedures and criteria for determining refugee status (1979) (Ackers 2005, p. 32). What is more, on appeal, the provisions it includes on judicial scrutiny go beyond the Handbook in requiring Member States to ensure an effective remedy before a court or tribunal as opposed to merely 'a formal reconsideration of the decision, either to the same or to a different authority, whether administrative or judicial, according to the prevailing system' (UNHCR 1979). Further, in a report published by the Refugee Council in 2007 on the UK's implementation of the Procedures Directive, the Refugee Council makes clear that the standards of the Directive would require an improvement of standards in the UK. Article 8(1), for example, states that 'Member States shall ensure that applications for asylum are neither rejected nor excluded from examination on the sole ground that they have not been made as soon as possible' (Refugee Council 2007, p. 7).

Return

The Directive on common standards and procedures in Member States for returning illegally staying third country nationals ('the Directive') was approved by the European Parliament on 18 June 2008, formally adopted by the Council on 9 December 2008 and published in the *Official Journal* on 24 December 2008. The Directive applies to all EU Member States except the UK, Ireland and Denmark.[4] It also covers Iceland, Norway, Switzerland and Liechtenstein. The Return Directive[5] is the most ambitious asylum instrument that the EU has adopted concerning return until now. The Directive provides for a set of rules to be applied throughout the return and removal process, for example, concerning the form of the relevant decisions, the use of coercive measures, detention and safeguards pending return. Although national legislation generally provides that the confinement of returnees should take place in special facilities, different to those in which ordinary prisoners are detained, this is not always the case in practice in all EU countries – in Ireland, for example, returnees are regularly held in prisons (Hailbronner 2005, p. 144). Significant differences also prevail in the Member States in relation to whether the detention of vulnerable groups, such as minors is permitted (Hailbronner 2005, European Parliament 2005). The Directive subjects detention to the principle of proportionality, providing that deprivation of liberty is justified 'only to prepare return or carry out the removal process and when the application of less coercive measures would not be sufficient' (Recital 16). Detention orders that are not issued by judicial authorities have to provide for the possibility of judicial review, although no deadlines are specified (Article 15.2). Custody should be sustained for as short a period as possible, and only as long as removal arrangements are in progress and executed 'with due diligence' (Article 15.1). In summary, not only are there powerful constraints on the downgrading of existing standards in the Member States, but we can also expect several protection-enhancing dynamics to result from the adoption of the Directive. In states where currently detention and entry bans can last indefinitely, Member States will have to change their national legislations in order to establish upper time limits.

The analysis of these two EU directives suggests that European cooperation and the development of the common asylum law on the basis of EU minimum standards in this area has curtailed regulatory competition and in doing so has largely halted the race to the bottom in protection standards in the EU. In more recent years, rather than leading to policy harmonisation at the 'lowest common denominator', EU asylum law has increasingly led to an upgrading of domestic asylum laws in several Member States, strengthening protection standards for forced migrants.

While there currently remain significant variations in Member States' implementation of EU asylum law, we expect that the ongoing 'communitarisation' of asylum policy will help to improve Member States' implementation records of EU asylum law and further strengthen refugee protection outcomes in Europe. This may already be seen to be taking place with the recent presentation of the European Commission's proposals for a second round of asylum directives, discussed in more detail below. Therefore, although the EU might have disappointed some of those who had hoped that it would do more to address the shortcomings of the international refugee regime, the evidence presented in this paper has shown that that the effects of European cooperation on asylum and refugee matters have not been invariably and uniquely negative and that on balance regional cooperation has strengthened rather than undermined refugee protection in Europe.[6]

EU refugee standards relative to those in other OECD countries

EU refugee policy has not become a uniquely restrictive policy as compared with other non-EU OECD countries. Restrictive practices found in the EU asylum regime are also found in the regimes of non-EU OECD countries. A number of elements of non-EU OECD countries' regimes will be examined here to determine their level of restriction as compared with the EU. The specific elements explored will be that of the 'safe third country' concept presently found in the EU Procedures Directive and return policy that finds its expression in the EU Return Directive.

Procedures

Perhaps the most contentious aspect of the Procedures Directive was its inclusion and expansion of the safe country concept. The concept, however, features in asylum regimes besides those of EU Member States. Norway operates a safe country provision. Since 1 January 2004, a '48-hour procedure' was introduced for asylum seekers originating from safe countries. The procedure involves the interviewing of the asylum seeker followed by the taking of a decision on the case by the Directorate of Immigration (UDI). The Norwegian Government asserts that this accelerated procedure 'does not entail less thorough processing of each individual application but that the case will be processed immediately by the UDI'.[7] In Norway, applicants subjected to the accelerated procedure are entitled to make an appeal and will receive legal assistance. However, such applicants cannot expect to remain in Norway while awaiting the outcome of their appeal. The government states that 'The police will transport most of them out of the country within three days' of the initial rejection of their application by the UDI.[7]

Australia also makes use of the safe country concept. The Australian Government asserts that it does not 'owe protection obligations' to asylum seekers who would otherwise be 'adequately protected in a safe third country' to which they can be sent (Department of Immigration, Procedures Advice Annual 3). Since 16 December 1999, Section 36(3) of Australia's Migration Act states that Australia is taken not to have protection obligations to a non-citizen who has not taken all possible steps to avail himself or herself of a right to enter and reside in, whether temporarily or permanently and, however, that right arose or is expressed, any country apart from Australia, including countries of which the non-citizen is a national. UNHCR's position is that Australia's reliance on the safe third country concept in such cases is potentially in breach of accepted international legal standards. According to UNHCR, the safe third country notion does not allow states to send individuals to countries with which they have no meaningful connection in the absence of a written guarantee from the receiving country that protection will be provided there.

The USA has also incorporated the safe country concept into its asylum legislation. A safe third country is defined as safe by the Secretary for Homeland Security as one in which an individual's 'life or freedom would not be threatened' on any Convention ground, and which provides 'access to a full and fair procedure for

determining a claim to asylum or equivalent temporary protection' (INA §
208(a)(2)(A), 8 USC § 1158(a)(2)(A)). In the USA, an applicant cannot appeal the
decision to bar the applicant from asylum on the basis of the safe third country
principle (INA § 208(a)(3), 8 USC § 1158(a)(3)). Canada also has a safe third country
agreement with the USA, effective since 2004. Under the agreement, a refugee must
claim protection in the first country of the two in which it arrives. Therefore, an
individual crossing the US–Canada border is liable to being sent back to the USA by
the Canadian authorities to claim protection there first.

Return

The 'return turn' is not a phenomenon exclusive to the EU, but one that affects other
Northern States (Gibney and Hansen 2003, pp. 11–12, Gibney 2008, p. 148). The
degree of restrictiveness of return policies in non-EU countries is comparable to that
of EU Member States, particularly as regards the detention of irregular migrants and
asylum seekers. Detention practices in Australia are illustrative of this point.
According to the Australian Department of Immigration and Citizenship, Australia's
1958 Migration Act provides that people who are unlawfully in Australia can be
detained indefinitely.[8] In 2005, Amnesty International (2005, p. 2) reported that
'Australia's longest serving immigration detainee, a rejected Kashmiri asylum seeker,
Peter Qasim, [had] been in detention since September 1998'. In December 2003, 'the
average detention time in the case of children was one year, eight months and eleven
days' (Amnesty International 2005, p. 2). The 'flexibilisation' of this policy which
took place in June 2005 included the introduction of some limited forms of non-
judicial revision in prolonged detention cases (Parliament of Australia 2005, p. 5).
Nevertheless, the lack of review by the courts has led the UN Human Rights
Committee to declare that Australia is in breach of Article 9 of the International
Covenant on Civil and Political Rights prohibiting arbitrary detention on a number
of occasions (Amnesty International 2005, p. 10).

In Canada, the 2001 Migration and Refugee Protection Act broadened the
circumstances allowing for detention.[9] Detention decisions are reviewed by the
officers of the Canada Borders Service Agency, first after 48 hours, then after 7 days
and then once a month. Detainees can also bring their cases before the Federal Court
of Canada at any time.[9] Nevertheless, there are no maximum time limits as to how
long a person can be held in custody.[9] Concerning the USA, the detention of asylum
seekers has risen in the political agenda after 11 September (Migration Information
Source 2005). In 2007, the Department of Immigration and Customs Enforcement
(ICE) detained 311,213 people for immigration violations, more than three times the
number detained in 2001 (Migration Information Source 2008). The Immigration
and Nationality Act provides for an initial detention period of 90 days, which can be
prolonged if the person concerned refuses to cooperate with the removal process.[10]
Nevertheless, while in 2003 the ICE reported an average stay in detention of 64 days,
it was estimated that persons subject to asylum procedures spent an average of 10
months in custody (Migration Information Source 2005).

Within the non-EU European context, the restrictiveness of detention policies in
Switzerland has also been increased recently. In September 2006, Swiss voters
decided in a referendum to introduce tough new laws allowing the detention of failed
asylum seekers, including children, for up to 2 years.[11] UNHCR condemned the new

laws as possibly being in breach of the United Nations Convention on the Rights of the Child.[11] In application of the Schengen Agreement, Switzerland must now bring its national legislation in line with the Returns Directive and thus reduce maximum deadlines for detention, an obligation which has been criticised by Swiss political parties favouring restrictive policies.[12] In contrast, rules regulating detention are significantly more lenient in Norway, where custody is limited to a maximum of 12 weeks and is reviewed automatically by a court every fortnight.[9]

The examples of the safe country concept and that of return policy have shown that EU policy in relation to asylum seekers is no more restrictive than that of non-EU countries in equivalent positions of wealth and development. In fact, as the previous section has shown, what the EU has succeeded in doing through its formulation of binding minimum standards is to halt the race to the bottom in asylum standards by preventing Member States from being able to adopt measures in the harmonised areas which go below the EU minimum standard. This is not the case for non-EU countries, which in theory can introduce new restrictive measures unfettered. Also discussed in the previous section is the likelihood that the role the EU plays in formulating common policy will in fact lead to improved standards of protection.

This is exemplified in the recent Commission proposals for a new round of legislative measures, which in their current form improve upon the present minimum standards. In respect of the proposal for a new Procedures Directive, the most contested of the initial directives, the changes introduced include reducing the exceptions to the procedural principles and guarantees provided for in the current Procedures Directive. UNHCR has pointed out that in some Member States, a personal interview is not conducted in cases subjected to accelerated procedures (UNHCR 2010). The possibility for this has been deleted in the Commission's recast proposal. The proposal also provides for additional guarantees, including the entitlement to free legal assistance for international protection applicants at first instance. In Article 27, the proposal revises the conditions for the use of accelerated procedures, delimiting a list of exhaustive grounds for the use of such procedures in manifestly unfounded cases. For vulnerable applicants, special guarantees are introduced, including their exemption from accelerated or border procedures. Furthermore, the proposal aims to broaden access to asylum procedures by broadening the scope of application of the directive, expressly including the territorial waters of Member States,[13] as well as clarifying the obligations of border guards, police and staff of detention centres in relation to asylum applicants.[14] The proposal deletes the notion of a common list of safe countries of origin.[7]

The proposal for the new Procedures Directive is not the only one to include rights-enhancing aspects. Through its proposal to recast the EU Reception Directive (COM(2008) 815 final), the Commission aims to establish higher common reception standards for asylum seekers across the EU. The changes proposed in the recast proposal are significant. For example, the scope of the directive would be extended to cover applicants for subsidiary protection. The recast proposal also seeks to facilitate access to the labour market for asylum seekers. Article 15(1) of the proposal provides that 'Member States shall ensure that applicants have access to the labour market no later than 6 months following the date when the application for international protection was lodged'. As for the Qualifications Directive, the Commission put forward its proposal for a new version in 2009. It provides for the creation of a uniform status for those qualifying as beneficiaries of subsidiary protection by prohibiting Member States from restricting the rights available to the latter. Article 2(h)(j) of the proposal extends the definition of family members to include married minor children, another adult relative responsible for a minor and minor unmarried siblings. It also provides that minor unmarried children no longer have to be dependent.

The Commission's proposals have proved contentious in their removal of Member State discretion over a number of aspects of asylum, particularly in relation to the proposal for a new Procedures Directive in an effort to achieve harmonisation (House of Commons European Scrutiny Committee 2010). The UK and Ireland have opted out of the new asylum Directives, the former expressing discomfort at the limiting of Member State discretion. It should be remembered, however, that the institutional framework in the context of which these new directives will be negotiated and perhaps adopted is very different to that in which the first set of directives were agreed. No longer will decision-making in the Council be on the basis of unanimity, but by qualified majority instead and the European Parliament will play the role of co-legislator under co-decision. The European Parliament has already expressed general approval for the Commission's proposals. As a result of these changes, we can perhaps expect more rights-oriented policies in the future.

European cooperation and the evolution of asylum numbers and protection contributions

The application of the collective action literature to refugee protection suggests that states have an incentive to enhance the restrictiveness of their refugee policies in order to shift responsibilities away from themselves onto others. In recent years we have seen a global trend in the implementation of restrictive measures designed to deflect and deter asylum seekers from being able to access territory and therefore protection in industrialised countries. Despite the frequent branding of European countries as being particularly restrictive in their building of a 'Fortress Europe', deflective measures such as carrier sanctions, visa regulations, safe country concepts and extraterritorial border checks and processing of claims are not merely European phenomena, but have been widely implemented by industrialised countries across the world in an effort to reduce access to territory. Although such measures are frequently justified on the ground that they are in an effort to prevent abuse of the asylum route by individuals who are seeking an economic status, they undoubtedly affect genuine refugees and irregular economic migrants alike. Not only do such measures severely affect the capacity of asylum seekers to access territories in which they can lodge protection claims, but such restrictions also impact heavily on host countries in regions of origin, which are primarily located in the south. There is no doubt that countries in the south host the vast majority of refugees. This is not merely due to their being geographically in close proximity to the majority of refugee-producing conflicts, but is also undeniably a result of the increasing limitation of access routes to protection in northern countries. In 2003, the European Commission recognised that the evident fall in recent years in the number of asylum claims made in European countries did 'not necessarily mean an overall reduction in the numbers of refugees and persons seeking international protection at a global level' (European Commission 2003, p. 7). Further, the Commission noted that 85 per cent of refugees are being hosted by countries in regions of origin struggling with limited resources, thus highlighting the fact that the distribution of forced migrants is highly unbalanced across countries and regions. The UNHCR provides comparative data on the total population of forced migrants around the world. In 2007, it estimated that there were just under 10 million refugees and almost 32 million 'individuals of concern' to the UNHCR worldwide.[15] The quantitative analysis of this paper focuses on refugee protection efforts in industrialised (OECD) countries as classified by the UNHCR.[16] While this provides for a sample of countries for which there is good comparative data, it is worth remembering that the world's richest countries are hosts only to about 20 per cent of the world's forced migrants and refugees (see Figure 1).

At a general level, there can be little doubt that restrictive practices in the north have been partly responsible for the continuation of disproportionate refugee responsibilities in the south. While north/south burden-shirking has clearly been taking place, the question we ask here is whether there is also evidence that would allow one to single the EU out as being particularly notorious – as the 'Fortress Europe' thesis implies? In other words, is there evidence to suggest that EU Member States have successfully used EU asylum and refugee policy initiatives to limit their responsibilities relative to those of comparable OECD countries? If EU protection standards have not become more restrictive relative to those of other industrialised states, as shown earlier, one would naturally doubt such a claim. And indeed, comparative analysis of UNHCR data allows us to reject the suggestion that EU refugee protection contributions have declined in relation to other OECD countries. The data confirm that there is no evidence to suggest that asylum seekers who are in a position to seek protection in industrialised countries have increasingly applied for, or been granted, protection in non-EU industrialised countries.

When looking at the evolution of total asylum applications in industrialised countries (Figure 2), one observes that the total number of asylum requests have been in decline since the early 1990s. Applications peaked during the Bosnian wars and even during the refugee producing conflicts in Kosovo, Afghanistan and Iraq in the late 1990s and in early 2000, applications remained below those of the early 1990s. To what extent this overall decline in asylum applications is the result of increasingly restrictive policy measures or simply a reflection of fewer persons seeking refugee protection is difficult to ascertain given that we have no comparable data on the evolution of refugee producing conflicts. What is clear, however, is that applications in the EU have fallen more rapidly from a much higher peak compared to other

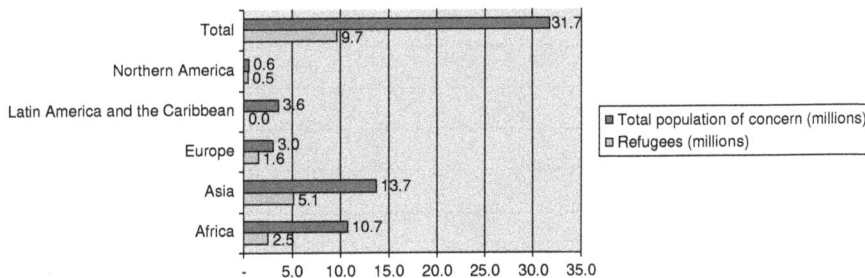

Figure 1. Population of concern to UNHCR in 2007.

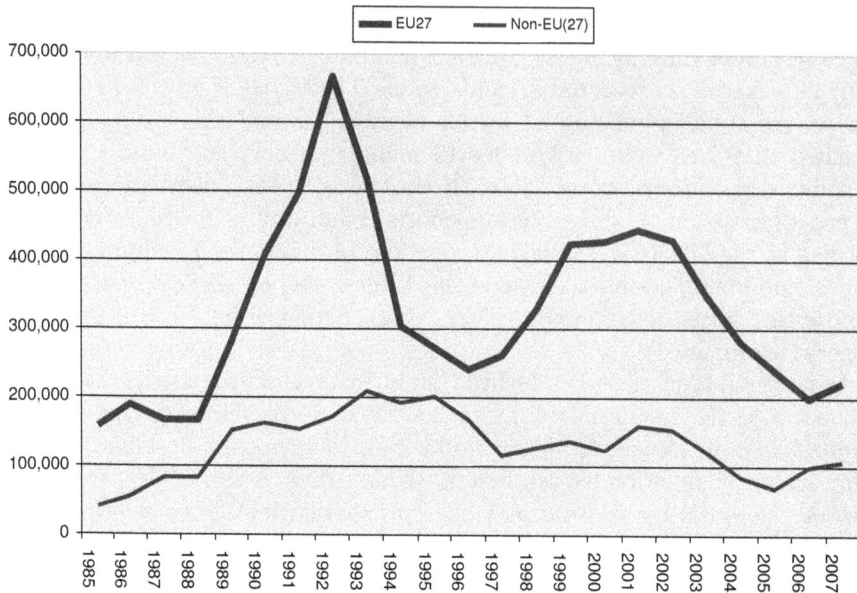

Figure 2.   Total number of asylum applications in OECD countries, 1985–2007.

industrialised countries (the most significant recipients being the USA, Canada and Australia). This can at least in part be explained by the fact that the two principal refugee producing conflicts of the 1990s (in Bosnia and Kosovo) were taking place in Europe and that more recently most of the principal countries of origin for asylum seekers have been non-European ones, for example Iraq, Afghanistan and Somalia.

A look at the evolution of application shares across industrialised countries (Figure 3) shows that the EU's share of asylum applications in the industrialised world has fluctuated, but today is similar to its share in the late 1980s.

However, a closer look at intra-EU trends (Figure 4) reveals two opposing trends among the current EU Member States. While the share of the old EU Member States

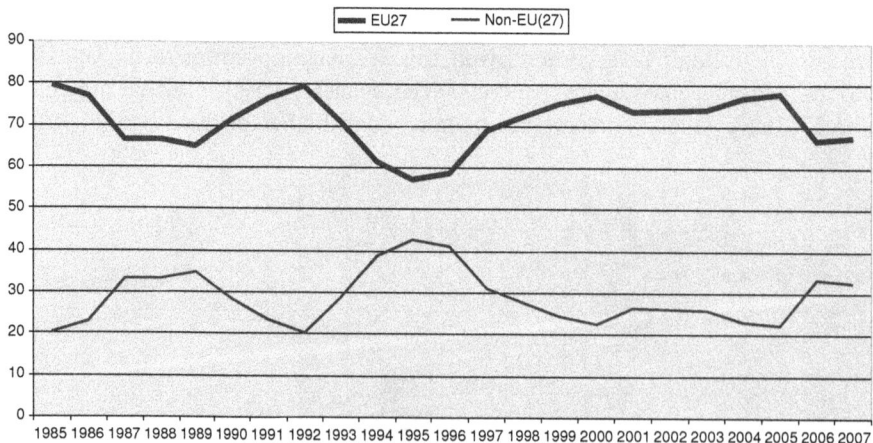

Figure 3.   Relative shares of asylum applications in OECD countries, 1985–2007.

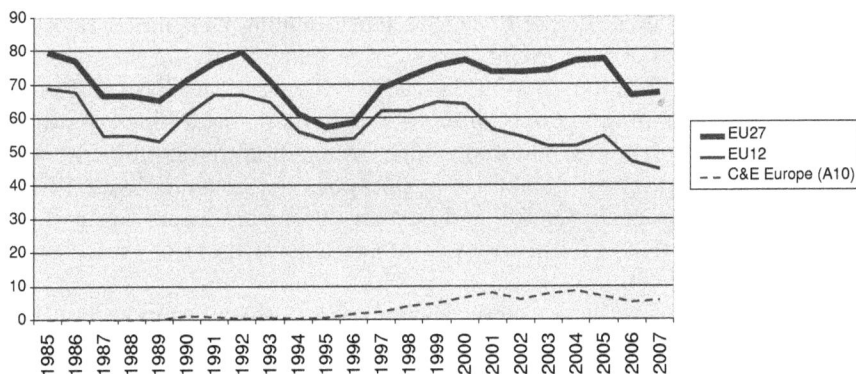

Figure 4.   Relative shares of asylum applications in Europe, 1985–2007.

has declined, it has been the increasing share of the Central and Eastern European Member States that has kept the overall EU share stable. The extent to which that trend is clear evidence of burden-shifting dynamics from west to east in the EU is, however, not clear, given that asylum applications in Eastern European countries are well below average both in terms of absolute numbers and relative to population size.

When comparing recognition rates (Figure 5), one observes a much more pronounced downward trend in the EU than in the rest of the world. In non-EU states, recognition rates have remained relatively stable, fluctuating at around 35 per cent with recognition rates being traditionally higher in North America than in the Pacific. This means that on average 35 per cent of all applicants in non-EU countries have received either refugee status or some other subsidiary protection status that has allowed them to remain legally on their territory. Recognition rates in the EU have dropped from 60 to 25 per cent over the period 1985–2005. A closer look suggests that the EU figures have converged to the lower recognition rates in Australia and New Zealand while rates in the USA and Canada have remained quite stable at a higher level (which might in part be explained by lower applications in North America compared to Europe).

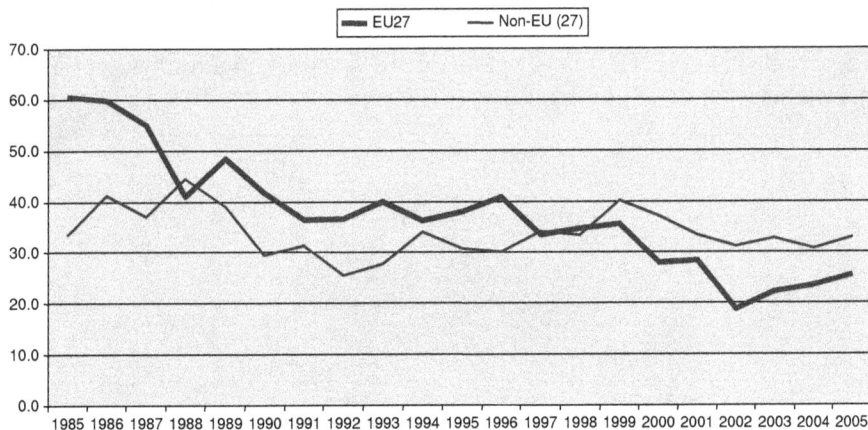

Figure 5.   Refugee recognition rates in OECD countries, 1985–2005.

The European figures (Figure 6) suggest that declining recognition rates inside the EU (27) are due to a large extent to rapidly declining figures in the countries of Central and Eastern Europe. During the early 1990s when the Eastern European states were only beginning to establish their own domestic institutions to deal with asylum-seekers and refugees, unusually high recognition rates probably were a reflection of the very small number of applications at the time. Since then, the number of asylum seekers in Central and Eastern Europe has increased significantly and recognition rates have fallen to levels comparable to those of West European states.

In order to obtain a more complete picture of host-state responsibilities, the analysis of asylum figures needs to be complemented by the examination of resettlement data.[17] While Europe continues to attract the largest share of asylum seekers in the industrialised world, it has traditionally played a minor role in resettling refugees.

If one combines the data on recognised asylum seekers and resettled refugees, one can create a measure of overall protection willingness/generosity that captures the total number of forced migrants who have been allowed to stay (Figure 7). This suggests that the protection willingness in the industrialised world was at its peak during the early and late 1990s. Non-EU states started to accept very large numbers of refugees during the Bosnian war when they gave protection status to almost twice as many forced migrants than the EU27. It appears that EU Member States were trying not to strengthen further already strong pull factors to their countries by keeping recognition rates as low as possible (some offering only temporary protection status). Since then, refugee numbers in non-EU states have declined, but have consistently (with the year 1999 being the single exception) remained above those in the EU. Accepted responsibilities temporarily increased in the 1990s in the EU (compared to the 1980s), reaching an exceptional peak during the time of the Kosovo war. Since then, however, accepted responsibilities have again declined sharply, stabilising today at levels that characterised those observed during the 1980s.

In terms of the evolution of the EU's share of overall accepted responsibilities for refugees in the industrialised world (Figure 8), one observes that the EU's shares which constituted between 60 and 90 per cent of the overall total in the 1980s, have fluctuated between 30 and just over 50 per cent since the early 1990s.

In terms of relative accepted protection responsibilities (in relation to population size, i.e. protection capacity) depicted in Figure 9, the EU figures have consistently remained below those of non-EU states over the past 20 years. This gap between EU

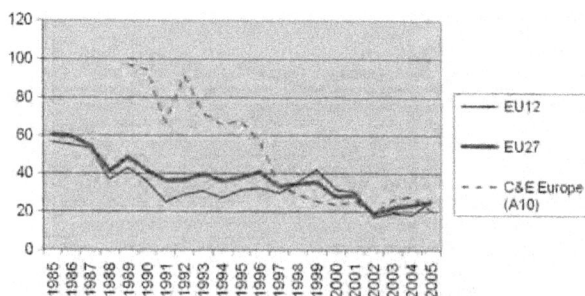

Figure 6.   Refugee recognition rates in Europe, 1985–2005.

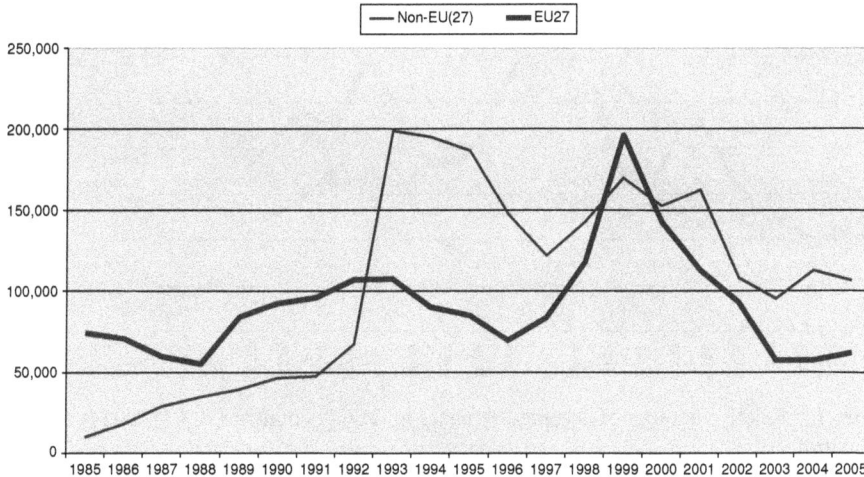

Figure 7. Total number of accepted refugees in OECD countries, 1985–2005 (recognised asylum seekers[18] and resettled refugees).

and non-EU states was widest during the early 1990s but has narrowed since. In most recent years, there has been little difference in the numbers of refugees accepted relative per population size in industrialised states which have converged to a figure of about 0.3 refugees per 1000 of population. Overall in the EU27, one can observe an upward trend (due to development in the new Member States), but compared to countries in North America and the Pacific, the EU continues to accept smaller relative responsibilities.

The analysis of the aggregate data across comparable OECD countries therefore shows that no straightforward picture emerges with regard to the impact of European integration on asylum and refugee policy outcomes in Europe. Overall, the broader impression that emerges over the past 20 years is one of stability rather than of dramatic change. There is no evidence to suggest that European integration

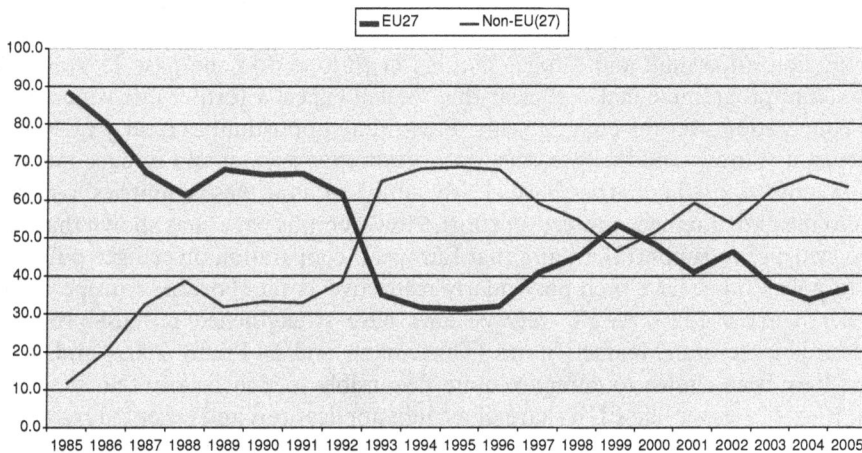

Figure 8. Total shares of accepted refugees in OECD countries, 1985–2005.

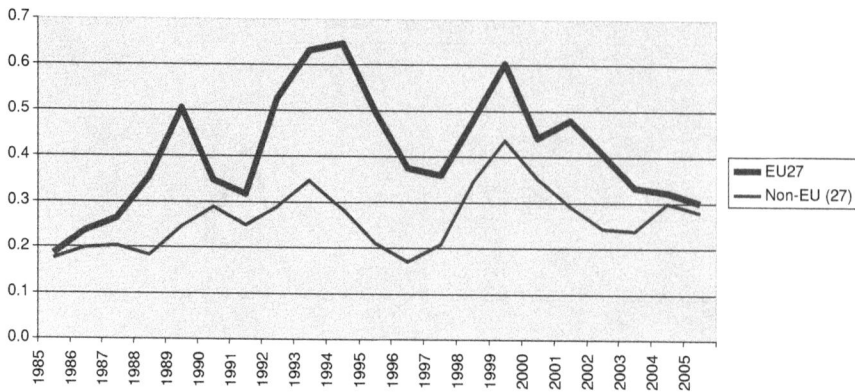

Figure 9. Relative number of accepted refugees in OECD countries, 1985–2005 (per 1000 of population).

has had a uniquely restrictive impact relative to other industrialised countries. Differences in application, resettlement and recognition figures among EU and non-EU states continue to exist partly due to country-specific factors (such as geographic, historical and political), but the above analysis has provided no evidence to suggest that there have been divergent trends of policy outcome in EU and non-EU states as a result of the European integration process. While there are clearly limits as to the EU's willingness to accept protection seekers, we do not observe a significant shift in the EU's relative figures or a rupture in EU Member States' willingness to provide protection as a result of European cooperation in this area. Within the EU we observes some redistribution of responsibilities between old Member States and new Members States with overall EU figures remaining quite stable.

Conclusion

This paper has shown how international refugee protection efforts suffer from collective action problems as states/regions have incentives to shift responsibilities for refugees to others. We have argued that the literature on collective action is useful when trying to explain the unprecedented scope and intensity of international cooperation on asylum and refugee matters in Europe over the past 25 years. The Stockholm programme makes it clear that we can expect a further intensification of this cooperation over the coming years. Free-riding opportunities clearly exist in the international arena and the introduction of restrictive asylum and refugee measures across industrialised countries have clearly aimed to limit these countries' contribution to the global refugee protection effort. However, this paper has shown that there is no evidence to support the claim that European cooperation on refugee policy has led to policies that have been particularly restrictive as the 'Fortress Europe' notion implies. On the contrary, EU refugee laws have strengthened refugee protection standards in several Member States (Thielemann and El-Enany 2009) and in key areas have been shown to compare quite favourably to policies of other developed countries. Moreover, the EU's share of asylum applications and accepted refugees in the overall OECD figures relative to other industrialised countries has not declined since the start of EU cooperation. Relative to population size, the EU today accepts protection responsibilities that are 50 per cent higher than they were in the 1980s. This analysis should divert attention away from the fact that restrictive refugee measures in the north continue to be at least partly responsible for vastly disproportionate refugee responsibilities being borne by the south. However, the walls that have been erected around the developed world stretch far beyond Europe across all OECD countries. They are clearly not 'made in the EU' nor unique to Europe as the notion of an emerging 'Fortress Europe' suggests. On the contrary, one might reasonably expect that with the additional safeguards of EU law in place, refugee protection standards behind the EU's walls will prove more resistant to calls for new restrictions than those in other OECD countries.

Notes

1. Brussels, 2 June 2004, COM(2004) 401 final, Communication from the Commission to the Council and the European Parliament, Area of Freedom, Security and Justice: assessment of the Tampere programme and future orientations, {SEC(2004)680 et SEC(2004)693}, p. 10.
2. Council Directive 2001/55/EC of 20 July 2001 on minimum standards for giving temporary protection in the event of a mass influx of displaced persons and on measures promoting a balance of efforts between Member States in receiving such persons and bearing the consequences thereof.
3. Council Directive 2003/9/EC of 27 January 2003; Council Directive 2004/83/EC of 29 April 2004 and Council Directive 2005/85/EC of 1 December 2005.
4. In accordance with Article 5 of the protocol on the position of Denmark annexed to the Treaty of the European Union, this Member State will decide within a period of 6 months from the adoption of the Directive whether to implement it in its national law.
5. Directive 2008/115/EC of 16 December 2008. *Official Journal* L348/98.
6. For a more extensive discussion, see Thielemann and El-Enany (2009).
7. See http://www.regjeringen.no/en/dep/aid/Topics/andre/asylum-and-refugee-policy/differ ential-treatment-of-asylum-seekers.html?id = 85864 [Accessed 11 September 2008.
8]. http://www.immi.gov.au/managing-australias-borders/detention/about/background.htm [Accessed 19 September 2008].
9. http://www.humanrightsfirst.org/refugees/reports/cntry_rev_02/Canada.pdf [Accessed 21 September 2008].
10. INA, Act 241.
11. 'UN condemns Swiss vote to detain failed asylum-seekers'. *The Independent*, 25 September 2006. http://www.independent.co.uk/news/world/europe/un-condemns-swiss-vote-to-detain-failed-asylumseekers-417484.html [Accessed 21 September 2008].
12. 'EU migration law has an impact on Switzerland', *Swissinfo*, 18 June 2008. http://www.swissinfo.ch/eng/front/EU_migration_law_has_an_impact_on_Switzerland.html?site Sect =105&sid =9236426&cKey =1213867867000&ty =st [Accessed 21 September 2008].
13. Article 3, Recast Procedures Directive proposal.
14. European Commission Explanatory Memorandum, note 44 above, 5, para. 3.1.2.
15. The 'population of concern to the UNHCR' includes refugees, asylum seekers, internally displaced persons (IDPs), returnees (refugees and IDPs), stateless persons.
16. The statistics of the UNHCR include data on the following 38 industrialised countries: the 27 countries of the EU, Australia, Canada, Iceland, Japan, Liechtenstein, New Zealand, Norway, Republic of Korea, Switzerland, Turkey and the USA.
17. Resettlement refers to decisions by host countries to allow individuals which have been recognised as refugees in their region of origin to relocate permanently to their territory.
18. Geneva recognition and subsidiary protection status.

Notes on contributors

Dr Eiko R. Thielemann has a Ph.D. from the University of Cambridge and is a Senior Lecturer in European Politics & Policy in the Department of Government and the European Institute of the London School of Economics. He is also the director of the LSE Migration Studies Unit (MSU) and a visiting professor at New York University (NYU). His research focuses on EU- and comparative policy-making, in particular with regard to asylum and refugee issues. He has been a guest editor for the *Journal of Common Market Studies* as well as the *Journal of Refugee Studies* and serves on as an editorial board member for the latter.

Nadine El-Enany is Lecturer in Law at Brunel University. She completed her LLB at the London School of Economics (LSE) before undertaking doctoral research at the European University Institute in Florence. She has taught European Union Law at the LSE and is presently a Research Associate at the LSE Migration Studies Unit. Her current research considers the protection implications of European refugee and migration law and policy in the context of both the European Union and the UK.

References

Ackers, D., 2005. The negotiations on the Asylum Procedures Directive. *European journal of migration and law*, 7, 1.

Amnesty International, 2005. *The impact of indefinite detention: the case to change Australia's mandatory detention regime.* Available from: http://www.amnesty.org/en/library/info/ASA12/001/2005 [Accessed 15 May 2010].

Betts, A., 2003. Public goods theory and the provision of refugee protection: the role of the joint-product model in burden-sharing theory. *Journal of refugee studies*, 16 (3), 274–296.

Byrne, R., Noll, G., and Vedsted-Hansen, J., 2002. *New asylum countries? Migration control and refugee protection in an enlarged European Union.* The Hague: Kluwer Law International.

Commission of the European Communities (Commission), 2007. *Green paper on the future common asylum system.* COM (2007) 301 final. Brussels: European Commission.

Costello, C., 2005. The Asylum Procedures Directive and the proliferation of safe country practices: deterrence, deflection and the dismantling of international protection? *European journal of migration law*, 7 (1), 35–70.

ECRE, 2004. *ILGA Europe, Amnesty International, Pac Christi International, Quaker Council for European Affairs, Human Rights Watch, CARITAS-Europe, Médecins Sans Frontières, Churches' Commission for Migrants, Save the Children in Europe, Call for withdrawal of the Asylum Procedures Directive (22 March 2004).* ECRE Country report.

European Commission, 2003. *Commission Communication of June 2003, Towards more accessible, equitable and managed asylum systems.* p. 7.

European Parliament, 2004. *European Parliament legislative resolution on the amended proposal for a council directive on minimum standards on procedures in Member States for granting and withdrawing refugee status (14203/2004 – C6-0200/2004 – 2000/0238(CNS)).*

European Parliament, 2005. *Asylum in the European Union Member States: reception of asylum seekers and examination of asylum applications.* Available from: http://www.europarl.europa.eu/activities/committees/studies/download.do?file=8959 [Accessed 15 May 2010].

Geddes, A., 2000. *Immigration and European integration, towards fortress Europe?.* Manchester: Manchester University Press.

Gibney, M.J., 2008. Asylum and the expansion of deportation in the United Kingdom. *Government and opposition*, 43 (2), 146–167.

Gibney, M.J. and Hansen, R., 2003. *Asylum policies in the west: past trends, future possibilities.* Discussion Paper No. 2003/68. World Institute for Development Economic Research.

Guiraudon, V., 2000. European integration and migration policy: vertical policy-making as venue shopping. *Journal of common market studies*, 8 (2), 251–271.

Hailbronner, K., 2005. *Refugee status in EU Member States and return policies: study.* Brussels: European Parliament.

House of Commons European Scrutiny Committee, 2010. 27 January, para. 2.3. Available from: http://www.publications.parliament.uk/pa/cm200910/cmselect/cmeuleg/5-viii/504.htm [Accessed 15 May 2010].

Huysmans, J., 2000. The European Union and the securitization of migration. *Journal of common market studies*, 38 (5), 751–757.

Lavenex, S., 2001. *The Europeanisation of refugee policies*. Aldershot: Ashgate.

Luedtke, A., 2009. Fortifying fortress Europe? The effect of September 11 on EU immigration policy. *In*: T. Givens, G. Freeman, and D.L. Leal, eds. *Immigration policy and security: US, European and commonwealth perspectives*. New York: Routledge, 130–137.

Migration Information Source, 2005. *US detention of asylum seekers and human rights*, March 2005. Available from: http://www.migrationinformation.org/usfocus/display.cfm?ID=296 [Accessed 15 May 2010].

Olson, M. and Zeckhauser, R., 1966. An economic theory of alliances. *Review of economics and statistics*, 48, 266–279.

Oneal, J.R., 1990. The theory of collective action and burden sharing in NATO. *International organization*, 44, 379–402.

Parliament of Australia, 2005. *Migration amendment (detention arrangements) bill*. No 190. Available from: http://www.aph.gov.au/library/Pubs/bd/2004-05/05bd190.pdf [Accessed 15 May 2010].

Refugee Council, 2007. *Refugee Council response to UK implementation of council directive 2005/85/EC of 1 December 2005 laying down minimum standards on procedures in Member States for granting and withdrawing refugee status*. Refugee Council.

Roper, S.D. and Barria, L.A., 2010. Burden sharing in the funding of the UNHCR: refugee protection as an impure public good. *Journal of Conflict Resolution*, 54 (4), 616–637.

Shimizu, H. and Sandler, T., 2002. Peacekeeping and burden sharing: 1999–2000. *Journal of peace research*, 39 (6), 651–568.

Shuck, P., 1997. Refugee burden-sharing: a modest proposal. *Yale journal of international law*, 22.

Suhrke, A., 1998. Burden-sharing during refugee emergencies: the logic of collective versus national action. *Journal of refugee studies*, 11 (4), 396–415.

Thielemann, E., 2003. Between interests and norms: explaining patterns of burden-sharing in Europe. *Journal of refugee studies*, 16 (3), 253–273.

Thielemann, E. and Dewan, T., 2006. The myth of free-riding: refugee protection and implicit burden-sharing. *West European politics*, 29 (2), 351–369.

Thielemann, E. and El-Enany, N., 2009. Beyond fortress Europe: how European cooperation has strengthened refugee protection. *Paper presented at European Union Studies Association's 11th Biennial International Conference*, 23–25 April 2009. Marina Del Rey, Los Angeles.

UNHCR, 1979. *Handbook on procedures and criteria for determinig refugee status under the 1951 Convention and the 1967 Protocol relating to the status of refugees*. HCR/IP/4/Eng/ REV.1 Reedited, Geneva, January 1992.

UNHCR, 2004. *Press release, lubbers calls for EU asylum laws not to contravene international law* (29 March 2004).

UNHCR, 2010. *Improving asylum procedures: comparative analysis and recommendations for law and practice*. Brussels: UNHCR.

EU border security and migration into the European Union: FRONTEX and securitisation through practices

Sarah Léonard[a,b]

[a]School of ESPaCH, University of Salford, Crescent House, Salford M5 4WT, UK; [b]Centre d'études européennes, Sciences Po Paris, 27 rue Saint Guillaume, 75337 Paris Cedex 07, France

This article examines the contribution of the activities of FRONTEX, the Agency in charge of managing operational cooperation at the external borders of the European Union (EU), to the securitisation of asylum and migration in the EU. It does so by applying a sociological approach to the study of securitisation processes, which, it argues, is particularly well-suited to the study of securitisation processes in the EU. Such an approach privileges the study of securitising practices over securitising 'speech acts' in securitisation processes. After identifying two main types of securitising practices in general, the article systematically examines the activities of FRONTEX and the extent to which they can be seen as securitising practices on the basis of these two (non-mutually exclusive) criteria. The article shows that all the main activities of FRONTEX can be considered to be securitising practices. The article therefore concludes that the activities of FRONTEX contribute to a significant extent to the ongoing securitisation of asylum and migration in the EU. It also highlights that this does not automatically make FRONTEX a significant securitising actor in its own right and that more research is needed on the relations between FRONTEX and the EU institutions, especially in the light of the current negotiations aiming to amend the founding Regulation of FRONTEX.

Introduction

Migration is one of the most contentious issues in Europe. Migratory flows, be the flows of asylum-seekers, labour migrants or irregular migrants, have been associated with various problems, including terrorism, criminality and social unrest (Weiner 1992/93, Lohrmann 2000). As a consequence, migration and asylum issues have become important topics of contemporary security politics in Europe, both in the 'real world' of policies and in the scholarly literature on the subject (Bigo 1998a, 1998b, 2001a, 2002, Huysmans 2000, 2006, Guild 2003a, 2003b, 2003c, 2009, but see also Kaunert 2009). This trend has often been referred to as 'the securitisation of migration', that is, the extreme politicisation of migration and its presentation as a security threat. There is a widespread view in the existing scholarly literature that this trend has been particularly visible in the EU asylum and migration policy (Huysmans 2000, 2006, Guild 2003a, 2003b, 2003c, Pellerin 2005, Colman 2006,

Chebel d'Appollonia and Reich 2008, van Munster 2009).[1] In other words, it is generally believed that asylum and migration have been securitised in the EU and that this evolution has had a negative impact on the status of asylum-seekers and migrants, including the protection of their human rights (Brouwer and Catz 2003, Baldaccini and Guild 2007, Chebel d'Appollonia and Reich 2008, Guild 2009).

It is in this specific context of securitisation of asylum and migration that EU Member States decided to establish the European Agency for the Management of Operational Cooperation at the External Borders of the Member States of the EU, which is better known under its acronym FRONTEX.[2] It was created by Council Regulation EC 2007/2004 of 26 October 2004 with the main aim of supporting operational cooperation amongst EU Member States with regard to the management of the external borders. One of the most remarkable aspects of FRONTEX is the considerable amount of attention that it has attracted since its operational start in 2005. Its activities have generated much controversy and have been heavily criticised especially by human rights activists and pro-migrant groups. Several blogs and websites that are critical of the actions of European states and the EU towards migrants and asylum-seekers specifically focus on FRONTEX, such as the blog entitled *Frontexwatch*[3] and the website of the Noborder network.[4] Several pro-migrant associations have rallied around a 'Shut down FRONTEX!' slogan, whilst demonstrations have taken place not only in front of the seat of the Agency in Warsaw, but also in other towns and cities where FRONTEX training sessions took place, such as in Lübeck in August 2008.[5] The German non-governmental organisation (NGO) PRO ASYL handed in a petition to the European Parliament in December 2008 that demanded notably the following: 'Stop the deathtrap at the EU borders! FRONTEX activities which violate human rights must cease!' (PRO ASYL 2008). The organisers of the actions in Lübeck denounced the 'standardisation and militarisation' of border politics represented by FRONTEX. Thus, whilst criticisms of the EU asylum and migration policy are certainly not new, it appears that, in the last few years, FRONTEX has become the focal point for the sharp criticisms of pro-migrant and human rights groups.

Given that there is a widespread view in the scholarly literature that asylum and migration have been securitised in the EU, whilst, at the same time, FRONTEX has often been depicted by human rights NGOs as having launched a 'war against migrants' (see, for example, Noborder Network 2006), it is surprising that little attention has been given to the potentially significant contribution of FRONTEX's activities to the securitisation of asylum and migration in the EU. This article precisely seeks to address the relative neglect of this issue in the existing scholarship. It is premised on the idea that, as argued by many scholars, asylum and migration had already been securitised in the EU at the time of the establishment of FRONTEX. Thus, the article does not seek to analyse how the activities of FRONTEX securitised asylum and migration in the EU for the first time, for they had already been securitised, but rather examines FRONTEX's contribution to the perpetuation of the securitisation of asylum and migration in the EU. It argues that it is necessary to do so for several reasons. First of all, the criticisms levelled at FRONTEX by pro-migrant and human rights NGOs, as well as asylum and migration law experts (see Standing Committee of Experts on International Immigration, Refugee and Criminal Law 2006) suggest that the activities of the Agency may be playing a significant role in the securitisation of asylum and migration. This role has not been fully comprehended yet, as the few existing academic articles on FRONTEX have focused on other aspects of the Agency than its potential contribution to the securitisation of asylum and migration in the EU (see Carrera 2007, Jorry 2007, Pollak and Slominski 2009). Only Neal (2009) has examined FRONTEX through the lenses of securitisation theory, but he has focused on the origins of the Agency, rather than its practices once it was established. Thus, it is necessary to systematically analyse the activities of FRONTEX and assess the extent to and the ways in which they can be viewed as constituting securitising practices. Moreover, it is important to deepen the existing knowledge of the securitisation of asylum and migration in the EU. To date, most studies of securitisation processes have tended to consider the EU as a monolithic actor and have not examined the EU internal institutional dynamics of securitisation. An examination of FRONTEX's activities, which are likely to contribute to the securitisation of asylum and migration according to NGOs' reports, constitutes a first step towards opening the 'black box' of the securitisation of asylum and migration in the EU. In addition to further developing knowledge on FRONTEX and the securitisation of asylum and migration in the EU, the article also contributes to the literature on securitisation, in particular the so-called 'sociological' approach to securitisation (Balzacq 2010) pioneered by Bigo (1998a, 1998b, 2000, 2001a, 2001b, 2002, 2008, see also Bigo and Tsoukala 2008), which privileges the role of practices over that of discourses in securitisation processes. In particular, it seeks to further refine the idea of securitising practice by developing two criteria to identify securitising practices.

The article is structured as follows. It opens with a presentation of FRONTEX, which is situated in the context of the development of the EU asylum and migration policy that has been taking place since the mid-1990s. Then, the article presents the theoretical framework that will underpin the analysis, which is embedded in securitisation theory. It explains why a so-called 'sociological' approach to securitisation (Balzacq 2010), which privileges practices over discourses, is the most adequate in this case. The next section of the article applies the theoretical framework to the activities of FRONTEX and examines the ways in and the extent to which FRONTEX has been securitising asylum and migration in the EU. The article offers some conclusions with respect to FRONTEX and the securitisation of asylum and migration in the EU, as well as the study of securitisation processes more generally.

FRONTEX and the EU asylum and migration policy

FRONTEX was created by Council Regulation EC 2007/2004 of 26 October 2004[6] with the main objective of coordinating operational cooperation amongst Member States to strengthen security at the external borders of the EU Member States. Whilst EU cooperation on asylum and migration matters started with the Maastricht Treaty in 1993, cooperation regarding the control of the external borders of the Member States of the EU originally developed amongst some EU Member States within the Schengen group from 1985 onwards and especially after the entry into force of the Schengen Convention in 1995 (Monar 2006, pp. 74–75). The so-called 'Schengen *acquis*' was finally incorporated into the EU institutional framework with the entry into force of the Amsterdam Treaty in 1999, which also enacted a partial and gradual shift from intergovernmentalism to a more communitarised approach in this policy area (Kaunert 2005, Peers and Rogers 2006, p. 169).[7] It is also that year that, EU cooperation on migration, asylum and external borders received an important impetus with the adoption of the 'Tampere Programme', a five-year work programme for the development of internal security policies in the EU. It notably called for the EU 'to develop common policies on asylum and immigration, while taking into account the need for a consistent control of external borders to stop illegal immigration and to combat those who organise it and commit related international crimes' (European Council 1999).

The willingness to strengthen cooperation amongst EU Member States with regard to external border controls – which was to ultimately lead to the creation of FRONTEX – was prompted by three main factors (see Léonard 2009). First of all, as already mentioned earlier in this article, migration flows have become an increasingly contentious issue in Europe, especially since the end of the Cold War. This has led European states to take various measures in a bid to curb the number of migrants, including the strengthening of border controls to restrict the access of migrants and asylum-seekers to their territory (Collinson 1993, Joly 1996, Guild 2006, Chebel d'Appollonia and Reich 2008). In addition, in the run-up to the 2004 'big bang' enlargement of the EU, some concerns were voiced about the alleged inability of the future Member States to effectively control the new external borders of the EU. From such a viewpoint, strengthening cooperation amongst EU Member States on border controls was seen as the most effective way to address the perceived lack of border control capabilities of the future EU Member States and their difficulties to meet the Schengen/EU border control standards (Monar 2006, p. 75). Finally, the tightening up of external border controls was also seen as an important contribution to the fight against terrorism in the aftermath of the terrorist attacks on 11 September 2001 (Monar 2005, p. 147, Mitsilegas 2007, p. 362, Léonard 2010). The decision to establish an Agency, i.e. FRONTEX, to increase cooperation on the management of external borders amongst EU Member States came after a few years of intense debates, during which other institutional forms of cooperation were also considered and temporarily implemented in some cases. However, a detailed examination of the evolution of these arrangements is beyond the scope of the present article (see Léonard 2009). It is nevertheless important to highlight that FRONTEX has been given a key-role by the EU Member States in implementing the concept of 'integrated border management' (IBM). This concept has underpinned the development of EU cooperation on border controls since the Tampere programme in 1999 and refers to the idea of joining up all the activities of the public authorities of the Member States relating to border control and surveillance including border checks, the analysis of risks at the borders, and the planning of the personnel and facilities required.[8]

Having briefly outlined the origins of FRONTEX and the broader context of the EU asylum and migration policy in which it operates, it is now possible to consider the theoretical framework that will underpin the subsequent analysis of the activities of FRONTEX. It is embedded in what has often been presented as one of the most promising approaches to the study of 'new' security issues such as migration, namely securitisation theory (Huysmans 1997, Williams 2003).

Securitisation theory

Securitisation theory is an approach to the study of security that was originally developed by Ole Wæver in collaboration with other researchers, who have come to be known as the 'Copenhagen School'.[9] It is premised on the idea that the world, including security threats, is socially constructed, which means that it is impossible to ever fully assess whether threats are 'real' or not. Therefore, what security scholars can and should study is the process through which an issue becomes socially constructed and recognised as a security threat. According to Wæver and his colleagues, security issues come into being through a discursive process that dramatises and prioritises them. More precisely, in a successful securitisation process, a 'speech act' by a securitising actor presents an issue as an existential threat to the survival of a 'referent object' (e.g. a state, national identity, etc.) and is accepted as such by the 'audience' of the speech act (e.g. the government, public opinion, etc.). Moreover, according to the Copenhagen School, the securitisation of an issue allows the successful securitising actor to claim that the issue '[requires] emergency measures and [justifies] actions outside the normal bounds of political procedure' (Buzan et al. 1998, p. 25). In other words, by labelling an issue a 'security issue', the securitising actor 'moves a particular development into a specific area, and thereby claims a special right to use whatever means are necessary to block it' (Wæver 1995, p. 55). Thus, for Wæver and his colleagues, there are no security issues in themselves, but only issues that have been 'securitised', i.e. constructed as such through securitising *speech acts*. Also, as indicated by the borrowing of the concept of 'speech act' from linguistics, the Copenhagen School's understanding of securitisation is centred on discourse.[10]

The Copenhagen School's work on securitisation has generated an intense debate in security studies in recent years, as various scholars have put forward suggestions for further developing and refining the original version of the securitisation framework. Whereas some scholars have retained the emphasis on the role of discourses in securitisation processes (see, for example, Vuori 2008, Atland and Ven Bruusgaard 2009), other scholars led by Didier Bigo have developed a different approach to the study of securitisation processes, which emphasises the importance of practices, rather than discourses, in such processes. According to Bigo (2000, p. 194), '[i]t is possible to securiti[s]e certain problems without speech or discourse and the military and the police have known that for a long time. The practical work, discipline and expertise are as important as all forms of discourse.' In other words, the acts of the bureaucratic structures or networks linked to security practices and the specific technologies that they use (Huysmans 2004) may play a more active role in securitisation processes than securitising speech acts.[11] Bigo (2002, pp. 65–66) has also made this point precisely with reference to the issue of migration, as he claims that

> [t]he securitization of immigration (. . .) emerges from the correlation between some successful speech acts of political leaders, the mobilization they create for and against some groups of people, and the specific field of security professionals (. . .). It comes also from a range of administrative practices such as population profiling, risk assessment, statistical calculation, category creation, proactive preparation, and what may be termed a specific *habitus* of the 'security professional' with its ethos of secrecy and concern for the management of fear or unease.

Thus, in sum, the Copenhagen School's approach to securitisation processes privileges the study of speech acts, whereas the approach pioneered by Bigo highlights the role of practices. Another difference is that the Copenhagen School's framework is based on a relatively precise definition of the securitising speech act, whereas Bigo's work does not offer any precise definition of 'securitising practice'. This is because the securitising speech act is the fixed unit of analysis in the Copenhagen School's analytical framework, whilst they leave open the question of who exactly can be a securitising actor. In contrast, the fixed unit of analysis in Bigo's approach is the security professionals, whose practices he studies without seeking to precisely define what securitising practices are and by which criteria they can be identified.

It has been argued that it is possible to combine insights from the two approaches outlined above to study both the discourses and practices of securitisation (Léonard 2007). As noted by Bigo, such a strategy can reveal interesting differences between everyday practices on the one hand and official discourses and policies on the other hand (Bigo 1998a, 2001b). However, notably because of space constraints, this article will focus on analysing practices, rather than discourses, of securitisation. It is argued that a focus on practices, rather than discourses, is also more adequate when analysing securitisation processes in the EU asylum and migration policy for two main reasons. Firstly, in cases where there is a persistent or recurrent security threat, a new drama establishing securitisation is no longer necessary as securitisation has become institutionalised over time (Buzan *et al.* 1998, pp. 27–28). A focus on discourses is therefore misguided in such cases, as they are not likely to indicate the existence of securitisation dynamics, which can only be revealed through an analysis of the practices of the institutions that have been established to deal with a given issue. This argument is particularly relevant for the case examined in this article, as FRONTEX was created in a context where the EU asylum and migration policy had already been shaped by a securitisation trend for a certain number of years (see Huysmans 2000, 2006). When one considers recent official discourses by the EU institutions on asylum and migration, one is struck by the fact that they tend to frame these issues mainly as humanitarian issues (Léonard 2007, Gammeltoft-Hansen 2008, Hernández-Carretero 2009, p. 1). For this reason, it is therefore necessary to consider the practices of the EU institutions and agencies such as FRONTEX in order to assess the extent to and the ways in which they securitise asylum and migration. Secondly, it is argued that it is also more adequate to focus on practices, rather than discourses, when analysing securitisation processes (regarding not only migration and asylum, but also other issues) in the EU. As even acknowledged by the Copenhagen School itself, there are cases where a logic of security is at play, even though no securitising discourse is uttered in the public sphere to justify it (Buzan *et al.* 1998, p. 28). Actually, this specific situation regularly occurs in the EU context, because of its unique political and institutional features. The EU is evidently not a state; it has no government or president to make the kind of dramatic securitising speech acts that can be identified in national contexts – such as those made by the British Government in 2002 to construct Iraq as a threat to the UK (see Roe 2008). This view is notably shared by Balzacq (2008). Analysing the EU's counter-terrorism policy, he observes that '[on] occasions, securitisation changes in scope and scale – for example, a new threat is identified – in the absence of a discursive articulation' (Balzacq 2008, p. 76). This leads him to suggest a shift in the study of securitisation processes 'away from discourse and towards the "empirical referents of policy" – policy tools or instruments – that the EU utilizes to alleviate public problems defined as threats' (*idem*). For these two main reasons, this article will therefore analyse the role of the practices (or activities) of FRONTEX, rather than its discourses, in the securitisation of asylum and migration in the EU.

Once it has been decided to focus on the analysis of securitising practices, rather than securitising discourses, it becomes necessary to define what is meant by 'securitising practices' in the context of the EU asylum and migration policy in order to be able to identify these securitising practices empirically. As Bigo's writings do not offer any precise definition of securitising practices, this article will build upon ideas developed by Balzacq (2008). In contrast with Bigo, Balzacq does not use the term 'practice', but rather the concept of 'tool of securitization', which he also uses interchangeably with 'instrument of securitization'. Nevertheless, his use of the concept seems to indicate that it is close to the idea of securitising practice as meant by Bigo – and which will be used in this article as it is more commonly used than securitisation 'tool' or 'instrument'. Balzacq (2008, p. 79) defines a 'tool of securitization' as 'an identifiable social and technical "dispositif" or device *embodying a specific threat image* through which public action is configured in order to address a security issue' (emphasis added). Thus, the key-idea to retain from this definition is that securitising practices are activities that, by their very intrinsic qualities, convey the idea to those who observe them, directly or indirectly, that the issue they are tackling is a security threat. When this general definition is applied to the case of the EU asylum and migration policy, it means that securitising practices can be defined as activities that, in themselves, convey the idea that asylum-seekers and migrants are a security threat to the EU.

The next necessary step is then to identify criteria for the identification of these securitising practices empirically. If these practices embody a 'specific threat image', to use Balzacq's words, then it means that these practices have characteristics that allow those who become aware of them to know that their deployment aims to tackle a security threat and is therefore justified by the existence of such a threat. This article puts forward the idea that there are two main types of practices which, when they are deployed, strongly suggest that there exists a security threat to be tackled and can therefore be considered 'securitising practices'. The first type of such practices refers to practices that are usually deployed to tackle issues that are widely considered to be security threats, such as a foreign armed attack or terrorism. For example, the deployment of military troops and military equipment such as tanks to tackle an issue conveys the message that this issue is a security threat that needs to be tackled urgently, thereby socially constructing this issue as a security threat.[12] The second type of securitising practices is 'extraordinary' practices. Their exceptional character suggests that the problem they are tackling is also exceptional and cannot be dealt with by 'normal' or 'ordinary' measures. The deployment of such extraordinary measures therefore constructs the issue that they are addressing as a security threat. 'Extraordinary' here is not only understood as 'outside the normal bounds of political procedure' or 'above politics' as suggested by the Copenhagen School (Buzan *et al.* 1998), who appears to have been strongly influenced by Schmitt's ideas on this point (Williams 2003). Rather, 'extraordinary' is understood more broadly as 'out of the ordinary' in order for the analytical framework to be able to capture the fact that not all securitising practices necessary involve emergency, exceptionalism or illegality, as suggested by Wæver and his colleagues. Also, the extraordinary character of a measure has to be assessed with regard to a specific issue in a certain political context. In other words, for a measure to be identified as 'out of the ordinary', it is not required that it has never been implemented before, but rather that is has not been previously applied to a specific policy issue in a given political context. This broad understanding of 'extraordinary measures' echoes the broad understanding of security underpinning this article, in line with the work of scholars such as Bigo (1998a, 2002) and Abrahamsen (2005, p. 59), who conceptualises security as involving a 'continuum from normalcy to worrisome/troublesome to risk and to existential threat'. As a result of this broad conceptualisation of security, which differs from a narrower definition that would focus on existential threats and exceptionalism, some practices will be interpreted as securitising practices in the subsequent analysis, whereas scholars drawing upon a narrower understanding of security may have seen these practices as merely embodying a 'risk approach' to the policy issue concerned.

In the context of the EU asylum and migration policy, and drawing upon the insights above, securitising practices can therefore be identified as activities concerning asylum and migration that (1) have traditionally been implemented to tackle issues that are largely perceived to be security issues (such as drug-trafficking, terrorism, a foreign invasion, etc.) and/or (2) are extraordinary, not only in the sense of 'exceptional' or 'illegal', but more broadly in the sense of 'out of the ordinary' (i.e. never or rarely applied previously to asylum and migration issues in the EU and its Member States). Although only one of these criteria needs to be fulfilled for a specific activity to be considered a securitising practice in this framework, they are not mutually exclusive, which means that a specific activity can fulfil both criteria at the same time. Having defined the criteria for the identification of securitising practices, one can now apply them to FRONTEX through a systematic and detailed analysis of its activities. Before doing so, it is important to add that this analysis is premised on the understanding that securitisation does not occur at one specific moment in time, but is a more diffuse and long-term process (Abrahamsen 2005). It also requires regular 'positive reinforcements', such as the regular enactment of securitising practices; otherwise, securitisation will likely fade away, as other social constructions of the issue at hand will take priority. Therefore, as previously noted, this article does not seek to analyse how FRONTEX securitised asylum and migration in the EU for the first time, for it did not, but rather examines the extent to and the specific ways in which this Agency contributes to the ongoing securitisation of asylum and migration in the EU.

The activities of FRONTEX: securitising practices?

EU Member States decided to establish FRONTEX in 2004, with the main aim of '[facilitating] the application of existing and future Community measures relating to the management of external borders by ensuring the coordination of Member States' actions in the implementation of those measures' (recital 4 of Council Regulation (EC) No 2007/2004). The Agency started its work in October 2005 and has its headquarters in Warsaw (Baldaccini 2010, p. 230). Its budget has four strands, the most important of which is by far a Community subsidy, which, incidentally, gives the European Parliament a substantial financial leverage on the Agency (Léonard

2009). According to its founding Regulation, FRONTEX has six 'main tasks': (1) coordinating operational cooperation between Member States regarding the management of external borders; (2) assisting Member States in the training of national border guards, including establishing common training standards; (3) conducting risk analyses; (4) following up on developments in research relevant for the control and surveillance of external borders; (5) assisting Member States when increased technical and operational assistance at external borders is required; and (6) assisting Member States in organising joint return operations. The remainder of this section examines each of these tasks of FRONTEX to assess the ways in and the extent to which the Agency's activities have amounted to securitising practices and have thereby contributed to the securitisation of asylum and migration in the EU.

The coordination of operational cooperation between Member States regarding the management of external borders

Amongst all of FRONTEX's tasks, the coordination of joint operations at the external borders of the Member States of the EU is certainly the task that has attracted most attention, especially from pro-migrant NGOs and the media, as well as scholars (Carrera 2007, Wolff 2008, Baldaccini 2010, Rijpma 2010). It is also the type of operational activities on which FRONTEX spends, by far, most of its budget (e.g. about €40 million in 2009) (FRONTEX 2009b, p. 10). FRONTEX has been given competences to coordinate joint operations at the air, land and sea external borders, which can be proposed by Member States or initiated by the Agency itself in agreement with the Member State(s) concerned (Article 3 of Regulation (EC) No 2007/2004). These joint operations bring together border guards and technical equipment from various Member States and Schengen Associated Countries to conduct joint reinforced border controls for a certain period of time. Decisions on launching operations are normally based on the results of the risk analyses conducted by the Agency (see below), although political considerations seem to sometimes prevail (COWI 2009, p. 41). The deployment of the joint operations is facilitated by the existence of the 'Central Record of Available Technical Equipment' (CRATE), which lists items of surveillance and control equipment that Member States are willing to put at the disposal of another Member State for a temporary period of time. At the beginning of 2010, the CRATE comprised 26 helicopters, 113 vessels, 22 fixed-wing aircrafts, and 476 other items, such as vehicles, mobile radar units, thermal cameras and heartbeat detectors (FRONTEX 2010b). Finally, an interesting point to note is that the exact division of responsibilities between the Agency and the EU Member States in the course of such operations has been a very controversial topic, in particular in cases where migrants have drowned at sea during the deployment of a joint operation coordinated by FRONTEX (FRONTEX 2007b). In line with its founding Regulation, FRONTEX's official position has consistently been that the Agency's role is strictly limited to that of a coordinator of the actions of the EU Member States, with which the responsibility for the control of the external borders fully remains. However, some scholars such as Baldaccini (2010, p. 234) have argued that the planning and coordinating role of FRONTEX also gives the Agency a certain degree of responsibility for the events occurring during the joint operations that it coordinates.

Whatever stance one takes over this complex issue, it can be argued that the joint operations coordinated by FRONTEX are securitising practices on two accounts. First of all, such coordinated actions amongst various states, particularly in the case of the sea joint operations, have traditionally been deployed to address more traditional security issues such as a military attack from a third state, piracy or drug-trafficking (Lutterbeck 2006). Given that some of the actors involved in these joint operations have a semi-military status in their country, such as the *Guardia Civil* in Spain or the *Guardia di Finanza* in Italy (Lutterbeck 2006), these joint operations that aim to stem migration flows can be seen as a 'semi-militarisation' of border controls and thereby a securitisation of migration flows given the traditional role of the military in addressing security issues. In addition, the joint operations coordinated by FRONTEX can also be seen as securitising practices because they are extraordinary practices. Let us focus on the joint operations at sea to develop this argument. Firstly, such operations are extraordinary in the broadest sense of the word, i.e. 'out of the ordinary'. Although such operations are not entirely new, as several countries such as Italy, the USA and Australia have already conducted naval operations to stem migration flows (Kneebone 2006, Kneebone 2010, Legomsky 2006, Lutterbeck 2006, di Pascale 2010, Frenzen 2010), the sophistication of the operations coordinated by FRONTEX, notably with respect to the intelligence gathered prior to the operations, the number of states involved on the EU side, the participation of some states of origin and transit through various agreements, the existence of the CRATE and the increasing length of the operations, puts them in a league of their own (despite the difficulties and limitations that have affected some operations, such as linguistic problems (COWI 2009, p. 36)).

Secondly, these joint operations at sea can also be considered extraordinary because the legality of some of their aspects has been called into question. It is impossible in this article to fully do justice to such a complex topic, as these joint operations take place at the intersection of various legal instruments from both the European Community and international legal orders. It suffices to say here that there are several aspects of the joint operations at sea coordinated by FRONTEX that are contentious from a legal point of view (see Gil-Bazo 2006, Commission of the European Communities 2007, Fischer-Lescano *et al.* 2009, Hernández-Carretero 2009, Trevisanut 2009, Baldaccini 2010, den Heijer 2010, Guild and Bigo 2010, Papastavridis 2010). The most problematic aspect of the operations is that their organisation does not seem to ensure respect for the '*non-refoulement*' principle, which is a cornerstone of the international protection regime. As explained by Klug and Howe (2010, p. 70), it 'prohibits States from acting to "expel" or "return" individuals to situations where they may face persecution or where their fundamental human rights may be at risk'. As argued by Papastavridis (2010, p. 75) in relation to the joint operations coordinated by FRONTEX, 'the application of the [principle of *non-refoulement*] appears to be especially problematic in the majority of these operations since it is very likely that the persons onboard the intercepted vessels would be forced to return to their countries of origin, where they may be subjected to torture or inhuman or degrading treatment'. All the persons that are intercepted, returned or otherwise prevented to reach the EU's territory as a result of the operations coordinated by FRONTEX are treated as if they were all illegal immigrants. No provision is made for the potential asylum-seekers amongst them, which can lead to situations where the EU Member States do not fully respect their international obligations.

Thus, in summary, this section has demonstrated that the joint operations coordinated by FRONTEX, which represent its most important activity from a budgetary point of view, can be considered securitising practices on several grounds. They are a type of practices that have traditionally been deployed to deal with security threats, whilst they can also be seen as 'out of the ordinary' and illegal in some respects.

Assistance to the training of national border guards

Another important task of FRONTEX is to assist Member States with the training of national border guards, including the establishment of common training standards. To date, FRONTEX has harmonised basic training for national border guards across the EU through the development of a Common Core Curriculum (CCC) and a Mid-Level Course (MLC). In addition, it has developed targeted specialised courses on a variety of issues such as the detection of falsified documents and stolen cars, joint return operations, dog handling, and air-naval cooperation for pilots performing surveillance operations. The 2008 FRONTEX Annual Report also mentions that 'during [that year] more emphasis was given to training on fundamental rights issues, which were included in training programmes' (FRONTEX 2009a), but no details on the contents of such training have been made publicly available.[13] In addition, FRONTEX also runs regular 'Rapid Border Intervention Team' (RABIT) training events (see below). The aims of these training activities are to enhance the competence of national borders guards in the EU and to develop common standards, which will strengthen operational cooperation during the joint operations coordinated by FRONTEX. With regard to the delivery of the training, the rather small size of the FRONTEX Training Unit has led it to outsource a significant amount of training. It has established a network of training coordinators, which implement common training tools in national contexts, as well as a 'partnership academy system' that is based on the training offers made by the EU Member States.

Evidently, the content of the training activities organised by FRONTEX – in particular the training sessions relating to the detection of false documents and air-naval cooperation in surveillance operations – reinforces the idea that the external borders of the EU Member States are under threat by irregular migration and need to be protected through the use of sophisticated technological means, such as aerial surveillance operations. The harmonisation of the border guards training curriculum through the CCC project and the lead taken by those with the highest level of expertise in the provision of training (i.e. existing training academies already specialising in tackling specific types of threats to the borders) have led to a general increase in the level of perception of the threat to the EU external borders, as well as in the levels of professionalism and expertise amongst border guards. Change has been particularly significant in countries that did not have much experience in dealing with incoming flows of migrants, in particular the new EU Member States. It is also striking to see that, despite the fact that no state has ever asked for the deployment of a RABIT, a significant number of RABIT exercises regularly take place. For example, in 2009, four RABIT training courses took place, involving 19

Member States (FRONTEX 2010a, p. 46). They reinforce the perception and the representation of migration flows as a threat that could become so acute that it would require emergency action. For these reasons, it can be concluded that, although it appears that the issues of human rights and international protection are being slowly and gradually integrated into the curriculum, FRONTEX's activities that aim to assist Member States in the training of their border guards have contributed to the securitisation of asylum and migration in the EU.

Conduct of risk analyses

Another of the main tasks of FRONTEX is, in its own words, 'to gather situational pictures based on intelligence and by analysing the situation to assess changes, risks and threats with possible impact on the security of the EU's external borders' (FRONTEX 2009b, p. 29). The Agency often presents itself as an 'intelligence-driven organisation'. The use of the concept of 'intelligence', which is of widespread use in FRONTEX documents, although it was not included in the founding Regulation, is interesting in itself. Given that 'intelligence' has traditionally referred to information concerning threats to (national) security (Gill and Phythian 2006, p. 1), the use of this concept, rather than more neutral concepts such as 'data' or 'information', already contributes to securitising asylum and migration in the EU. This is reinforced by the increasingly sophisticated structures developed by FRONTEX to gather, produce and exchange information on the migration flows towards the EU, which are reminiscent of the structures that have been developed to continuously monitor traditional security threats, such as foreign armed attacks.

Within FRONTEX, risk analysis is carried out by the Risk Analysis Unit (RAU) using the Common Integrated Risk Management Model (CIRAM), which was initially developed by a European Council Expert Group in 2002 before being updated in 2007 (COWI 2009, p. 47). FRONTEX produces various types of reports aiming to assess the extent and evolution of irregular migration flows, as well as the 'risk' that they pose to the security of the EU external borders. In particular, it releases an Annual Risk Assessment (ARA) covering the EU external borders in general, which provides strategic long-term analysis and constitutes the basis for the Agency's annual work plan. This report is circulated within FRONTEX and is also sent to the Management Board and the FRONTEX Risk Analysis Network (FRAN), which consists of the RAUs of the EU Member States ad the Schengen Associated Countries. The ARA reports are complemented and updated by 'Interim Annual Risk Analysis' (I-ARA) reports, as well as operational short-term risk analyses that support the joint operations coordinated by FRONTEX (COWI 2009, p. 46). In addition, the Agency produces tailored risk analyses (TRAs), which focus on a specific country, geographical region or specific phenomenon. For example, in 2007, FRONTEX released TRAs on irregular migration from China to the EU and on the Black Sea as a potential route for irregular migration into the EU (FRONTEX 2008). FRONTEX also prepares joint risk analyses with other organisations. In particular, FRONTEX has developed a close working relationship with Europol. Both agencies contribute to each other's analytical bulletins and have delivered joint reports, such as that on the 'determination of high risk routes regarding illegal migration in the Western Balkan countries' (FRONTEX 2008). In addition, FRONTEX has cooperated with the countries involved in the 'Western

Balkans Risk Analysis Network' that it has helped establish[14] to produce the first FRONTEX-Western Balkans joint illegal migration risk assessment on the Balkans in 2010 (FRONTEX 2010a, p. 25). The Agency is also interested in developing 'data collection plans' with third countries such as Russia, the Ukraine and Moldova (FRONTEX 2009b, pp. 25–26).

Finally, a particularly interesting development from the point of view of securitisation studies has been the establishment of the FRONTEX Situation Centre (FSC), which took up its functions at the beginning of 2009. Its main aim is to provide a 'real time' picture of the situation at the external borders of the EU with regard to irregular migration. It can also initiate a '24/7 emergency response mechanism' 'when a situation is critical and needs a high level of attention' (FRONTEX 2009a, p. 18). This is an interesting development because, until then, existing Situation Centres such as those of the North-Atlantic Treaty Organisation (NATO), the United Nations in the field of peacekeeping (Peacekeeping Situation Centre) and the EU (Joint Situation Centre) had always been tasked with monitoring and providing intelligence regarding more traditional security threats. For example, the EU Joint Situation Centre, which is located within the General Secretariat of the Council of the EU, continuously monitors and provides intelligence on issues that have traditionally been viewed as security threats such as the proliferation of weapons of mass destruction or terrorism to the Council of the EU. It also contributes to early warning and provides facilities for crisis task force. The FRONTEX Joint Situation Centre can therefore be seen as another example of the application of specific practices to migration, which had hitherto only been applied to issues widely considered to be security threats. Thus, this section has demonstrated that FRONTEX has been active in developing increasingly sophisticated structures to gather, produce and disseminate amongst EU Member States what it calls 'intelligence' on irregular migration flows. Given that such intelligence structures have only traditionally been developed to monitor security threats, the activities of FRONTEX in the field of risk analysis can also be seen as securitising practices that contribute to the securitisation of asylum and migration in the EU.[15]

Follow up on developments in research relevant for external border controls and surveillance

Research and development is another area where the activities of FRONTEX can be seen as securitisation practices. The Directive establishing FRONTEX gave the Agency the competence to follow up on developments in research that are relevant for external border surveillance and controls and to disseminate such information to the Member States and the European Commission. In practice, a Research and Development Unit has been established, which aims to act as a 'coordinator and facilitator' in border-related research and development activities (FRONTEX 2007a, p. 18). It follows such activities and disseminates research results through the release of studies, such as that on automated border controls, and information bulletins. Moreover, it organises events that bring together representatives of the Member States, the industry, the research community and 'end-users' to discuss the 'operational needs' of the Member States (FRONTEX 2007a, p. 18). For example, in 2009, it organised a conference on the use of biometric technologies in border controls (FRONTEX 2010a, p. 30), whilst it ran a workshop on the use of unmanned aircraft systems – more commonly known as 'drones' – in border surveillance in 2007 (FRONTEX 2008, p. 53). In developing increasingly close relations with private sector companies specialising in security and surveillance technologies, FRONTEX contributes to the securitisation of asylum and migration in the EU by signalling that surveillance and control technologies traditionally used to address security problems are adequate to deal with migrants and asylum-seekers. In addition, FRONTEX also seeks to influence the development of the EU research agenda (FRONTEX 2009b, p. 11), notably to ensure the availability of research funding for research projects on 'border security'. The Head of FRONTEX's Research and Development Unit is a member of the European Research and Innovation Forum (ESRIF), which works as an Advisory Board that influences the development of the EU security research agenda, and chairs its Committee on Border Security, in addition to participating in the evaluation of the proposals submitted for funding from the Seventh Framework Programme (FP7) managed by the European Commission (COWI 2009, pp. 49–50). Thus, the Agency is active in ensuring that the issue of migration control is part of the EU security agenda and that funding is available to support border security-related research and development activities, which will further strengthen the linkage between migration and security. This section has therefore demonstrated that the activities of FRONTEX at various stages of the research and development cycle can be identified as securitising practices, which contribute to the securitisation of asylum and migration in the EU.

Assistance to Member States in cases where increased technical and operational assistance at external borders is required

FRONTEX has also been tasked with assisting Member States in circumstances when they require increased technical and operational assistance. This specific task is particularly interesting from the point of view of the securitisation of asylum and migration in the EU. The founding Regulation foresaw in its Article 8 that 'one or more Member States confronted with circumstances requiring increased technical and operational assistance (...) may request the Agency for assistance'. Such assistance was to take the form of support from the Agency for the organisation of coordination between two or more Member States or the deployment of experts from FRONTEX to help the national authorities of the state making the request. However, in 2007, these provisions were amended by a Regulation establishing the new mechanism of the RABITs. This change was justified on the grounds that '[the] current possibilities for providing efficient practical assistance (...) at European level are not considered sufficient, in particular where Member States are faced with the arrival of large numbers of third-country nationals trying to enter the territory of the Member States illegally' (recital 5 of Regulation (EC) No 863/2007). In other words, according to that perspective, migration flows can be so threatening to some EU Member States that they would not be able to cope with them, even with the help of the cooperation mechanisms already in place. This perception led EU Member States to establish the RABITs, which are teams of 'specially trained experts from other Member States' that can be deployed on the territory of a Member State requiring assistance 'for a limited period of time (...) in exceptional and urgent situations' (Recitals 6 and 7 of Regulation (EC) 863/2007).

The RABITs are particularly remarkable in two respects. First of all, their creation has been presented as a contribution to 'increasing solidarity and mutual assistance between Member States' (recital 6 of Regulation (EC) 863/2007). Secondly, in contrast with the entirely voluntary participation in the joint operations coordinated by FRONTEX, RABITS are based on the principle of 'compulsory solidarity'. EU Member States are required to contribute border guards to the 'Rapid Pool' and are obliged to make them available for deployment at the request of FRONTEX, unless they are themselves faced with an exceptional situation (Article 4, Regulation (EC) 863/2007).

To date, no EU Member State has ever requested the deployment of a RABIT. However, as explained earlier, RABIT training exercises are regularly organised, which perpetuate the idea that, at any time, migration flows could constitute an emergency situation requiring a rapid response. Also, RABITs – the development and activation of which are the responsibility of FRONTEX – embody the application, for the first time to the issue of migration, of a type of mechanism that has traditionally been developed to deal with emergency and acute threats such as foreign armed attacks. The idea of mandatory participation of every Member State to tackle the emergency situation in the name of solidarity is reminiscent of the 'solidarity clause' of the North-Atlantic Treaty. For these reasons it can be argued that FRONTEX's activities in relation to the RABITs can also be seen as securitising practices.

Assistance to Member States for the organisation of joint return operations

The Council Regulation establishing FRONTEX has also given the Agency tasks relating to the so-called 'EU return policy', that is, the policy that aims to send back to their country or origin (or a country through which they have transited) those whose asylum application has been rejected or who have otherwise been found in an illegal situation on the territory of one of the EU Member States. More precisely, the Agency has been tasked with providing assistance in the organisation of joint return operations by the Member States – which, in practice, take place by air in most cases–and identifying best practices concerning the acquisition of travel documents for those to be expelled from the EU territory and the removal of third country nationals in an illegal situation. Article 9 of the Regulation also stipulates that FRONTEX 'may use Community financial means available in the field of return'.

After a rather slow start, especially compared to the area of joint operations at sea, this is an area of activities that has recently become increasingly important for the Agency (FRONTEX 2010a, p. 18). In addition to producing two documents outlining best practices in relation to both the acquisition of travel documents and the removal of illegally present third-country nationals by air, FRONTEX has developed a 'Return Section' on the ICONet – a secure web-based information and coordination network used by the migration management services of the EU Member States – to manage the assistance regarding joint return operations. It can be used by Member States to announce the return flights that they intend to organise so that other EU Member States can also participate in these return operations, by filling in the planes with other persons that they also intended to expel to the same country or region (Guild and Bigo 2010, pp. 271–272). For example, in 2009, Austria organised a joint return operation in which eight other EU Member States and

Schengen Associated Countries (Romania, Cyprus, the Netherlands, Poland, Finland, Germany, Norway and Sweden) participated, which resulted in the deportation of 50 persons back to Nigeria (FRONTEX 2009c). The overall responsibility for the implementation of any given return operation remains with the organising and leading country, and not FRONTEX. However, the Agency plays an increasingly important role in return operations. It uses its experience to assist EU Member States in coordinating them and co-finances some of them. It may also have staff participating in the advance mission sent to the destination country of the return flight or onboard the return flight (COWI 2009, pp. 57–58), whilst it is planned that it will charter aircrafts for joint return flights from 2010 onwards (COWI 2009, p. 58; FRONTEX 2010b). 'Needs and possibilities' for joint return operations are identified by FRONTEX and the so-called 'Core Country Group' (CCG), that has been identified as the 'group of core countries experienced in return operations' (FRONTEX 2010a, p. 18).

Thus, although FRONTEX does not have overall responsibility to organise joint return operations, it plays an increasingly important role in the EU return policy by facilitating the organisation of joint operations on the basis of its expertise and financial means. The activities of FRONTEX in this area can also be seen as securitising practices on the grounds that they are significantly 'out of the ordinary'. Nowhere else in the world, and never before, has there been such a high level of sophistication in the coordination of operations aiming to expel certain groups of migrants amongst such a large group of states. FRONTEX allows the EU Member States to plan and coordinate return operations more easily than before and can even assist them financially and logistically. What is also remarkable is that, in a similar fashion to what has been observed when analysing the joint surveillance and control operations and the training activities coordinated by FRONTEX, the lead is taken by the most experienced EU Member States, which then shares their experience and 'best practices' with the states that are less experienced in expelling migrants. For example, in 2009, all joint operations were organised by 'old' EU Member States that have had significant experience in dealing with migration flows over the last few years (as well as three operations by Switzerland), whilst some of them were joined in by several of the 'new' EU Member States, which have traditionally had little experience of immigration, such as Poland, the Czech Republic, Slovakia, Hungary, Romania, Latvia, Slovenia, Cyprus and Malta (FRONTEX 2009c). Consequently, it can be argued that FRONTEX's activities in the field of return operations can also be identified as securitising practices.

Conclusions

This article has demonstrated that all the main activities of FRONTEX can be considered to be securitising practices and have therefore significantly contributed to the ongoing securitisation of asylum and migration in the EU. From a theoretical point of view, this article has further developed the 'sociological' approach to securitisation, which privileges the role of practices over that of 'speech acts' in securitisation processes. It has argued that this approach to securitisation is particularly well-suited to the study of securitisation processes in the EU. The article has also sought to further refine and operationalise 'securitising practices' by identifying two main types of securitising practices, namely activities that have traditionally been implemented to tackle issues that are largely perceived to be security threats and extraordinary activities.

From an empirical point of view, the article has showed that all the main activities of FRONTEX fall into at least one of the two (non-mutually exclusive) categories of securitising practices identified earlier, i.e. practices that have traditionally been implemented to address issues largely considered to be security threats and extraordinary practices. The activities of FRONTEX relating to the training of national border guards, the conduct of risk analyses and the follow-up on border security-related research fall into the first category of securitising practices. Other important FRONTEX's activities, such as the coordination of joint surveillance and control operations at the external borders and the assistance for the organisation of joint return operations, fulfil both criteria and can therefore be considered securitising practices on these two accounts. Thus, it can be argued that, through the increasing coordination of practices spearheaded by FRONTEX, but with a strong involvement of some of the EU Member States with the most advanced securitising practices of asylum and migration, there has been an overall increase in securitising practices directed at asylum-seekers and migrants in the EU. This is because FRONTEX, through its expertise, its coordination activities and its funding capacities, has facilitated EU Member States' involvement in securitising practices. In particular, it has allowed some states that do not have much experience in or financial means for dealing with migration to participate in securitising practices that they would have found significantly more difficult to develop without FRONTEX's assistance (see COWI 2009, p. 59).

However, it is important to note that the deployment of a wide range of securitising practices does not automatically make FRONTEX an important securitising actor *in itself* with regard to the EU asylum and migration policy. Indeed, FRONTEX has been established by the EU Member States, which have also given the Agency its specific competences. At this stage in its development, it is a rather weak actor, whose autonomy is significantly limited. Despite spectacular growths in both its budget and its staff, the activities of FRONTEX are to a significant extent both controlled by the Member States and dependent upon them for their execution, whilst also depending upon the European Parliament from a financial point of view as FRONTEX is a Community Agency (Léonard 2009). Its role is mostly limited to the coordination of Member States' activities, for which those remain formally responsible. In that respect, it can be argued that the strong criticisms levelled at FRONTEX for the shortcomings of the EU asylum and migration policy, as illustrated at the beginning of this article, are somewhat misguided. It is true that most activities of FRONTEX contribute to the securitisation of asylum and migration in the EU, which can be criticised on human rights grounds. Nevertheless, the extent to which FRONTEX can be seen as a securitising actor in itself should not be overestimated. More research is needed to assess more precisely the extent to which FRONTEX is an autonomous actor in the EU asylum and migration policy, taking both the formal (or legal) and informal autonomy of this Agency into account (Groenleer 2009).

Finally, it will also be important to observe the evolution of FRONTEX, as negotiations to amend the Council Regulation that established FRONTEX are currently under way following the submission of a proposal by the Commission in February 2010 (European Commission 2010, see European Parliament 2008). The new Regulation, contrary to the founding Regulation, is to be adopted by both the European Parliament and the Council under the co-decision procedure. It could potentially enact significant changes regarding both the tasks attributed to FRONTEX and its relations with the EU institutions. The new FRONTEX Regulation could also reinforce the trend that is still modest, but that has recently developed in FRONTEX's activities, to also consider human rights issues when seeking to strengthen border security, as notably evidenced by the signing of working arrangements with the Office of the United Nations High Commissioner for Refugees (June 2008) and the EU Fundamental Rights Agency (May 2010).

In conclusion, this article has showed that all the main activities of FRONTEX can be seen as securitising practices. It can therefore be stated that FRONTEX's activities have significantly contributed to the ongoing securitisation of asylum and migration in the EU. Nevertheless, in the context of the strong criticisms levelled at FRONTEX by some pro-migrant groups, it is important not to conclude too hastily that FRONTEX is a significant securitising actor. It is mainly a coordinator of EU Member States' activities and its autonomy is significantly limited at present. However, important changes might be ahead. The outcome of the negotiations on the revised FRONTEX Regulation will therefore have a crucial impact on the contribution of FRONTEX's activities to the ongoing securitisation of asylum and migration in the EU.

Notes

1. A rare exception is Boswell (2007), who argues that there are other institutional dynamics at work in the development of asylum and migration policies in Europe, which can mitigate the securitisation trend. It is important to note that she does not focus on the development of the EU asylum and migration policy in particular, but considers the EU policy alongside national policies.
2. From '*frontières extérieures*' in French, i.e. 'external borders'.
3. Its URL is http://www.frontex.antira.info/frontexwatch [Accessed 1 June 2010].
4. Its URL is http://www.noborder.org/ [Accessed 1 June 2010].
5. More detailed information on these events, including pictures, is available at http://frontexplode.eu/action/ [Accessed 1 June 2010].
6. It was later amended by Regulation EC 863/2007 of the European Parliament and of the Council of 11 July 2007 establishing a mechanism for the creation of RABITs.
7. Article 62(2)(a), within Title IV of the Treaty on European Community that governs visas, asylum, immigration and other policies related to the free movement of persons, gave the Community the power to adopt measures concerning the 'standards and procedures to be followed by Member States in carrying out checks on persons' at the external borders. It enacted only a partial communitarisation of asylum and migration matters, since it also established a transition period of five years (i.e. until 1 May 2004). During that time, the Commission and the Member States were to share the right of initiative. In addition, decisions had to be taken unanimously in the Council, whereas the European Parliament was only consulted on legislative proposals, rather than being fully involved in the policy-making process through the co-decision procedure (Kaunert 2005, Peers and Rogers 2006).
8. This concept was precisely defined by the Council only in 2006. The Council Conclusions on IBM outlined the five main dimensions of IBM: (1) border control, which includes border checks, border surveillance and relevant risk analysis and crime intelligence; (2) the detection and investigation of cross-border crime; (3) the 'four-tier access control model' (which includes activities in third countries, cooperation with neighbouring third countries, controls at the external border sites and inland border control activities inside the Schengen area); (4) inter-agency cooperation for border management and

international cooperation; and (5) coordination and coherence of the activities of the Member States and institutions, as well as other bodies of the Community and the Union (Council of the European Union, 2006).

9. After the location of the now defunct Copenhagen Peace Research Institute (COPRI), where this research programme was initially developed.

10. The Copenhagen School often summarises the securitisation framework as having one 'distinguishing feature', which is 'a specific rhetorical structure (survival, priority of action (...))' (Buzan *et al.* 1998, p. 26).

11. It is interesting to note that, with this emphasis on the practices of bureaucracies in securitisation processes, Bigo's work can be seen as the first attempt to open up the securitisation framework to insights from risk analysis (Aradau and van Munster 2007). From that viewpoint, one can argue that the 'risk approach' and 'securitisation approach' to the study of security may not be so far apart, although they will diverge more or less according to one's definitions of 'risk' and 'security'. There are important debates on how to define 'security' in security studies (Sheehan 2005, Dannreuther 2007), whilst there is no widely accepted definition of 'risk' either. For example, Aradau and van Munster (2007, p. 91) state that their work draws upon a conceptualisation of risk as 'precautionary risk' inspired by Foucault's writings, whereas they interpret Bigo's approach as focusing on 'practices of proactive risk management' (see also Amoore and de Goede 2008).

12. This is not to say that the meaning of security or that of a specific practice is forever fixed. However, meanings evolve slowly.

13. In an interview, Michele Simone, the United Nations High Commissioner for Refugees (UNHCR) Liaison Officer with FRONTEX, also indicated that the UNHCR had contributed to training sessions for FRONTEX staff in order to take into account the issue of international protection in the work of the national border guards (UNHCR 2010).

14. This is the first of FRONTEX's regional Risk Analysis Networks, which aims to foster the exchange of intelligence on irregular migration in the Balkans between FRONTEX and Albania, Bosnia and Herzegovina, Croatia, the Former Republic of Macedonia, Montenegro and Serbia (FRONTEX 2010a, p. 25).

15. It is acknowledged that Neal (2009) has interpreted the importance of 'risk' and risk analysis in the work of FRONTEX differently than this article. In Neal's view (2009, p. 347), the 'risk model' of FRONTEX' can be interpreted as 'the opposite of securitization'. It is argued here that the interpretation of 'risk' in the activities of FRONTEX – as 'securitization' or its opposite – depends on one's definitions of securitisation and security. This article, in line with Bigo (2002), is underpinned by a broad definition of security, which does not limit security to the realm of existential threats and exceptionalism, but understands 'security politics [as being also] concerned with the more mundane management of risk' (Abrahamsen 2005, p. 59). As a result, practices such as the conduct of risk analyses and the establishment of the FRONTEX Situation Centre are interpreted as securitising practices. However, if one operates with a different definition of security, then one might have a different interpretation of the same practices.

Notes on contributor

Sarah Léonard is a Lecturer in International Security at the University of Salford, UK, and has also been a Marie Curie Research Fellow at Sciences Po Paris, Centre d'études européennes, France, since October 2010. Research for this article was conducted whilst the author was a Visiting Research Fellow at the 'Institut Barcelona d'Estudis Internacionals' (IBEI) in Spain, during a research stay supported by the Research and Innovation Strategic Fund of the Arts, Media & Social Sciences Faculty at the University of Salford. The author would like to thank the University of Salford for its financial support. She also would like to thank an anonymous reviewer, the participants to the IBEI research seminar, Christian Kaunert and Thierry Balzacq, for their helpful comments and suggestions.

References

Abrahamsen, R., 2005. Blair's Africa: the politics of securitization and fear. *Alternatives*, 30 (1), 55–80.

Amoore, L. and de Goede, M., eds., 2008. *Risk and the war on terror*. Abingdon: Routledge.

Aradau, C. and van Munster, R., 2007. Governing terrorism through risk: taking precautions, (un)knowing the future. *European journal of international relations*, 13 (1), 89–115.

Atland, K. and Ven Bruusgaard, K., 2009. When security speech acts misfire: Russia and the *Elektron* incident. *Security dialogue*, 40 (3), 333–354.

Baldaccini, A., 2010. Extraterritorial border controls in the EU: the role of FRONTEX in operations at sea. *In*: B. Ryan and V. Mitsilegas, eds. *Extraterritorial immigration control: legal challenges*. Leiden: Martinus Nijhoff.

Baldaccini, A. and Guild, E., eds., 2007. *Terrorism and the foreigner: a decade of tension around the rule of law in Europe*. Leiden: Martinus Nijhoff.

Balzacq, T., 2008. The policy tools of securitization: information exchange, EU foreign and interior policies. *Journal of common market studies*, 46 (1), 75–100.

Balzacq, T., 2010. Constructivism and securitization studies. *In*: M. Dunn Cavelty and V. Mauer, eds. *The Routledge handbook of security studies*. London: Routledge.

Bigo, D., 1998a. Europe passoire et Europe forteresse: La sécurisation/humanitarisation de l'immigration [Sieve Europe and fortress Europe: the securitisation/humanitarisation of immigration]. *In*: A. Rea, ed. *Immigration et racisme en Europe* [Immigration and racism in Europe]. Bruxelles: Complexe.

Bigo, D., 1998b. L'immigration à la croisée des chemins sécuritaires. *Revue Européenne des Migrations Internationales*, 14 (1), 25–46.

Bigo, D., 2000. When two become one: internal and external securitizations in Europe. *In*: M. Kelstrup and M.C. Williams, eds. *International relations theory and the politics of European integration: power, security and community*. London: Routledge.

Bigo, D., 2001a. Migration and security. *In*: V. Guiraudon and C. Joppke, eds. *Controlling a new migration world*. London: Routledge.

Bigo, D., 2001b. The Möbius ribbon of internal and external security(ies). *In*: M. Albert, D. Jacobson, and Y. Lapid, eds. *Identities, borders, orders: rethinking international relations theory*. Minneapolis, MN: University of Minnesota Press.

Bigo, D., 2002. Security and immigration: toward a critique of the governmentality of unease. *Alternatives*, 27 (Special Issue), 63–92.

Bigo, D., 2008. International political sociology. *In*: P. Williams, ed. *Security studies: an introduction*. London: Routledge.

Bigo, D. and Tsoukala, A., 2008. Understanding (in)security. *In*: D. Bigo and A. Tsoukala, eds. *Terror, insecurity and liberty: illiberal practices of liberal regimes after 9/11*. London: Routledge.

Boswell, C., 2007. Migration control in Europe after 9/11: explaining the absence of securitization. *Journal of common market studies*, 45 (3), 589–610.

Brouwer, E. and Catz, P., 2003. Terrorism and the struggle for competence in community law. *In*: E. Brouwer, P. Catz, and E. Guild, eds. *Immigration, asylum and terrorism: a changing dynamic in European law*. Nijmegen: Instituut voor Rechtssociologie/Centrum voor Migratierecht, KU Nijmegen.

Buzan, B., Wæver, O., and de Wilde, J., eds., 1998. *Security: a new framework for analysis*. Boulder, CO and London: Lynne Rienner.

Carrera, S., 2007. *The EU border management strategy: FRONTEX and the challenges of irregular immigration in the Canary Islands*. CEPS Working Document 261. Brussels: Centre for European Policy Studies.

Chebel d'Appollonia, A. and Reich, S., eds., 2008. *Immigration, integration, and security: America and Europe in comparative perspective*. Pittsburgh, PA: University of Pittsburgh Press.

Collinson, S., 1993. *Beyond borders: West European migration policy towards the 21st century*. London: Royal Institute of International Affairs.

Colman, N., 2006. From Gulf war to Gulf war: years of security concern in immigration and asylum policies at EU level. *In*: A. Baldaccini and E. Guild, eds. *Terrorism and the foreigner: a decade of tension around the rule of law in Europe*. Leiden: Martinus Nijhoff.

Commission of the European Communities, 2007. *Commission staff working document: study on the international law instruments in relation to illegal immigration by sea*. SEC(2007) 691, 15 May 2007. Brussels: Commission of the European Communities.

Council of the European Union, 2006. *Council conclusions on integrated border management*. 4–5 December 2006. Brussels: Council of the European Union.

COWI, 2009. *FRONTEX: external evaluation of the European agency for the management of operational coordination at the external borders of the Member States of the European Union*, final report. Kongens Lyngby: COWI A/S. Available from: http://www.frontex.europa.eu/ specific_documents/other/ [Accessed 1 June 2010].

Dannreuther, R., 2007. *International security: the contemporary agenda*. Cambridge: Polity.

Den Heijer, M., 2010. Europe beyond its borders: refugees and human rights protection in extraterritorial immigration control. *In*: B. Ryan and V. Mitsilegas, eds. *Extraterritorial immigration control: legal challenges*. Leiden: Martinus Nijhoff.

Di Pascale, A., 2010. Migration control at sea: the Italian case. *In*: B. Ryan and V. Mitsilegas, eds. *Extraterritorial immigration control: legal challenges*. Leiden: Martinus Nijhoff.

European Commission, 2010. *Proposal for a regulation of the European Parliament and the council amending council regulation (EC) No 2007/2004 establishing a European agency for the management of operational cooperation at the external borders of the Member States of the European Union (FRONTEX)*, COM(2010) 61, 24 February 2010. Brussels: European Commission.

European Council, 1999. *Presidency conclusions of the Tampere European Council*, 15–16 October 1999. Brussels: European Council.

European Parliament, 2008. *An analysis of the commission communications on the future development of FRONTEX and the creation of a European border surveillance system (EUROSUR)*, PE 408.295. Brussels: European Parliament, Directorate General Internal Policies of the Union, Policy Department C: Citizens' Rights and Constitutional Affairs, June 2008.

Fischer-Lescano, A., *et al.* 2009. Border controls at sea: requirements under international human rights and refugee law. *International journal of refugee law*, 21 (2), 256–296.

Frenzen, N., 2010. US migrant interdiction practices in international and territorial waters. *In*: B. Ryan and V. Mitsilegas, eds. *Extraterritorial immigration control: legal challenges*. Leiden: Martinus Nijhoff.

FRONTEX, 2007a. *FRONTEX annual report 2006*. Warsaw: FRONTEX. Available from: http://www.frontex.europa.eu/annual_report [Accessed 20 May 2010].

FRONTEX, 2007b. *FRONTEX: facts and myths*. News release, 11 June 2007. Warsaw: FRONTEX. Available from: http://www.frontex.europa.eu/newsroom/news_releases/art26. html [Accessed 1 June 2010].

FRONTEX, 2008. *FRONTEX general report 2007*. Warsaw: FRONTEX. Available from: http://www.frontex.europa.eu/annual_report [Accessed 20 May 2010].

FRONTEX, 2009a. *FRONTEX general report 2008*. Warsaw: FRONTEX. Available from: http://www.frontex.europa.eu/annual_report [Accessed 20 May 2010].

FRONTEX, 2009b. *FRONTEX programme of work 2010*. Warsaw: FRONTEX. Available from: http://www.frontex.europa.eu/work_programme [Accessed 1 June 2010].

FRONTEX, 2009c. *Activities of FRONTEX in the field of return: presentation of the return operations sector to the GDISC returns conference*. Visegrad, Hungary, 28–30 October 2009. Warsaw: FRONTEX.

FRONTEX, 2010a. *FRONTEX general report 2009*. Available from: http://www.frontex. europa.eu/annual_report [Accessed 20 May 2010].

FRONTEX, 2010b. *2010 Working programme and related aspects*. Presentation by Ilkka Laitinen, FRONTEX Executive Director, to the European Parliament, LIBE Committee, 11 January 2010. Available from: http://www.poptel.org.uk/statewatch/news/2010/jan/ eu-frontex-work-prog-2010.pdf [Accessed 1 June 2010].

Gammeltoft-Hansen, T., 2008. *The refugee, the sovereign and the sea: EU interdiction policies in the Mediterranean*. DIIS Working Paper 2008/6. Copenhagen: Danish Institute for International Studies.

Gil-Bazo, M.-T., 2006. The practice of Mediterranean states in the context of the European Union's Justice and Home Affairs External Dimension. *International journal of refugee law*, 18 (3–4), 571–600.

Gill, P. and Phythian, M., 2006. *Intelligence in an insecure world*. Cambridge: Polity.

Groenleer, M., 2009. *The autonomy of European Union agencies: a comparative study of institutional development*. Delft: Eburon.

Guild, E., 2003a. International terrorism and EU immigration, asylum and borders policy: the unexpected victims of 11 September 2001. *European foreign affairs review*, 8 (3), 331–346.

Guild, E., 2003b. Immigration, asylum, borders and terrorism: the unexpected victims of 11 September 2001. *In*: B. Gökay and R.B.J. Walker, eds. *11 September 2001: war, terror and judgement*. London: Frank Cass.

Guild, E., 2003c. The face of securitas: redefining the relationship of security and foreigners in Europe. *In*: P. Craig and R. Rawlings, eds. *Law and administration in Europe: essays in honour of Carol Harlow*. Oxford: Oxford University Press.

Guild, E., 2006. Danger-borders under construction: assessing the first five years of border policy in the area of freedom, security and justice. *In*: J.W. de Zwaan and F.A.N.J. Goudappel, eds. *Freedom, security and justice in the European Union: implementation of the Hague Programme*. The Hague: T.M.C. Asser Press.

Guild, E., 2009. *Security and migration in the 21st century*. Cambridge: Polity.

Guild, E. and Bigo, D., 2010. The transformation of European border controls. *In*: B. Ryan and V. Mitsilegas, eds. *Extraterritorial immigration control: legal challenges*. Leiden: Martinus Nijhoff.

Hernández-Carretero, M., 2009. *Reconciling border control with the human aspects of unauthorized migration*. PRIO Policy Brief 1/2009. Oslo: International Peace Research Institute Oslo. Available from: http://www.prio.no/sptrans/724731520/Reconciling-Border-Control.pdf [Accessed 1 June 2010].

Huysmans, J., 1997. Revisiting Copenhagen: or, on the creative development of a security studies agenda in Europe. *European journal of international relations*, 4 (4), 479–505.

Huysmans, J., 2000. The European Union and the securitization of migration. *Journal of common market studies*, 38 (5), 751–777.

Huysmans, J., 2004. A foucaultian view on spill-over: freedom and security in the EU. *Journal of international relations and development*, 7 (3), 294–318.

Huysmans, J., 2006. *The politics of insecurity: fear, migration and asylum in the EU*. London: Routledge.

Joly, D., 1996. *Haven or hell? Asylum policies and refuges in Europe*. Basingstoke: Macmillan.

Jorry, H., 2007. *Construction of a European model for managing operational cooperation at the EU's external borders: is the FRONTEX agency a decisive step forward?* Challenge research paper 6. Brussels: Centre for European Policy Studies.

Kaunert, C., 2005. The area of freedom, security and justice: the construction of a 'European public order'. *European security*, 14 (4), 459–483.

Kaunert, C., 2009. Liberty versus security? EU asylum policy and the European commission. *Journal of contemporary European research*, 5 (2), 148–170.

Klug, A. and Howe, T., 2010. The concept of state jurisdiction and the applicability of the *non-refoulement* principle to extraterritorial interception measures. *In*: B. Ryan and V. Mitsilegas, eds. *Extraterritorial immigration control: legal challenges*. Leiden: Martinus Nijhoff.

Kneebone, S., 2006. The Pacific plan: the provision of 'effective protection'? *International journal of refugee law*, 18 (3–4), 696–721.

Kneebone, S., 2010. Controlling migration by sea: the Australian case. *In*: B. Ryan and V. Mitsilegas, eds. *Extraterritorial immigration control: legal challenges*. Leiden: Martinus Nijhoff.

Legomsky, S., 2006. The USA and the Caribbean interdiction program. *International journal of refugee law*, 18 (3–4), 677–695.

Léonard, S., 2007. *The European Union and the 'securitization' of asylum and migration: beyond the Copenhagen school's framework*. Thesis (PhD). University of Wales, Aberystwyth.

Léonard, S., 2009. The creation of FRONTEX and the politics of institutionalisation in the EU external borders policy. *Journal of contemporary European research*, 5 (3), 371–388.

Léonard, S., 2010. The use and effectiveness of migration controls as a counter-terrorism instrument in the European Union. *Central European journal of international and security studies*, 4 (1), 32–50.

Lohrmann, R., 2000. Migrants, refugees and insecurity: current threats to peace? *International migration*, 38 (4), 3–22.

Lutterbeck, D., 2006. Policing migration in the Mediterranean. *Mediterranean politics*, 11 (1), 59–82.

Mitsilegas, V., 2007. Border security in the European Union: towards centralised controls and maximum surveillance. *In*: A. Baldaccini, E. Guild, and H. Toner, eds. *Whose freedom, security and justice? EU immigration and asylum law and policy*. Oxford: Hart.

Monar, J., 2005. The European Union's 'integrated management' of external borders. *In*: J. DeBardeleben, ed. *Soft or hard borders? Managing the divide in an enlarged Europe*. Aldershot: Ashgate.

Monar, J., 2006. The external shield of the area of freedom, security and justice: progress and deficits of the integrated management of external EU borders. *In*: J.W. de Zwaan and F.A.N.J. Goudappel, eds. *Freedom, security and justice in the European Union: implementation of the Hague programme*. The Hague: T.M.C. Asser Press.

Neal, A., 2009. Securitization and risk at the EU border: the origins of FRONTEX. *Journal of common market studies*, 47 (2), 333–356.

Noborder Network, 2006. Crossing borders: movements and struggles of migration. *Transnational newsletter, 1st issue*, October 2006. Available from: http://www.noborder.org/ [Accessed 1 June 2010].

Papastavridis, E., 2010. Fortress Europe' and FRONTEX: within or without international law? *Nordic journal of international law*, 79 (1), 75–111.

Peers, S. and Rogers, N., eds., 2006. *EU immigration and asylum law: text and commentary*. Leiden: Martinus Nijhoff.

Pellerin, H., 2005. Migration and border controls in the EU: economic and security factors. *In*: DeBardeleben J., ed. *Soft or hard borders? Managing the divide in an enlarged Europe*. Aldershot: Ashgate.

Pollak, J. and Slominski, P., 2009. Experimentalist but not accountable governance? The role of FRONTEX in managing the EU's external borders. *West European politics*, 32 (5), 904–924.

PRO ASYL, 2008. *Petition to the European parliament: year by year thousands die at Europe's borders. stop the deathtrap at the EU borders*. Frankfurt, 10 December 2008. Available from: http://www.proasyl.de/fileadmin/proasyl/fm_redakteure/Kampagnen/Stoppt_das_Sterben/Petition_engl..pdf [Accessed 1 June 2010].

Rijpma, J., 2010. *FRONTEX: successful blame shifting of the Member States?* ARI 69/2010, Real Instituto Elcano, 13 April 2010. Available from: http://www.realinstitutoelcano.org [Accessed 1 June 2010].

Roe, P., 2008. Actor, audience(s) and emergency measures: securitization and the UK's decision to invade Iraq. *Security dialogue*, 39 (6), 615–635.

Sheehan, M., 2005. *International security: an analytical framework*. Boulder, CO: Lynne Rienner.

Standing Committee of Experts on International Immigration, Refugee and Criminal Law, 2006. *Letter to the Committee on Civil Liberties, Justice and Home Affairs (LIBE) of the European Parliament regarding the proposal for a regulation establishing a mechanism for the creation of rapid border intervention teams and amending council regulation (EC) No 2007/2004 as regards that mechanism (COM (2006) 401 final*, CM06–14, 24 October 2006.

Trevisanut, S., 2009. Maritime border control and the protection of asylum-seekers in the European Union. *Touro international law review*, 12, 157–161.

United Nations High Commissioner for Refugees (UNHCR), 2010. *Working for refugees on Europe's outer borders*, 18 May 2010. Available from: http://www.unhcr.org/4bf29c8b6.html [Accessed 20 May 2010].

van Munster, R., 2009. *The politics of risk in the European Union: securitizing immigration*. Basingstoke: Palgrave.

Vuori, J.A., 2008. Illocutionary logic and strands of securitization: applying the theory of securitization to the study of non-democratic political orders. *European journal of international relations*, 14 (1), 65–99.

Wæver, O., 1995. Securitization and desecuritization. *In*: R.D. Lipschutz, ed. *On security*. New York, NY: Columbia University Press.

Weiner, M., 1992. 93. Security, stability, and international migration. *International security*, 17 (3), 91–126.

Williams, M., 2003. Words, images, enemies: securitization and international politics. *International studies quarterly*, 47, 511–531.

Wolff, S., 2008. Border management in the Mediterranean: internal, external and ethical challenges. *Cambridge review of international affairs*, 21 (2), 253–271.

Towards a common European border security policy

Vihar Georgiev

European Studies Department, Sofia University 'St. Kliment Ohridski', Sofia, Bulgaria

The internal abolition of borders in the European Union (EU) has created a security deficit that is supposed to be compensated by inventing a new border – the 'external frontier' – which is to protect the combined territory of the Member States. This article argues that the security deficit has not been fully compensated for due to uneven policy implementation. The overview of impending threats to the EU border security system stemming from climate change impacts and demographic pressures shows that the future holds even greater challenges to the implementation of the Schengen acquis. A new approach to border security is urgently needed. The introduction of a common European border security policy can become an adequate response to many of the otherwise imminent threats.

1. Introduction

Border security is currently a hot topic of political debate in the European Union (EU) and even more so in the USA. Various approaches to defining the objectives and instruments of border security policy are suggested, sometimes in direct contradiction. That is why reviewing both the current state of affairs and future challenges to the border security policy in the EU may provide useful and practical recommendations for policy-makers.

The adoption and implementation of the Schengen acquis is one of the cornerstones of the freedom of movement of persons in the EU.[1] However, relatively little is known about the actual effectiveness (or indeed performance) of the EU legal framework on border security. This fact can be explained by the general lack of consistent methodologies for measuring policy effectiveness.[2] The assessment of effectiveness of cooperation in Justice and Home Affairs is also a function of different political perspectives (Anderson *et al.* 2001, p. 22).

In the domain of EU policies, there has been a consistent conceptual debate on policy effectiveness as an instrument for 'output legitimacy' counterbalancing the democratic deficit of the EU.[3] But the efficiency of any EU policy should not be assessed in isolation. From a broader perspective, the border security framework is instrumental for various other policies such as foreign policy (Hill 2002, p. 95), security (Andreas 2003) and economic development (Gallup *et al.* 1999, p. 15). These dialectical relationships prove the assessment of the efficiency of the EU border security policy all the more pressing.

The internal abolition of borders in the EU has created a security deficit that is supposed to be compensated for by inventing a new border – the 'external frontier' – which is to protect the combined territory of the Member States (Walters 2004, p. 252). But to what extent has the security deficit been compensated for? This article intends to search for an answer.

The first part of the article examines the current state of play of EU border security policy with a specific focus on the actual performance of individual Member States. Available data are studied and some general conclusions are made on the level of performance of individual Member States that reveal a certain geographical pattern. The second part outlines some impending threats to the EU border security system based on the use of the preliminary hazard analysis technique. The third part proposes a comprehensive framework strategy for reform of the EU border security policy based on the findings of the previous parts.

This article was not able to examine the broader question of the limits of implementation of a border security policy – the limits imposed by the democratic setting of the EU, the practical limits of technology (Salter 2004), the unintended consequences of policy measures (Cornelius 2001), as well as the alternatives of classical border control. Due to the limitation of space, it was not possible to analyse in depth the underlying motives of the Member States and Community institutions in shaping the Schengen acquis and the current border security policy.[4] For the same reason, other EU policies that can contribute to mitigating the threats such as the development policy (Nyberg-Sørensen et al. 2002) were not explored. Instead, the article limits its research focus on the actual implementation of the existing legal framework as both an objective benchmark and a platform for future reform of the policy. The methodology of the literature studying the policy implementation deficit in the EU was used (Lampinen and Uusikylä 1998, Jordan 1999).

2. Border security in the European Union – the state of play

The history of the Schengen agreements and other forms of police cooperation in the EU is well documented and is not reproduced here (Anderson et al. 1995, Noll 2000, Walters 2002, Occhipinti 2003, Aden 2006, Peers 2006, Zaiotti 2007, Walsch 2008, Neal 2009). Only the relative and ex ante effectiveness of the Schengen institutional framework is studied.

Security agencies suffer from substantial gaps in accountability. The Schengen institutional framework is also prone to such gaps due to the secret investigation and intelligence strategies used in cross-border police cooperation, as well as the de facto autonomy of police work (Aden 2006, pp. 354–355). However, the effectiveness of an accountable policy set-up can be more readily measurable externally. The accountability of the EU border security policy at multiple levels thus is considered a necessary element of good governance (Hills 2002, pp. 22–23).

The academic literature on the implementation of the Schengen acquis is quite scarce. The institutional efforts on EU level are focused more on the development of sophisticated information sharing systems, rather than on assessing the actual implementation of common legal standards. Empirical data are needed to assess the adequacy of the existing arrangements for border security in the EU. Some directions for relevant criteria are known from the academic literature (Salter 2004, Wasem *et al.* 2004). Niemenkari (2002) has proposed a comprehensive list of EU requirements relating to border security.

A comprehensive framework for assessment should relate to all the aspects of border security (Wasem *et al.* 2004). This approach provides a holistic, policy-oriented and practical method of analysis, focusing on a set of activities that are crucial for effective border security as shown in Figure 1.

The three main elements of the proposed border security framework include immigration inspections (and the control of movement of human beings), customs inspections (and the control of movement of goods and information), and the animal and plant health control (as far as living organisms are treated differently by the relevant legislation). The related policies include aviation security, protection against communicable diseases, supply chain security, etc. Two policy issues appear outstanding for the assessment – the physical control of the flow of persons (immigration inspections) and goods (customs inspections and animal and plant health inspections). These two issues are selected due to their overall importance for other EU policies (security, external trade, economic development, climate policy, etc.) and the availability of some objective data for the quality of policy implementation.

Each sub-section examines the available data sources, tools for assessment and possible divergences in policy implementation, and the EU institutional assessment of policy implementation and initiatives for reform.

2.1. Border and customs control of goods

2.1.1. Available data sources

Probably the best tool to assess the actual performance of the border and customs control of the movement of goods is the quantitative and qualitative assessment of the statistical asymmetries in the external trade data.[5] Such studies explore the discrepancies in statistical accounts of external trade between two or more territories. Unfortunately these studies are not common in the EU and are not prepared on a systematic basis by Eurostat.

Existing studies reveal large discrepancies in the statistical data not only between EU Member States and third parties (Geyer-Schaefer 2007, Veronese and Tyrman 2009), but also among Member States themselves (Durnford 2007). At least some of the asymmetries are created by dysfunctions in the collection systems (Veronese and Tyrman 2009). Given the size of the asymmetries (sometimes reaching 30–40% or more of the bilateral trade volume),[6] this is a significant issue. The lack of systematic and thorough accounting of trade asymmetries is worrying on its own. More discrepancies can be expected in Member States with weaker collection systems (Schaffer and Turley 2001).

Figure 1. The border security policy framework.

Another dimension of the assessment of the efficiency of border control is the success rate in detecting and preventing the illegal traffic of some goods. The traffic of narcotic substances is especially well documented and monitored by international organisations. In its last World Drug Report 2009, the United Nations Office on Drugs and Crime (UNODC) notices the increase in drug possession/use in West and Central Europe. Most of the heroin seizures are proportionally larger in destination countries when compared to transit countries in South-East Europe, including Member States Bulgaria and Greece.[7] This observation points to significant discrepancies in drug traffic prevention between drug destination and transit Member States.[8] Data on tobacco smuggling also show serious discrepancies that are mainly explained by the relative ability of Member States to cut-off supply to the illicit market (Joossens and Raw 1998, 2008).

It is worth noting that gaps in the physical control of goods in one Member States can negatively affect other Member States due to the openness of the internal market.

2.1.2. Institutional assessment of policy implementation

The actual aggregate performance of border police, customs, tax authorities and other bodies that monitor external trade in the EU is widely unknown. The European Commission does not assess the quality of collection systems in Member States with the partial exception of Bulgaria and Romania under the Cooperation and Verification Mechanism, and only in terms of the fight against corruption and organised crime.[9] Under the Naples II Convention,[10] Member States only provide fact sheets on national legal restrictions for cooperation.

In terms of the fight against drug trafficking, a number of initiatives have been set-up. The first EU action plan on drugs was adopted in 1994.[11] The EU Drug Strategy and action plan on drugs was adopted in 1999.[12] An annex contained an evaluation of the previous efforts to prevent drug use and illegal drug trafficking in particular. The assessment focused on the application of different instruments for cooperation. The Commission did not discuss the performance of separate Member States. In December 2004, the European Council endorsed the EU Drugs Strategy (2005–2012)[8] which set the framework, objectives and priorities for two consecutive four-year action plans to be brought forward by the European Commission. The Commission also assessed the implementation of the EU Strategy on Drugs for 2000–2004.[13] For the first time, the Commission analysed the relative performance of Member States in policy implementation. It found that some Member States did not have formal structures for cooperation between national law enforcement agencies. The Commission appealed to Member States to establish joint investigation teams to deal with drug trafficking. The Commission conceded that the targets for reduction of drug use prevalence and the availability of drugs have not been reached.

In 2005, a new action plan was adopted for the period 2005–2008.[14] In 2008, the Commission assessed the implementation of the 2005–2008 action plan.[15] The Commission reported that seizure statistics were not always easy to obtain as some major destination countries accounting for large proportion of total EU seizures did not report at all or reported with a delay of over two years. In other words, the Commission often lacked sufficient data on one of the few objective indicators available for assessing the efficiency of drug trafficking prevention.

In addition, McLean *et al.* (2003) claim that police cooperation to combat small arms and light weapons (SALW) trafficking within the EU has tended to be accorded a low priority. This critique is to some extent corroborated by the lack of consistent analysis of illegal small arms trafficking in the last EU Organised Crime Threat Assessment by Europol.[16] The last annual report by the Commission on the implementation of the Council Joint Action on the EU's contribution to combating the spread of small arms and light weapons[17] does not contain any critical evaluation of the progress reported by Member States.

2.2. Immigration inspections and visa policy

Immigration control is an essential element of border security with serious implications for various other policies.[18] Controlling for illegal immigration is at the heart of the Schengen acquis.[19] However, even on a conceptual level, the Schengen legal framework was not designed to accommodate the needs and take into account the resources of all Member States. The 'South' of the EU had to fit in with Schengen requirements although it was impossible to implement them qualitatively (Baldwin-Edwards 2007). This problem was exacerbated with the fifth enlargement of the EU (Lavenex 1999, Mitsilegas 2002, Baldwin-Edwards 2007) in its two waves in 2004 (Czech Republic, Estonia, Hungary, Latvia, Lithuania, Poland, Slovakia, Slovenia, Malta and Cyprus) and 2007 (Bulgaria and Romania).

2.2.1. Available data sources

But how can one assess the efficiency of the border control in terms of visa and immigration policy? The question is more difficult given the size of the EU and the complexity of admission regimes. The effectiveness of the Schengen border security regime is probably best assessed through the relative permeation of illegal immigrants and the scope of human trafficking in the Schengen area. These criteria lack benchmarking against some best practice. The reason is that the immigration policy itself influences the rate of illegal immigration (Ethier 1986, pp. 56–57). Other economic policies of the host countries also influence the illegal immigration rate (Borjas 1999, Coppel *et al.* 2001). The economic policies of the source countries also impact illegal immigration rates (Bratsberg 1995).

Political actors in the field of illegal migration have their own interests in producing particular numbers, with damaging effects on policy formulation and implementation (Jandl 2004). A report by the Frontex Risk Analysis Unit in August 2009 clearly illustrates the problem of data collection and data quality. A questionnaire on the impact of economic crisis on Member States' border management was sent to all Member States in the first quarter of 2009. Most front-line Member States in terms of illegal migration did not return the questionnaire.[20]

One way to measure illegal migration is mapping irregular migration flows through border apprehension statistics. The analysis shows that the main direction of irregular migration flows is still from Eastern and South-Eastern to Western Europe (Jandl 2007, p. 299).

In 2006, the European Commission acknowledged that the illegal entry crisis as already seen and perceived at the time would increase both in qualitative and quantitative terms.[21] The Third Annual Report on Migration and Integration[22] by the European Commission said that in 2006 third-country nationals residing in the EU represented 3.8% of the total population of almost 493 million. In 2008, the Impact Assessment for the Communication on a Common Immigration Policy for Europe[23] said that the total number of illegally staying migrants is several million and the number of annual inflows into the EU at several hundreds of thousands up to 1 million people.[23]

A report from Europol on illegal immigration in 2009 outlines the main immigration pressure points in the EU, including the islands of Lampedusa, Sicily and Sardinia in Italy, Mainland Spain and the Canary Islands, as well as the coasts and islands of Greece.[24] The illegal trafficking of human beings to Italy, Greece and Spain now involves extremely flexible organisational structures that overwhelm national prevention capacities (Monzini 2007, p. 181).

A note from the presidency of the Council to the Member States on the trafficking of human beings[25] in September 2008 noted an apparent increase in recent years in the number of victims trafficked into the EU.

2.2.2. *Institutional assessment of policy implementation*

The Impact Assessment for the Communication on a Common Immigration Policy for Europe notes that Member States' legislation on returning illegal third-country nationals differs widely, as regards terminology, as well as substantive provisions. The Impact Assessment concludes that the core problem is related to enforcement of the law rather than the absence of legal rules.[24]

In February 2008, the European Commission issued three documents related to border management in the EU. The documents focused on the current activity of the Frontex agency,[26] the next steps in border management in the EU[27] and the creation of a European Border Surveillance System (EUROSUR).[28] The communications do not deal with the quality of implementation of relevant Community law, but rather advise on measures to improve and simplify the overall legislative framework. The European Parliament in its resolution on the communications recommended that the Commission should first of all analyse the effectiveness of the existing border management systems of the Member States.[29] The European Commission, however, continued to focus on supporting the Member States in their efforts to extend or upgrade their national infrastructures for border surveillance.[30]

In January 2009, the report by the consulting company COWI on the effectiveness of the Frontex agency found that most stakeholders had difficulties in seeing the value added by Frontex in research in border management issues.[31]

In September 2009, France proposed to the Council to strengthen Frontex operations and thereby make controls at the EU's external borders as effective as possible.[32] The note specifically points out that several Member States are facing an increasingly critical situation in the Mediterranean.

In October 2009, the European Council called for the enhancement of the operational capacities of Frontex, as well as progress in its development and invited the Commission to present proposals to that end early in 2010.[33]

The Stockholm programme[34] adopted by the European Council, 10–11 December 2009, called upon the Commission to present a proposal in early 2010, to clarify the mandate and enhance the role of Frontex. In January 2010, the Commission put forward a proposal for a Regulation amending the regulation on

Frontex.[35] The proposal was accompanied by an impact assessment (IA).[36] The IA is very important, because it reveals in some detail the analytical framework used by the Commission in drafting its proposal.

The IA acknowledges that migratory pressure remains high or is rising at certain border sections of the EU. Member States face unequal different workloads as well as critical situations at certain sections of the border. Four Member states – Italy, Greece, Spain, and Malta – registered the bulk of illegal border crossings in 2008. The IA finds that the operational cooperation among Member States is still inefficient and insufficient. The Commission also acknowledges that the risk analysis of Frontex remains weak when it comes to assessing the capacity of Member States' border management systems to manage the threats they are facing. As a general framework, the IA outlines a number of 'building blocks' of the reform. However, the detailed review of the relevant sub-options reveals some questionable strategic planning on behalf of the Commission.

The IA finds that some Member States dispose of excellent working relations to certain countries of return. The Commission thinks that these relations cannot be compensated by any kind of Frontex working arrangement with the country of return. This argument may wrongly imply that some Member States can and indeed should nurture exclusive relationships with the countries of origin to the detriment of other Member States that are not so well connected.

The IA is critical towards giving Frontex an explicit role with regard to Member States' compliance with EC law during joint operations. It is true that the Commission must ensure the application of the acquis communautaire (art. 17, para. 1 TEU). However, the Commission has not considered assigning a signalling function for Frontex that would, in the case of a possible infringement, refer the case to the Commission.

The proposed mandate for Frontex to carry out inspections in Member States is a positive step forward. This mandate includes evaluating Member States' capacity to face threats and pressure at the external borders, and more particularly their capacity in terms of national structures, equipment and resources. Unfortunately, the IA does not stipulate who and how will actually use this information.

Overall the Commission proposals represent a step in the right direction, but are quite subdued and lack strategic depth. Some existing discrepancies of the border security system of the EU are not addressed, while other problems are tackled only partially.

The Council reacted quickly to the Commission proposal and also outlined a number of policy measures for reinforcing the protection of the external borders and combating illegal immigration.[37] However, apart from the creation of an operational office in the eastern Mediterranean and the creation of a network of national Coordination Centres, the Council conclusions fail to identify any deadlines and specific benchmarks for the relevant measures.

Also in February 2010, the Council adopted the Internal Security Strategy for the EU.[38] The strategy says that the feasibility of the creation of a European system of border guards must be explored on the basis of a prior analysis.

In conclusion, the EU institutions and the Member States do recognise the threats of illegal immigration and do attempt to enhance and coordinate the border security management systems of the Member States. As the European Parliament has rightly pointed out, this is done in the absence of an impartial analysis of the current effectiveness of the border security systems. The problem is that the Member States that have experienced difficulties with implementing the Schengen acquis happen to be also the main pressure points for illegal migration and human trafficking. Law enforcement in such pressure points can be successful only at the condition of constantly broadening its international horizon (Pastore *et al.* 2006, p. 115).

2.3. *General conclusions on the state of play*

The findings from the previous sections show that:

(1) Data on the effectiveness of the border security systems of the EU Member States are scarce and inconsistent.
(2) The institutions of the EU are focused on enhancing the cooperation among Member States on border security issues, but fail to assess in a transparent and consistent manner the individual performance of separate Member States, as well as the overall impact of the discrepancies of performance (Guild *et al.* 2009, p. 3).
(3) Certain Member States in Central and Eastern Europe and the Mediterranean have had more difficulties in implementing the Schengen acquis.
(4) The same Member States are also the main pressure points for illegal drug trafficking, small arms trafficking and human trafficking into the EU.

One may argue that although there are serious challenges to border security in the EU, the institutional evolution of border control cooperation among Member States will succeed in answering these challenges. But the border security system of the EU is not a static structure. It should be able to meet and overcome future challenges, developing dynamic approaches and robust capabilities based on a participatory framework of decision-making (Forester 1999). In the next part, an attempt has been made to evaluate the imminent challenges to the EU border security system.

3. The future challenges for border security in the European Union

This part now approaches the essential question about the future challenges of border security policy in the EU. The separate challenges (threats or hazards) have been reviewed in their entirety. This holistic approach allows mapping the challenges to a shifting institutional paradigm of border control. It is based on an understanding of border security risk as a credible threat of attack on a vulnerable target that would result in unwanted consequences (Wermuth and Riley 2007, p. 2).

The threats are assessed borrowing from the preliminary hazard analysis technique.[39] A number of hazards were pre-selected based on the research provided by the report Global Risks 2010 by the World Economic Forum.[40] This particular risk framework was chosen because it explores a set of risks that share a potential for wider systemic impact and are strongly linked to a number of significant, long-term trends.

The threats may also be regarded from a broader systemic perspective, encroaching security policy in general, as well as various other EU policies, such as immigration, development, humanitarian aid, human rights protection, the internal market, etc. The preliminary hazard analysis points to some considerable risks for those policies that deserve future research and evaluation.

The major challenges (or threats) were identified based on an understanding of two fundamental factors affecting human security[41] – the changing climate (Stern 2007) and the global demographic trends (Lee 2003). The threats were split into sub-categories or hazards from the viewpoint of border security policy in order to maintain clarity.

3.1. Climate change

Climate change is an overall challenge for basically all EU policies. This has recently been illustrated by the inclusion of a 'Climate Action' portfolio in the new European Commission.[42] There are ongoing debates in the scientific community on various aspects of climate change causality, scale and intensity (Hulme 2009). Nevertheless, the prevailing number of experts in the Intergovernmental Panel on Climate Change (IPCC) does forecast significant impacts resulting from climate change events (Parry et al. 2007). In terms of border security, two issues stand out – the increasing immigration pressures and the possible limitations of trade. This analysis focuses on immigration pressures due to climate change, while noting the possibility of emerging new trade regimes that seek to mitigate carbon leakage.

Climate change may undermine human security by reducing access to essential natural resources (Parry et al. 2007, pp. 81–82). This may in turn result in violent conflict (Barnett and Adger 2007, Nordåsa and Gleditsch 2007) and migration (Clark 2008). Climate change is likely to be a significant factor leading to mass exodus from increasingly uninhabitable areas, and population shifts stemming from environmental pressures can place significant burdens on migrant-receiving areas (Gleditsch et al. 2007, p. 1).

The multi-causality of all migration should be considered first, including forced migration (Kolmannskog 2008, p. 11). The impacts of climate are more significant when the different factors of migration, demography and climate change coincide (Kolmannskog 2008, p. 13). That is why it is reasonable to investigate geographic areas that are both affected by climate change and are under strong demographic pressures. A comparative review of demographic stress (Cincotta et al. 2003), climate change risk[43] and physical water scarcity[44] shows that major affected areas overlap.

Some of these areas (sub-Saharan and Northern Africa, the Middle East and Central Asia) are also net sources of migration towards the EU. The International Organization on Migration (IOM) forecasts that by 2050 between 25 million and as many as 1 billion people may migrate or be displaced due to environmental degradation and climate change events.[45] The level of uncertainty is high, but the magnitude of impact in the upper scale clearly indentifies the risk as severe. Climate change is most likely to exacerbate existing migration patterns more than creating entirely new flows (Barnett and Webber 2009, p. 17). Even today up to 80% of young people in countries in Northern Africa and the Middle East would consider immigrating to the EU.[46]

The climate change impact on migration pressures probably reinforces other 'push' factors for migration discussed below (McGregor 1994). The ethical implications of climate-induced migration are especially important for the present assessment. The notion of fairness and justice is questioned probably often when dealing with climate change (Adger *et al.* 2006). One option is to accept 'climate refugees'. Assessing which countries are best suited to discharge some of their climate change obligations by resettling climate refugees depends on pre-existing relations or practical capacity (Risse 2009, p. 297). Not everyone will concur on the criteria used or the scope of contribution. That is why climate change migration pressures and deteriorating quality of life may fuel old and new terrorism movements (Tol 2008, p. 453).

Some authors believe that climate change will affect predominantly internal migration away from rural areas within developing countries (Barnett and Weber 2009, p. 17). Others point out that climate change might be a somewhat amorphous contributory factor that exacerbates a number of existing problems (Brown and McLeman 2009, p. 299).

3.2. Rising commodity prices

The likely relative rise of prices of various commodities caused by demographic processes and economic growth mainly in developing countries may pose a significant challenge to the EU border security system. The report 'The World in 2025' by the Commission Directorate-General for Research anticipates increasing distributional issues with significant shifts in the terms of trade in favour of countries well endowed with natural resources and low-income groups in society becoming confronted with difficulties in getting access to basic subsistence commodities.[47] The U.S. National Intelligence Council says that the demand for highly strategic resources, including energy, food and water, is projected to outstrip easily available supplies over the next decade.[48] This trend can influence negatively both immigration pressures and the border regime for physical goods.

Immigration pressures may increase in positive correlation with the rise in prices of subsistence commodities. Profits from rises in commodity prices are typically not distributed to the general population in resource-rich developing countries. In sub-Saharan Africa, ruling elites are likely to continue to accrue greater income and wealth, while poverty persists or worsens in rural areas and sprawling urban centres.[49]

Some commodities, such as rare metals (Ragnarsdóttir 2008), may become so scarce that their trade may become subject to serious restrictions, while the demand for related products remains high. This asymmetry can fuel organised crime schemes to illegally import (or export) such goods to the EU internal market.

3.3. Failing and sailed states

Failing and failed states are of particular interest due to their declining ability to control their own borders (Rotberg 2003, p. 5). Pressures from climate change impacts, commodity price rises and demographic pressures may further weaken the fragile statehood in many of the EU neighbouring countries (Burke *et al.* 2009). In 2025, three of every four youth-bulge countries will be located in sub-Saharan Africa; nearly all of the remainder will be located in the core of the Middle East.[48]

The weakness of these states may result in negative spill-over effects, such as terrorism, drugs trade and migration into rich democracies (Marton 2008, p. 102). One could argue that the EU is effectively managing such threats in the moment with a certain number of failed states in its proximity. A scenario of mass state failure in critical regions is not impossible, though, especially in the case of severe climate change impacts on the subsistence agriculture (Alley *et al.* 2003, Burke *et al.* 2009). The use of military forces for deterring or managing human flows may become necessary (Smith 2007).

3.4. Regional conflicts

In the future, the EU will probably face a number of challenges posed by regional conflicts, given the existing pressures in the Middle East, the Caucuses and Central Asia. Regional conflicts have intensified over the last few decades. They have been made more complex by the introduction of a nuclear weapons dynamic (Raghavan 2008, p. 2). An increase of the number of refugees seeking access to the EU may be expected, as well as other negative spill-over effects, such as proliferation of terrorism, drug trafficking activities, illegal weapons trade and even attempts to smuggle weapons of mass destruction (WMD) (Sopko 1996, Halden 2007, p. 128). Regional conflicts pose a serious threat even when not considered from a climate change perspective.

3.5. Summary of findings

The brief overview of future challenges for the border security policy of the EU points mainly to a likely and substantial increase of current flows of illegal migration into the EU as the main threat. Given the current difficulties of some Member States to manage and prevent illegal migration flows, the gap in capabilities and resources for addressing the future challenges is worrying, especially bearing in mind the existing limitations of border security policy instruments.

4. Emerging institutional guidelines for a common border security policy

The lack of consistent data on the present efficiency of the Schengen institutional framework does not provide a reliable framework for extrapolating future trends (and threats) to border security policy in the EU. The analysis could have ended at that point and should have appealed for a thorough and transparent review of the actual performance of the Schengen acquis and the EU border security system in achieving their objectives. Such a review should include a clear set of benchmarks that measure the performance of the border security system of each and every Member State across all objectives (Thym 2005).

Instead, this article summarised existing knowledge about the major future challenges to the EU border security policy. The overview suggests that the magnitude of future threats is probably greater than the capacity of some Member States to unilaterally sustain the various pressures that may (and probably will) emerge. The current pace of institutional evolution of border security cooperation does not entail sufficient resources that may be targeted to help separate overstretched Member States in their strive to address increasing challenges (Wolff 2008). That is why a truly common approach to border security in the EU is needed.

4.1. The benefits of a common EU border security system

Some of the benefits of such an approach are self-evident. The common system allows for a more justified distribution of burdens among Member States based on necessity. Today some Member States, such as Austria, Belgium and the Czech Republic are practically insulated from direct exposure to border security risks, while Italy, Spain, Malta, Cyprus, Bulgaria and Greece face increasing challenges that are already detrimental to their national security (Wilson 2005). Second, a unified border regime system levels the playing field among national security infrastructures of the Member States and negates detrimental effects of the varying degrees of effectiveness of the border security systems. This in turn streamlines police cooperation in transnational investigations – a crucial task in the face of globalised organised crime. Third, this approach provides an indispensable tool for the promotion of internal market and customs policies especially in the light of future developments of the climate policy. Fourth, this development fosters the efficient implementation of common immigration and asylum policies to the extent that they exist. Fifth, it leads to a streamlined protection of fundamental human rights and relevant non-discrimination policies (Luedtke 2008, p. 3).

4.2. The obstacles

Many will not agree that a common EU border security system is indeed necessary. Given the recent events surrounding the ratification of the Treaty of Lisbon, including the restrictive decision of the German Constitutional Court,[50] it may appear unlikely that the public opinion and the relevant institutions of the Member States will be able to accommodate such an idea (Jorry 2007, p. 25).

The recent academic literature is somewhat sceptical due to variations in cultures of law enforcement, border control, intelligence and diplomacy, and new cultures of fear and prudence of Member States (Burgess 2009). The challenges to implementation even of existing provisions are manifold, extending beyond the level of legal alignment with the EU requirements (Mitsilegas 2002, pp. 675–678).

On the other hand, the Schengen agreement was not, initially, a 'genuine' Community project. Even when the communautarisation of the Schengen acquis was proposed, some Member States chose not to participate in the system (Wiener 1999). In that sense, the initial Schengen experience is instructive in its practical approach to the question of border security. The Treaty of Lisbon provides sufficient legal instruments for the gradual and flexible development of a common border security policy (Ladenburger 2008).

The further communautarisation of the border security policy can be considered by some as controversial. But should the practical benefits of such communautarisation be visible to policy-makers and the public opinion, the support should develop. The external dimension of border security informs debates on the common European foreign and security policy (Duke and Ojanen 2006).

4.3. The practical steps forward

This section includes practically oriented steps for developing a common EU border security policy based on the findings for the current weaknesses and future challenges to the security of EU borders.

The initial political debate should focus on the current effectiveness of the Schengen institutional framework (Jorry 2007, Jeandesboz 2008). This analysis is instrumental in deciding whether and to what extent the implementation of the

Schengen acquis by individual Member States is in line with the relevant objectives. An assessment of the effectiveness of the institutional framework should address the inherent gaps of policy implementation among Member States and the extent to which the existing legal and institutional frameworks can overcome these gaps. The issue of implementation deficit is extremely relevant in this case (Jordan 1999).

A second step is to bridge the gaps of understanding about future challenges to the border security of the EU. Although there are numerous strategic documents of the EU, OECD and NATO on this subject, the debate may be enhanced and focused more on the practical implications of these challenges and threats for the border security of the EU. Some may not agree on the significance or magnitude of challenges themselves. Risk assessment methodologies are abundant, but policy-makers often fail to apprehend their limitations and ambiguities (Leiter 2008).

A third step then is to evaluate the necessary degree of integration of border security management. This will probably be a gradual process that will largely depend on the realisation of threats themselves. The main risk here is that policy planning exercises may tend to focus on issues of technical cooperation and training.

But what should the outcome be? This article borrows from a vision that, although created for a single country, proposes a comprehensive framework strategy for reform (Wermuth and Riley 2007). The authors outline some indispensable elements of the strategy. These are applicable in their entirety for the future common European border security policy, since they relate to the overall border management effectiveness on a large scale. The strategy includes:

- Establishment of quantified benchmarks and performance and effectiveness metrics.
- Development of a comprehensive border technology road map.
- Integration of planning and coordination among border security entities.
- Creation of crisis response border management plans.
- Coordination and alignment of border security with other EU policies.
- Protection of human rights.

These elements of the framework strategy should be pursued incrementally based on available instruments for policy development and policy implementation.

5. Concluding remarks

This article has shown that the security deficit created by the abolition of internal borders in the EU has not been fully compensated for. The existing indicators for the quality of the physical control of the flow of persons and goods in the EU were examined. The data are insufficient for a full assessment of the actual performance of the EU border security system and national sub-systems, but the analysis points to substantial weaknesses.

The specific threats for the border security of the EU were then evaluated based on a selection of findings from available interdisciplinary research of climate change impacts and demographic pressures. The future pressures on the border security system combined with current deficiencies and implementation deficits may pose overwhelming threats to the security of the EU. That is why a true common

European border security policy is urgently needed in order to develop and implement adequate holistic solutions for mitigating those threats.

The Treaty of Lisbon provides sufficient instruments for Member States to gradually develop a framework strategy for the introduction of a common European border security policy. The process should be interactive and inclusive, and this article should be viewed as a conversation starter.

Notes

1. Guild (2005) provides a useful overview of the legal regulation of the freedom of movement in the EU and the role of the Schengen acquis. Carrera (2005) asks important questions regarding the role of pro-security policies such as the Schengen Information System II towards (or rather against) the free movement paradigm. See also Connor (2010).
2. See a rare example in Behrman and Skoufias (2006) about practical measures for policy evaluation in poverty reduction. Potter and Harries (2006) note that there are limiting factors to the effectiveness of public policy such as the realities of the public administration system, the local training and educational systems and how they prepare professionals; and the prevailing cultural and economic values.
3. See Scharpf (1999, pp. 7–21) and the classification of input and output legitimacy dimensions in Lord and Magnette (2004, p. 188).
4. See the excellent study of Neal (2009) on the political debate surrounding the establishment of FRONTEX.
5. Nitsch (2009) is one of the very few papers that systemically assesses the asymmetry in partner country trade statistics due to mispricing.
6. Veronese and Tyrman (2009) have established large asymmetries, sometimes reaching 200% of the registered trade volume. Geyer-Schaefer (2007) claims that asymmetries worth hundreds of millions of euro remain unaccounted for.
7. See Addiction, Crime and Insurgency. The transnational threat of Afghan opium. UNODOC, 2009.
8. See EU Drugs Strategy (2005–2012), Council of the European Union 15074/04, Brussels, 22 November 2004.
9. See Commission Decision C (2006) 6570 final for Bulgaria and Commission Decision C (2006) 6569 final for Romania.
10. Council Act of 18 December 1997 drawing up, on the basis of Article K.3 of the Treaty on European Union, the Convention on mutual assistance and cooperation between customs administrations, in *Official Journal of the European Communities* (OJEC) 1998, No C 24, 01.
11. Communication from the Commission to the Council and the European Parliament on a EU action plan to combat drugs (1995–1999). COM (1994) 234 final, 23 June 1994.
12. EU action plan to combat drugs (2000–2004). COM (99) 239 final, 26 May 1999.
13. Communication on the results of the final evaluation of the EU Drugs Strategy and Action Plan on Drugs (2000–2004). COM (2004) 707 final, 22 October 2004.
14. EU Drugs Action Plan (2005–2008), in *Official Journal of the European Communities* (OJEC), 2005 No C 168, 1.
15. Accompanying document to the Communication from the Commission to the Council and the European Parliament on an EU Drugs Action Plan 2009–2012. SEC(2008) 2456, 18 September 2008.
16. OCTA 2009 EU Organised Crime Threat Assessment, European Police Office, 2009.
17. Eighth annual report on the implementation of the Council Joint Action of 12 July 2002 on the EU's contribution to combating the destabilising accumulation and spread of small arms and light weapons (2002/589/CFSP), OJ 2010 C-14/35.
18. See the landmark economic research of Borjas (1994) and Hammar (1985). Guiraudon (2000) analyses European cooperation in this area through a venue-shopping framework. Luedtke (2008) reviews recent developments in the European immigration policy.

19. See the considerations in European Parliament, resolution on the Schengen agreement and political asylum (6 April 1995), in *Official Journal of the European Communities* (OJEC). 01 May 1995, No C 109, 169.
20. The impact of the global economic crisis on illegal migration to the EU. Frontex Risk Analysis Unit, Warsaw, August 2009.
21. Communication from the Commission on policy priorities in the fight against illegal immigration of third-country nationals (COM/2006/0402 final), 5.
22. Third annual report on migration and integration (COM(2007) 512 final).
23. Commission staff working document accompanying the Communication on a Common Immigration Policy for Europe: Principles, Actions and Tools. Impact Assessment (SEC(2008) 2026).
24. Facilitated illegal immigration into the EU. Europol, September 2009.
25. Note from the Presidency to the Delegations. Action-oriented paper on strengthening the EU external dimension on action against trafficking in human beings; towards global EU action against trafficking in human beings. 11450/2/09 REV 2. Available from: http://www.statewatch.org/news/2009/sep/eu-council-action-paper-on-trafficking.pdf
26. Commission Communication of 13 February 2008 'Report on the evaluation and future development of the FRONTEX Agency' (COM (2008) 0067).
27. Commission Communication of 13 February 2008 'Preparing the next steps in border management in the European Union' (COM (2008) 69 final).
28. Commission Communication of 13 February 2008 'Examining the creation of a European Border Surveillance System (EUROSUR)' (COM (2008) 0068).
29. European Parliament resolution of 18 December 2008 on the evaluation and future development of the Frontex Agency and of the European Border Surveillance System (Eurosur), in *Official Journal of the European Communities* (OJEC), 23.2.2010, No. C 45, E/41.
30. Report on progress made in developing the European Border Surveillance System (EUROSUR) (SEC (2009) 1265 final).
31. External evaluation of the European agency for the management of operational cooperation at the external borders of the Member States of the EU – final report 2009, 7.
32. Note from French delegation to: Coreper/Council. Strengthening the operations of the FRONTEX Agency, particularly in the Mediterranean. 13226/09. Available from: http://www.statewatch.org/news/2009/sep/eu-council-strengthening-FRONTEX-13226-09.pdf
33. Brussels European Council, 29–30 October 2009, 15265/09.
34. The Stockholm programme – an open and secure Europe serving and protecting the citizens. Conclusions of the European Council (10/11 December 2009).
35. Proposal for a Regulation amending Council Regulation (EC) No 2007/2004 establishing a European Agency for the Management of Operational Cooperation at the External Borders of the Member States of the European Union (FRONTEX). COM (2010) 61 final.
36. IA accompanying the proposal for a regulation of the European Parliament and of the Council amending Council Regulation (EC) No 2007/2004 establishing a European agency for the management of operational cooperation at the external borders of the Member States of the EU (FRONTEX). COM (2010) 61 final.
37. Council conclusions on 29 measures for reinforcing the protection of the external borders and combating illegal immigration (25 and 26 February 2010).
38. Internal security strategy for the EU: 'Towards a European Security Model'. Council conclusions, 23 February 2010.
39. See Ericson (2005, pp. 73–93). Concrete worksheets were developed for the different elements of the EU border security system and evaluated the possible impact of separate hazards, accounting for their severity and probability. Feedback loops were also considered.
40. Global risks 2010. A global risk network report. World Economic Forum, 2010. Available from: http://www.weforum.org/pdf/globalrisk/globalrisks2010.pdf
41. See on the dialectic of environment and demographic processes of Matthews (1989, pp. 163–168).

42. President Barroso unveils his new team. IP/09/1837. Brussels, 27 November 2009.
43. See the Maplecroft climate change risk report 2009/2010 for a comprehensive methodology and empirical assessment of current and pending climate change risks.
44. See the comprehensive assessment of water management in agriculture. International Water Management Institute, 2007.
45. Climate change, environmental degradation and migration: addressing vulnerabilities and harnessing opportunities. Report from the conference. IOM, Geneva, 19 February 2008.
46. Mediterranean migration 2008–2009 report, European University Institute 2009, 21–22.
47. The world in 2025. Contributions from an expert group. Directorate-General for Research, 2009, 47.
48. Global trends 2025: a transformed world. National Intelligence Council, 2008, viii.
49. Global trends 2025, 56. See also Le Billon (2001, p. 567).
50. BVerfG, 2 BvE 2/08 vom 30.6.2009, Absatz-Nr. (1-421). Available from: http://www.bverfg.de/entscheidungen/es20090630_2bve000208en.html

Notes on contributor

Vihar Georgiev is a Ph.D. student at the European Studies Department of the Sofia University 'St. Kliment Ohridski'. The main focus of his research is the procedures for execution of the implementing powers of the European Commission (comitology). Additionally Mr. Georgiev has academic interests in European environmental law, security policy and climate policy of the European Union. Mr. Georgiev has a LLM degree from the Faculty of Law, Sofia University 'St. Kliment Ohridski'. He is also a lecturer at the Center for European Programs of the American University in Bulgaria, the Bulgarian Institute for Public Administration and the Faculty of Legal Studies at the Burgas Free University. He maintains a bilingual blog in Bulgarian and English about European Union law.

References

Aden, H., 2006. Administrative governance in the fields of EU police and judicial co-operation. *In*: H. Hofmann and A. Türk, eds. *EU administrative governance*. Cheltenham: Edward Elgar, 341–360.

Adger, W.N., *et al.*, 2006. *Fairness in adaptation to climate change*. Cambridge, MA: MIT Press.

Alley, R.B., *et al.*, 2003. Abrupt climate change. *Science*, 299, 2005–2010.

Anderson, M., *et al.*, 1995. *Policing the European Union*. Oxford: Clarendon Press.

Anderson, M., Apap, J., and Mulkins, C., 2001. Policy alternatives to Schengen border controls on the future EU external frontier. *Proceedings of an expert seminar*, 23–24 February, Warsaw. Available from: http://new.ceps.eu/files/book/159.pdf

Andreas, P., 2003. Redrawing the line: borders and security in the twenty-first century. *International security*, 28 (2), 78–111.

Baldwin-Edwards, M., 2007. Navigating between Scylla and Charybdis: migration policies for a Romania within the European Union. *Journal of southeast European & Black Sea studies*, 7 (1), 5–35.

Barnett, J. and Adger, W.N., 2007. Climate change, human security and violent conflict. *Political geography*, 26 (6), 639–655.

Barnett, J. and Webber, M., 2009. *Accommodating migration to promote adaptation to climate change*. Policy brief prepared for the Secretariat of the Swedish Commission on Climate Change, March 2009. Sweden: Commission on Climate Change and Development.

Behrman, J.R. and Skoufias, E., 2006. Mitigating myths about policy effectiveness: evaluation of Mexico's antipoverty and human resource investment program. *The annals of the American Academy of Political and Social Science*, 606 (1), 244–275.

Borjas, G.J., 1994. The economics of immigration. *Journal of economic literature*, XXXII, 1667–1717.

Borjas, G.J., 1999. *Economic research on the determinants of immigration: lessons for the European Union*. World Bank Technical Paper 438. Washington, DC: World Bank Publications.

Bratsberg, B., 1995. Legal versus illegal U.S. immigration and source country characteristics. *Southern economic journal*, 61 (3), 715–727.

Brown, O. and McLeman, R., 2009. A recurring anarchy? The emergence of climate change as a threat to international peace and security. *Conflict, security & development*, 9 (3), 289–305.

Burgess, J.P., 2009. There is no European security, only European securities. *Cooperation and conflict*, 44 (3), 309–328.

Burke, M.B., *et al.*, 2009. Warming increases the risk of Civil War in Africa. *PNAS*, 106 (49), 20670–20674.

Carrera, S., 2005. What does free movement mean in theory and practice in an enlarged EU? *European law journal*, 11 (6), 699–721.

Cincotta, R.P., Engelman, R., and Anastasion, D., 2003. *The security demographic: population and civil conflict after the Cold War*. Washington, DC: Population Action International.

Clark, W.A.V., 2008. Environmentally induced migration and conflict. Externe expertise für das WBGU-Hauptgutachten. *Welt im Wandel: Sicherheitsrisiko Klimawandel* [World in the change: security risk climate change]. Berlin, Heidelberg: Springer-Verlag.

Connor, T., 2010. Goods, persons, services and capital in the European Union: jurisprudential routes to free movement. *German law journal*, 11 (2), 159–209.

Coppel, J., Dumont, J-C., and Visco, I., 2001. *Trends in immigration and economic consequences*. OECD Economics Department Working Papers, No. 284. Paris: OECD.

Cornelius, W.A., 2001. Death at the border: efficacy and unintended consequences of US immigration control policy. *Population and development review*, 27 (4), 661–685.

Duke, S. and Ojanen, H., 2006. Bridging internal and external security: lessons from the European security and defence policy. *European integration*, 28 (5), 477–494.

Durnford, J., 2007. *A reconciliation of differences in trade statistics*. Working Paper, September 2007. European Union Member States. Southend-on-Sea: HM Revenue & Customs.

Ericson, C.A., 2005. *Hazard analysis techniques for system safety*. Hoboken, NJ: John Wiley.

Ethier, W.E., 1986. Illegal immigration: the host-country problem. *The American economic review*, 76 (1), 56–71.

Forester, J., 1999. *The deliberative practicioner. Encouraging participatory planning processes*. Cambridge, MA: MIT Press.

Gallup, J.L., Sachs, J.D., and Mellinger, A.D., 1999. Geography and economic development. *International regional science review*, 22 (2), 179–232.

Geyer-Schaefer, K., 2007. *Analysis of asymmetries of trade statistics between Germany and China*. OECD Working Paper STD/NAES/TASS/ITS(2007)22. Paris: OECD.

Gleditsch, N.P., Nordås, R., and Salehyan, I., 2007. *Climate change and conflict: the migration link. Coping with crisis*. Working Paper Series. New York: International Peace Academy.

Guild, E., 2005. The legal framework: who is entitled to move? *In*: D. Bigo and E. Guild, eds., *Controlling frontiers: free movement into and within Europe*. Aldershot: Ashgate, 14–48.

Guild, E., Carrera, S., and Eggenschwiler, A., 2009. *Informing the borders debate*. Justice and Home Affairs CEPS special reports, 18 May 2009. Brussels: CEPS.

Guiraudon, V., 2000. European integration and migration policy: vertical policy-making as venue shopping. *Journal of common market studies*, 38 (2), 251–271.

Halden, P., 2007. *The geopolitics of climate change*. Stockholm: Swedish Defense Research Agency.

Hammar, T., 1985. *European immigration policy: a comparative study*. Cambridge: Cambridge University Press.

Hill, C., 2002. The geopolitical implications of enlargement in Europe. *In*: J. Zielonka, ed. *Unbound: enlarging and reshaping the boundaries of the European Union*. London and New York: Routledge, 95–116.

Hills, A., 2002. *Border control services and security sector reform*. Geneva Centre for The Democratic Control of Armed Forces Working Paper Series 37. Geneva: DCAF.

Hulme, M., 2009. *Why we disagree about climate change: understanding controversy, inaction and opportunity*. Cambridge: Cambridge University Press.

Jandl, M., 2004. The estimation of illegal migration in Europe. *Studi Emigrazione/migration studies*, XLI (153), 141–155.

Jandl, M., 2007. Irregular migration, human smuggling, and the eastern enlargement of the European Union. *International migration review*, 41 (2), 291–315.

Jeandesboz, J., 2008. *Reinforcing the surveillance of EU borders: the future development of FRONTEX and EUROSUR*. CEPS Challenge Research paper no. 11, August 2008. Brussels: CEPS.

Joossens, L. and Raw, M., 1998. Cigarette smuggling in Europe: who really benefits. *Tobacco control*, 7, 66–71.

Joossens, L. and Raw, M., 2008. Progress in combating cigarette smuggling: controlling the supply chain. *Tobacco control*, 17 (6), 399–404.

Jordan, A., 1999. The implementation of EU environmental policy: a policy problem without a political solution? *Environment and planning C: government and policy*, 17 (1), 69–90.

Jorry, H., 2007. *Construction of a European institutional model for managing operational cooperation at the EU's external borders: is the FRONTEX agency a decisive step forward?* CEPS Challenge Research paper no 6, March 2007. Brussels: CEPS.

Kolmannskog, V.O., 2008. *Future floods of refugees. A comment on climate change, conflict and forced migration*. Oslo: Norwegian Refugee Council.

Ladenburger, C., 2008. Police and criminal law in the treaty of Lisbon. *European constitutional law review*, 4, 20–40.

Lampinen, R. and Uusikylä, P., 1998. Implementation deficit – why member states do not comply with EU directives? *Scandinavian political studies*, 21 (3), 231–251.

Lavenex, S., 1999. *Safe third countries: extending the EU asylum and immigration policies to Central and Eastern Europe*. Budapest: Central European University Press.

Le Billon, P., 2001. The political ecology of war: natural resources and armed conflicts. *Political geography*, 20, 561–584.

Lee, R., 2003. The demographic transition: three centuries of fundamental change. *The journal of economic perspectives*, 17 (4), 167–190.

Leiter, A., 2008. The perils of a half-built bridge: risk perception, shifting majorities, and the nuclear power debate. *Ecology law quarterly*, 35 (1), 31–72.

Lord, C. and Magnette, P., 2004. E Pluribus Unum? Creative disagreement about legitimacy in the EU. *Journal of common market studies*, 42 (1), 183–202.

Luedtke, A., 2008. Why a European Union immigration policy? A comparative study of national immigration politics and incentives for supranational delegation. *Paper presented at the annual meeting of the ISA's 49th annual convention, bridging multiple divides*. San Francisco, CA. Available from: http://www.allacademic.com/meta/p253921_index.html

Marton, P., 2008. Global governance vs. state failure. *Perspectives*, 16 (1), 85–107.

Matthews, J.T., 1989. Redefining security. *Foreign affairs*, 68, 162–177.

McGregor, J., 1994. Climate change and involuntary migration: implications for food security. *Food policy*, 19 (2), 120–132.

McLean, A., Mariani, B., and Vatanka, A., 2003. *Enhancing EU action to prevent illicit small arms trafficking*. Background Paper Prepared for the Project European Action on Small Arms and Light Weapons and Explosive Remnants of War. Geneva: United Nations Institute for Disarmament Research.

Mitsilegas, V., 2002. The implementation of the EU acquis on illegal immigration by the candidate countries of Central and Eastern Europe: challenges and contradictions. *Journal of ethnic and migration studies*, 28 (4), 665–682.

Monzini, P., 2007. Sea-border crossings: the organization of irregular migration to Italy. *Mediterranean politics*, 12 (2), 163–184.

Neal, A.W., 2009. Securitization and risk at the EU border: the origins of FRONTEX. *Journal of common market studies*, 47 (2), 333–356.

Niemenkari, A., 2002. *Eu/Schengen requirements for national border security systems*. Working Paper Series 8. Geneva: Geneva Centre for the Democratic Control of Armed Forces (Dcaf).

Nitsch, V., 2009. Trade mispricing and illicit flows. *Paper prepared for a World Bank conference on "The Dynamics of Illicit Flows from Developing Countries"*, 14–15 September 2009. Available from: http://www.publicpolicy.umd.edu/files.php/faculty/reuter/IllicitFlows/Nitsch.pdf

Noll, G., 2000. *Negotiating asylum: the EU acquis, extraterritorial protection, and the common market of deflection*. The Hague: Martinus Nijhoff.

Nordåsa, R. and Gleditsch, N.P., 2007. Climate change and conflict. *Political geography*, 26 (6), 627–638.

Nyberg-Sørensen, N., Hear, N.V., and Engberg-Pedersen, P., 2002. The migration–development nexus evidence and policy options state-of-the-art overview. *International migration*, 40 (5), 3–47.

Occhipinti, J.D., 2003. *The politics of EU police cooperation: toward a European FBI?* London and Boulder, CO: Lynne Rienner.

Parry, M.L., *et al.*, 2007. *Climate change 2007: impacts, adaptation and vulnerability. Contribution of working group II to the fourth assessment report of the Intergovernmental Panel on Climate Change.* Cambridge, New York, Melbourne, Madrid, Cape Town, Singapore, São Paolo, Delhi: Cambridge University Press.

Pastore, F., Monzini, P., and Sciortino, G., 2006. Schengen's soft underbelly? Irregular migration and human smuggling across land and sea borders to Italy. *International migration*, 44 (4), 96–119.

Peers, S., 2006. From black market to constitution: the development of the institutional framework for EC immigration and asylum law. *In*: S. Peers and N. Rogers, eds. *EU immigration and asylum law: text and commentary.* Leiden: Martinus Nijhoff, 19–46.

Potter, C.C. and Harries, J., 2006. The determinants of policy effectiveness. *Bulletin of the World Health Organization*, 84 (11), 843.

Raghavan, V.R., 2008. Regional conflicts & their impact on reducing nuclear dangers. *Paper prepared for the international conference on nuclear disarmament*, 26–27 February 2008, Oslo. Available from: http://disarmament.nrpa.no/wp-content/uploads/2008/02/Paper_Raghavan.pdf

Ragnarsdóttir, K.V., 2008. Rare metals getting rarer. *Nature geoscience*, 1, 720–721.

Risse, M., 2009. The right to relocation: disappearing island nations and common ownership of the earth. *Ethics & international affairs*, 23 (3), 281–300.

Rotberg, R.I., 2003. Failed states, collapsed states, weak states: causes and indicators. *In*: R.I. Rotberg, ed. *State failure and state weakness in a time of terror.* Washington, DC: Brookings Institution Press, 1–25.

Salter, M.B., 2004. Passports, mobility and security: how smart can the border be? *International studies perspectives*, 5, 71–91.

Schaffer, M. and Turley, G., 2001. *Effective versus statutory taxation: measuring effective tax administration in transition economies.* Working Paper no. 62. London: European Bank for Reconstruction and Development.

Scharpf, F.W., 1999. *Governing in Europe: effective and democratic?* Oxford: Oxford University Press.

Smith, P.J., 2007. Climate change, mass migration and the military response. *Orbis*, 51 (4), 617–633.

Sopko, J.F., 1996. The changing proliferation threat. *Foreign policy*, 105, 3–20.

Stern, N., 2007. *The economics of climate change: the stern review.* Cambridge: Cambridge University Press.

Thym, D., 2005. The Schengen Law: a challenge for legal accountability in the European Union. *European law journal*, 8 (2), 218–245.

Tol, R.S.J., 2008. Why worry about climate change? A research agenda. *Environmental values*, 17, 437–470.

Veronese, N. and Tyrman, H., 2009. *MEDSTAT II: Asymmetry in foreign trade statistics in Mediterranean partner countries.* EUROSTAT methodologies and Working Papers, 2009. Luxembourg: Office for Official Publications of the European Communities.

Walters, W., 2002. Mapping Schengenland: denaturalizing the border. *Environment and planning D: society and space*, 20 (5), 561–580.

Walters, W., 2004. Secure borders, safe haven, domopolitics. *Citizenship studies*, 8 (3), 237–260.

Wasem, R.E., *et al.*, 2004. *Border security: inspections practices, policies, and issues.* CRS report for Congress. Washington, DC: Congressional Research Service.

Wermuth, M.A. and Riley, K.J., 2007. *The strategic challenge of border security.* Testimony presented before the House Homeland Security Committee, Subcommittee on Border,

Maritime and Global Counterterrorism of the US Congress on March 8, 2007. Santa Monica, CA: Rand Corporation.

Wiener, A., 1999. Forging flexibility – the British 'No' to Schengen. *European journal of migration and law*, 1, 441–463.

Wilson, L., 2005. Challenging sovereignty: international refugee flows as a threat to national security. *Paper presented at the annual meeting of the International Studies Association*, March 2005. Hilton Hawaiian Village, Honolulu, Hawaii. Available from: http://www.all academic.com/meta/p_mla_apa_research_citation/0/6/9/5/1/p69514_index.html

Wolff, S., 2008. Border management in the mediterranean: internal, external and ethical challenges. *Cambridge review of international affairs*, 21 (2), 253–271.

Zaiotti, R., 2007. Revisiting Schengen: Europe and the emergence of a new culture of border control. *Perspectives on European politics & society*, 8 (1), 31–54.

Post-9/11 EU counter-terrorist financing cooperation: differentiating supranational policy entrepreneurship by the Commission and the Council Secretariat

Christian Kaunert[a,b,] and Marina Della Giovanna[c]

[a]Centre for European Security, ESPaCH, University of Salford, Salford, UK; [b]European University Institute, Florence, Italy; [c]University of Siena, Italy

The European Union counter-terrorist financing (EU-CTF) regime has experienced significant developments since 2001. This article builds on the notion of supranational policy entrepreneurship (SPE) in order to investigate the post-9/11 development of EU-CTF regime. Admittedly, counter-terrorism is a policy area in which supranational institutions have rarely taken the lead, nor consistently been very active. However, the article suggests that, despite the centrality that member states maintain in the policy-making process, European institutions, notably the European Commission and the Council Secretariat, have been significant in EU-CTF cooperation. While the European Commission and the Council Secretariat both played the role of an SPE, the article outlines the different ways in which this occurred. Empirically, the article challenges an intergovernmentalist perspective by examining the implementation of United Nations Security Council resolutions and Financial Action Task Force recommendations on countering terrorist financing at the EU level.

Introduction

Since 2001, the funding of terrorist groups has developed into one of the most important policy areas in the fight against global terrorism. In the immediate aftermath of the terrorist attacks on the United States (US), it became apparent that the question of how to finance the daily activity of terrorist networks, the necessary propaganda, and, ultimately, specific terrorist actions, was of crucial importance to the survival of Islamist fundamentalist organisations such as Al Qaeda. Hence, post-9/11 international and regional counter-terrorism strategies prioritised the enhancement of counter-terrorist financing (CTF) measures with the primary aim to tighten control over the international banking circuit, disrupting the lifeblood of terrorist groups and gathering important information from financial transactions for the identification and prosecution of terrorists.

The United Nations (UN) and the Financial Action Task Force (FATF)[1] were the international fora who took the lead in the design of globally binding standards[2]

against the misuse of the international financial system by terrorist organisations. All UN member states have thus acquired a legal obligation in international law to implement these standards, which also applies to European Union (EU) member states. Accordingly, the 9/11 attacks have provided EU policy-makers with an opportunity to endorse new initiatives, new EU competences and institutional arrangements, which has acted as a catalyst for the significant development of EU counter-terrorist financing (EU-CTF) cooperation.

The EU is a 'good' implementer of UN Security Council (SC) sanctions, despite the fact that the EU itself is not a member of the UN. Despite the fact that international legal obligations apply to UN member states, and not the EU, the EU nonetheless implements these obligations in order to ensure that, in areas of EU competence, its legislation does not contradict these international legal obligations. Lavranos (2007) outlines the two step procedure of EU implementation: (1) a Common Foreign and Security Policy (CFSP) common position is adopted by the Council, followed by (2) an EC regulation adopted in the European Community Pillar (pre-Lisbon Pillar 1) in order to give a legally binding effect to the common position. This regulation is directly applicable in all EU member states according to European Court of Justice (ECJ) jurisprudence. The European Commission is subsequently tasked with the enforcement of the sanctions regime by updating automatically the listing of suspected targets in accordance with the list of the UN Sanctions Committee. Lavranos (2007, p. 7) calls this the 'communitarisation of UN Security Council resolutions (UNSCRs) within the Community legal order'. The FATF special recommendations on counter-terrorism financing can arguably be seen as extensions to already existing anti-money laundering recommendations, with the first special recommendation simply directing ratification of the 1999 International Convention for the Suppression of the Financing of Terrorism. Consequently, that first special recommendation, viewed through UNSCR 1617 (2005) which strongly urges the member states to implement the FATF recommendations, produces a circular logic between the UN and FATF measures to address terrorist finance (de Goede 2003, 2007, 2008, Heupel 2007, 2009, Guild 2008, Vlcek 2007, 2008, 2009, Heng and McDonagh 2008). In effect, to extend Lavranos argument, this implies a certain 'communitarisation of UN and FATF obligations'.

EU counter-terrorism policy has received increasing scholarly attention over the past few years (Reinares 2000, den Boer and Monar 2002, Dubois 2002, Gilmore 2003, Occhipinti 2003, Friedrichs 2005, Gregory 2005, Kaunert 2005, 2007, 2009, 2010a, 2010b, Bures 2006, 2008, Deflem 2006, Spence 2006, Zimmermann 2006, Mitsilegas and Gilmore 2007, Monar 2007, Bossong 2008, den Boer et al. 2008, Edwards and Meyer 2008, Müller-Wille 2008, Keohane 2008, Argomaniz 2009). Students of EU counter-terrorism, however, disagree on the extent to which EU competences matter in the fight against the global terrorist threat. Some commentators describe the EU as a 'paper tiger' (Bures 2006, p. 57) and an ineffective counter-terrorism actor; while others point to the progress the EU has made towards encouraging cooperation between its member states and increasing integration in the field. According to Edwards and Meyer (2008, p. 1) the entire 'governance of the European Union has been changed through its responses to international terrorism'. Zimmermann (2006, p. 123) argues that 'on 21 September 2001, the Union prioritised the fight against terrorism, and accelerated the development and implementation of measures deliberated on prior to the events of 9/11'.

Concurrently, Zimmermann (2006, p. 126) also makes it clear that '(...) the Union does not have a "normal" government at the supranational level with all the requisite powers, competences, and hence, capabilities of a regular government; it is not a federal European state'. This means that, a priori, one would not necessarily expect EU institutions to provide significant leadership in counter-terrorism. Admittedly, counter-terrorism is a policy area in which European institutions have rarely taken the lead, nor consistently been very active. Yet, increasingly, this view has become challenged (Kaunert 2007). This article reconceptualises the notion of supranational policy entrepreneurship (SPE) in order to explore and assess the role played by EU supranational actors in implementing post-2001 UN and FATF standards on countering terrorist financing at EU level. The argument is advanced that, despite the centrality that member states maintain in the EU policy-making process, EU supranational actors, in particular the European Commission and the Council Secretariat,[3] have exerted considerable influence in shaping the current design of EU-CTF regime. Thus, the article provides new insights as to the different ways in which international bureaucracies can work together in order to build an alliance of different SPEs, such as the Council Secretariat and the European Commission in this case. How does this work in practice? What institutional tools do they have at their disposal in order to do so? Furthermore, the article explains why counter-terrorism financing was pushed so strongly at the level of the EU, despite the fact that, a priori, the EU level does not have the international legal obligations through the UN and the FATF. These obligations could have been complied with through the national EU member states level alone; yet, the EU developed a strong counter-terrorism financing regime nonetheless. Thus, this article provides for a supranational explanation for this empirical development.

The remainder of the article is structured as follows. The first section introduces the theoretical debate on SPE and the analytical framework used for the article, outlining the differences in providing policy entrepreneurship by the Commission and the Council Secretariat. The second section briefly presents scope and content of post-9/11 global CTF standards. The third section analyses the empirical evidence within the case study of EU-CTF by examining the transposition of global standards at the EU level, and the role of European institutions in the process. The last section is dedicated to some final reflections concerning key findings, implications on how to regard the powers of EU supranational actors in counter-terrorism policy and the most relevant changes introduced by the entry into force of the Lisbon Treaty.

Supranational policy entrepreneurship

Agency is a long-standing and central question within the theoretical debate concerning the importance of supranational institutions in European integration. Early neo-functionalist arguments about incrementalism and 'spill-over' dynamics assigned a primary role to supranational actors in this process (Haas 1958, Lindberg 1963). Intergovernmentalists (Moravcsik 1993, 1998), supranationalists (Sandholtz and Stone Sweet 1998) and institutionalists positioned 'somewhere in between' (Pollack 2003, Beach 2005, Kaunert 2007), however, hold competing opinions about original neo-functionalist ideas and actual powers of European institutions. Intergovernmentalists view European integration as a process largely determined by interests and preferences of rational domestic policy-makers. Supranational institutions are seen as merely functional to reinforcing inter-state commitments. Conversely, supranationalists, despite recognising the political power of member states at the bargaining stage of decision-making, emphasise the activism of European actors in promoting and facilitating more cooperation among national governments. The European Commission, in particular, is often portrayed as a skilful SPE: eager to introduce innovative ideas into policy-making and capable to create supportive coalitions around its preferred solutions.

The SPE notion is rooted in the original conceptualisation of 'policy entrepreneurs' which dates back to Kingdon (1995, originally published in 1984). Kingdon's approach to US policy-making consists of three major separate streams (problem identification, generation of policy proposals and political processes) flowing simultaneously through the political system. At a critical point in time, when a certain problem is defined in the problem stream, feasible solutions are available in the policy stream, and the balance of forces in the political stream is favourable, all streams may be 'coupled' together (Kingdon 1995, p. 20). Chances for such convergence to occur increases when a so-called 'policy window' is opened, often by the efforts of a 'policy entrepreneur' who stands at that window to profit by the most propitious time to rally support for his own policy proposal (Kingdon 1995, p. 20). Policy entrepreneurs are very experienced actors, willing to invest their resources – time, energy, reputation and money – to sustain a policy from which they expect a future return (Kingdon 1995, p. 180). There are three fundamental characteristics of a successful policy entrepreneur: he/she must 'have some claim to a hearing', he/she must be well-known for his/her political relations and/or negotiation ability, he/she must be very persistent in waiting for a policy window to open (Kingdon 1995, p. 181). This article further elaborates on Kingdon's 'multiple streams' model and its conceptualisation of 'policy entrepreneurs' to which it incorporates constructivist insights about the significance of norms in international institutions. The 'constructivist turn' in international relations pointed out that norm construction and strategic bargaining are closely inter-linked, and it convincingly demonstrated that norms and values can shape national interests and determine state behaviour (Finnemore 1996a, 1996b, Finnemore and Sikkink 1998).

An inclusion of the concept of norms is highly beneficial for the realities of EU policy-making. More often than not, the nature of the EU between a fully fledged state and an international organisation means that different norms are competing with one another, unlike an established domestic polity. National sovereignty is the prevailing and generally accepted norm within the international system. Yet, within the EU system this norm is constantly competing with the norm to pool national sovereignty at the EU level, and to drive forward the process of European integration. A successful SPE needs to push for an alignment of these norms, before any serious policy proposal be suggested. The differences between these approaches are greater than normally found within established systems, such as within states or on the international level. Thus, a successful SPE in the EU has to be able to realign these norms as well as pushing for a new substantive policy. The argument here is that norms in effect guide the other three (Kingdon) streams, i.e. the problem, policy and politics stream. These normative frames constrain actors as they provide limits to the establishment of new norms and also interpretation bands, which an SPE can use when he/she acts as a first mover. They are guiding devices for the recognition and appreciation of extraordinary crises and indicators, as well as for the search for policy alternatives, and the search for coalition partners. At the same time, norms do not determine precise outcomes. Actors still have a substantial degree of freedom within which to be guided by norms. At the point where all streams are coupled, the SPE provides the impetus to push for detailed policy proposals which fit the other three streams. As soon as a policy window opens, the SPE gets an opportunity to succeed.

Kaunert (2007, 2009) suggests the ways in which political entrepreneurs can achieve this:

(1) First mover advantage: SPEs need to come in faster with their proposals than their rivals.
(2) Persuasion strategy: as mentioned above, in order to achieve acceptance, other actors need to be convinced by the reasons for the action proposed.
(3) Alliances: it is vital for the SPE to form initial alliances with other powerful actors to create a bandwagon effect, whereby more actors will join the 'winning team'.

Hülsse (2007) has analysed the emergence of money laundering as a global problem, which provides an interesting example of policy entrepreneurship at the global level, and in many ways following on from the conception by Kaunert (2007, 2009). His study focused on the area of money laundering and counter-terrorist finance, which he analysed using the concept of supranational policy entrepreneurs. In his study, SPEs first problematise an issue, i.e. they are intrinsically important for the construction of a policy problem, to which they then present a policy solution. In other words, his study shows that SPEs first had to construct their 'window of opportunity', given the lack of a specific trigger event in the policy area and subsequently applied their policy solutions to the political problem they had themselves constructed.

Applying this empirically, one needs to note that the potential for SPE is different amongst the different EU institutions. The Commission can be conceptualised as having a much more direct impact on the negotiations due to its institutional powers. It is responsible for initiating and implementing EU policy; however, it is also, as the Union's bureaucracy, responsible for the detailed drafting of legislation. The Commission acts as the conscience of the Community, as it is formally the Guardian of the Treaties and responsible for determining whether policy proposals fall within the EU's competence (Wallace *et al.* 2005). It also plays a crucial mediating role between the institutions and amongst the member states within the Council (Edwards and Spence 2005).

On the other hand, the Council General Secretariat is much more reliant on persuasive force, and thus potentially a less powerful SPE. It conducts the administrative work of the Council. Officials from the Secretariat have the responsibility for drafting agendas, keeping records, providing legal advice, processing and circulating documentation, and translating and monitoring policy decisions (Nugent 2000, pp. 152–153). At a basic level the General Secretariat provides consistent policy advice and support for the rotating Presidencies. Thus, the general functions of the Council Secretariat imply that it needs to resort to more 'soft' tools, such as persuasion and the power of the pen in the negotiations. Often, it might even be conceptualised as a 'contributing' SPE, or an ally for the Commission, depending on their own rivalries during specific negotiations. As the Council Secretariat has been 'successful in gaining an executive role in the more intergovernmental policy areas of the Union', this has led to a redefinition of its relations with the European Commission in some policy areas (Christiansen 2006, p. 165). Consequently, for the area of CTF, either institution is more likely to be successful as an SPE if they act together in unison, and avoids falling into the trap of inter-institutional rivalries.

Post-2001 international counter-terrorist financing action

The financing of terrorism has become a major target of international counter-terrorism action since 9/11. Arguably, two main factors explain the significance of CTF. Firstly, under conditions of globalisation, increasingly, terrorists benefit from modern technologies to recruit new affiliates and carry out terrorist attacks. Terrorist financing covers both the funding of terrorist networks, including propaganda and recruitment, and that of terrorist actions. Similarly to what happens with money laundering and organised crime, terrorist groups resort to complex transactions across the international financial system in order to elude national controls (Mitsilegas and Gilmore 2007). Secondly, the organisation of the economy and the banking systems in the Middle East, which is seen as the core of Al-Qaida's financial structure (Gardner 2007), together with the role therein played by Islamic charities and the hawala networks (de Moraes Ruehsen 2007, Gunning 2008), makes terrorist financing a very sensitive issue.

Yet, what makes countering terrorist finances such a sensitive issue? The two main issues in that respect are the role of Islamic charities and the importance of hawalas (Gardner 2007, p. 342). Charitable giving (zakat) is an obligation for all practising Muslims, which means that sometimes considerable amounts of money are given to charities, often in cash and with very little regulation. According to some Western officials, some of the donations made to Islamic charities have financed terrorism (de Moraes Ruehsen 2007, p. 165; see also Gunning 2008). Hawala networks are informal value transfer systems based on trust and operating completely outside the formal banking system. Despite this potential for negative use, they are often equally used by bona fide emigrated workers who only aim to send remittances back home (de Moraes Ruehsen 2007). Other scholars have also commented that charities and hawala have not been demonstrated as actual significant sources for terrorist finance (de Goede 2003, 2007, 2008, Gilmore 2004, Heupel 2007, 2009, Sykes 2007, Vlcek 2007, 2008, 2009, Guild 2008, Heng and McDonagh 2008, Razavy and Haggerty 2009).

Accordingly, more coordinated international action and long-term prevention were identified as key measures to inhibit the passage of terrorist financial flows through domestic financial institutions. The UN and the FATF were the leading international organisations in the process of setting global CTF standards and promoting full compliance of their respective members (Thony and Png 2007). At the beginning of the process, Resolutions 1267 and 1373 were adopted by the UN Security Council (UN 1999, 2001). Resolution 1267 was adopted in 1999 in order to establish sanctions against the Taliban regime in Afghanistan which was suspected of supporting Osama bin Laden and Al-Qaeda. The scope of Resolution 1373 is broader since it does not target any specific individuals or organisations, but all forms of terrorism. It requires states to take concerted action to prevent the support of terrorist organisations, including financial support. It also imposes the criminalisation of terrorist financing and the immediate freezing of all funds and assets of terrorists and terrorist groups. This far-reaching and binding resolution was adopted by the United Nations Security Council (UNSC) under Chapter VII of the UN Charter on 28 September 2001, emphasising the massive threat posed to international peace and security. Observers point out that Resolution 1373 is one of the strongest acts ever taken by the UN because of the unprecedented reach into many sectors of domestic legislation and security policy (Eling 2006). This text has a pronounced law-making character which is detectable in the imposition of strict anti-terrorist financing obligations. In addition, it calls for the implementation of already existing international conventions on terrorism, including the 1999 UN International Convention for the Suppression of the Financing of Terrorism, and it sets up a special Counter-Terrorism Committee charged with monitoring UN member states' compliance (Cameron 2002, 2003, 2006, Lavranos 2006, 2007, Eckes 2008a, 2008b, Klabbers 2008). This committee regularly updates the list of designated persons and entities in order to enforce the sanctions; it is charged with the listing and de-listing requests. Individuals and entities can submit requests for de-listing through their countries of residence or citizenship. The UN Security Council produces reports through its Analytical Support and Sanctions Monitoring Team concerning the progress made by the UN member states. It is important to note that the UN reports provide the perspective that compliance within the EU is no better and no worse than the rest of the UN member states[4] (Cameron 2002, 2003, 2006, Lavranos 2006, 2007, Eckes 2008a, 2008b, Klabbers 2008).

While the precise EU legal regime to give effect to these SC resolutions will be explained in the next section, it is important to note at this stage that the implementation of UN financial sanctions against alleged terrorist financiers can bring up considerable Human Rights questions (van Thiel 2008), as the case of Mr Kadi and the case of the People's Mojahedin Organisation of Iran (PMOI) shows. On 3 September 2008, the ECJ delivered judgement in the cases of P Kadi and Al Barakaat International Foundation vs. Council and Commission. Mr Kadi was listed, as a person suspected of supporting terrorism whose funds and resources should be frozen, by the UN in 2001 under the UNSCR 1267 (Al Qaeda and Taliban list). In December 2001, Mr Kadi appealed to the Court of First Instance against the inclusion on this list on the basis that his fundamental rights had been violated, e.g. the right of a fair hearing, respect for property, the principle of proportionality, the right to effective judicial review, etc. On appeal to the ECJ, the latter annulled the EC Regulation aimed at transposing the UN obligation in so far as Mr Kadi was concerned, on the grounds that their procedural and fundamental rights had not been sufficiently respected. The story is similar regarding the PMOI, an Iranian opposition group.

As the most important international player beside the UNSC, the FATF also emerged as a proactive international standard-setter against the misuse of the global financial system by terrorist groups. The FATF's main task is to develop and promote anti-money laundering and CTF recommendations. Its membership currently comprises 32 countries and territories and two regional organisations, including the EU 15 'old' member states and the European Commission. Since the beginning of its activity, the FATF has drawn up Forty Recommendations, which set out the basic framework for international action against money laundering, and whose implementation is monitored through a 'mutual evaluation process'. These recommendations were subsequently updated, in particular in October 2001, when the FATF's overall remit was extended beyond money laundering as to also include the fight against terrorist financing.

The so-called 'Eight Special Recommendations' on terrorist financing (FATF 2001) were adopted at the extraordinary plenary session held in Washington in October 2001, following the adoption of the 'International Money Laundering Abatement and Anti-Terrorist Financing Act' by the US Congress, which increased pressure on other governments to tighten their own anti-money laundering and CTF legislations (Allen 2003, Eling 2006). These eight Recommendations, to which a ninth was added in 2004, established new, firm international standards to detect, prevent and suppress the financing of terrorism and terrorist acts by denying terrorists and their supporters access to the international financial system, with specific regard to: (1) ratifying and implementing UN instruments; (2) criminalising the financing of terrorism and associated money laundering; (3) freezing and confiscating terrorist assets; (4) reporting suspicious transactions potentially linked to terrorism; (5) cooperating at international level in terrorist financing investigations; (6) imposing anti-money laundering requirements on alternative remittance systems; (7) strengthening customer identification measures in international and domestic wire transfers; (8) preventing non-profit organisations from being misused to finance terrorism; and (9) detecting and stopping cash couriers. Yet, it is important to emphasise, as noted in the introduction, that, given the first special recommendation demanding ratification of the 1999 International Convention for the Suppression of the Financing of Terrorism, the FATF recommendations produce a circular logic between the UN and FATF measures to address terrorist finance (de Goede 2003, 2007, 2008, Heupel 2007, 2009, Vlcek 2007, 2008, 2009, Guild 2008, Heng and McDonagh 2008).

Post-9/11 EU-CTF cooperation

This section analyses the developments of EU-CTF cooperation by focusing on the role played by EU supranational actors in the process. It is worthwhile recalling the fact that both issues, terrorism and money laundering, have been embedded in the policy domain of Justice and Home Affairs (JHA) since its inclusion into the EU treaty settlement by the Maastricht Treaty in the early 1990s. However, the specific question of terrorist financing did not get on the EU priority agenda prior to 2001.

Hülsse's (2007) study is particularly relevant in this regard because the measures undertaken to combat terrorist finance are grounded on a pre-existing foundation of anti-money laundering measures. According to him, SPEs had to first problematise anti-money laundering as a policy issue in order to be able to present a policy solution to this problem. Kingdon (1995) suggests two ways for a political problem to achieve recognition on the formal agenda: (1) a sudden rise in a particular statistical indicator; or (2) crisis or a prominent event. In this definition, a crisis is an event with extraordinary consequences. However, as Hülsse (2007) suggests, due to the lack of a triggering event in anti-money laundering, SPEs themselves had to construct their 'window of opportunity' and subsequently applied their policy solutions to this political problem.

This can be contrasted to the events of 11 September 2001, and the subsequent creation of measures to combat terrorist finance. The 9/11 attacks certainly represented a crisis with extraordinary consequences. Thus in its wake a 'window of opportunity' opened (den Boer 2006) through the extraordinary nature of the attacks and acted as a catalyst for the incremental development of EU-CTF cooperation. It also managed to incrementally change a fundamental political norm of European counter-terrorism prior to 9/11 – national sovereignty as sacrosanct. However, it needs to be mentioned that it built on pre-exisiting policy problem understanding provided by the fight against anti-money laundering (Hülsse 2007).

At the extraordinary meeting of 21 September 2001, the European Council launched an ambitious 'Action Plan to Combat Terrorism'. The Plan's cornerstones were 'close cooperation between all the member states of the EU' and the adoption of a 'coordinated and interdisciplinary approach embracing all Union's policies' (European Council 2001, p. 1). The European Council called for the use of all tools at the EU's disposal, including legislative, operational, repressive, preventive, internal and external measures. The primary purpose was to make the EU's collective response as comprehensive as possible, and essentially multidimensional (Monar 2007).

Following the US, UN and FATF drive, the European Council declared that '(...) combating the funding of terrorism is a decisive aspect. Energetic international action is required to ensure that that fight is fully effective. The European Union will contribute to the full' (European Council 2001, p. 2). On the basis of such statements, the JHA as well as the Economic and Financial Affairs (ECOFIN) Councils of Ministers were instructed to 'take all the necessary measures to combat any form of financing for terrorist activities' (European Council 2001, p. 2). As a result, the Action Plan which was finally adopted in November 2001, included many provisions specifically focused on preventing the acquisition, retention and use of funds or assets by terrorist groups.

In practice, the implementation of the Plan was strongly linked to the transposition of UN and FATF international CTF standards into EU legislation, and required a pooling of national sovereignty. In response to the 'war on terror' in the aftermath of the 9/11 attacks, EU member states wanted to demonstrate their solidarity with the USA, and former President G.W. Bush Jr. made it clear that his government would divide the world into two camps: either you are with us or against us. This made an unambiguous EU response crucial. Nonetheless surprisingly, EU member states, despite their traditional reluctance to hand over powers to European institutions in areas as deeply entrenched into national sovereignty as counter-terrorism, recognised that collective implementation at EU level could contribute to a more effective response[5] to the 'war on terror'. Two other factors strengthened such perception of the importance of a European added value. On the one hand, some national governments, which were not previously familiar with terrorism, lacked the original primary legislation necessary to adopt some of the instruments to implement the provisions. On the other hand, the EU had consistently been committed in the past to aligning itself to FATF and UN decisions, as well as implementing both UNSC resolutions and FATF recommendations into EU legislation. The aforementioned reasons help to explain why the EU as a whole sought to be 'an exemplary implementer' (Eling 2006). More importantly, the response to the 'war on terror' was starting to incrementally change one fundamental norm in European counter-terrorism – national sovereignty (Kaunert 2007).

Subsequently, the EU-CTF commitment was reinforced by the shock of the terrorist attacks in Madrid on 11 March 2004 – the first European '9/11', subsequently termed the '3/11 attacks' in Spain. The 'solidarity' Declaration on Combating Terrorism, which was agreed upon by the European Heads of State and Government on 29 March 2004, once again emphasised the need 'to reduce the access of terrorists to financial and other economic resources' and 'to address the factors contributing to the support for and recruitment into terrorism' (European Council 2004a). Accordingly, the European Council held in June 2004 included the combating of terrorist financing among the four priority areas of action.[6] The subsequent revised Counter-Terrorism Action Plan set out new proposals aimed at more effectively tackling terrorist funding, and it prompted the quick development of an EU ad hoc strategy. The strategy on terrorist financing was swiftly drawn up by the Council on the basis of a proposal made jointly by the Council Secretariat and the European Commission, and then adopted by the European Council in December 2004 (European Council 2004b). The strategy provided a critical overview of the actions undertaken until then concerning the fight against terrorist financing. It also recommended a number of initiatives to be adopted to strengthen EU efforts.

The European Commission and the Council Secretariat in action

This section argues that the European Commission and the Council Secretariat have played a significant role in the transposition of CTF international standards into EU legislation, and, overall, in the design of the EU-CTF regime. While the European Commission exerted considerable influence in promoting EU cooperation with regards to FATF recommendations, the Council Secretariat constructed its influence predominantly within the intergovernmental context of implementing UN resolutions through the Council of Ministers. Thus, the Commission and the Council Secretariat both managed to play the role of an SPE, in different ways, and persuaded member states to promote European integration in countering terrorism financing matters. Yet, as conceptualised in the first section of this article, the use of the term 'persuasion' here is applied differently to both EU institutions. While the Commission had to persuade the member states of the merits of the policy, the Council Secretariat acted more as a facilitator, given that UN resolution 1373 is binding in international law on UN member states. However, despite this, EU member states needed to be convinced to use the framework of the Union in order to fulfil their international legal obligations. They could have easily implemented their international legal obligations through domestic legislations alone. What is the benefit for member states to fulfil their international legal obligations through the EU? Despite the fact they apply to UN member states, and not the EU level, these obligations can beneficially be implemented through the EU in order to ensure that, in areas of EU competence, its legislation does not contradict these international legal obligations. In effect, as outlined at the beginning of the article, this implies a certain 'communitarisation of UN and FATF obligations'. In the context of the Kadi and al Barakaat cases, the European Commission considered that it was necessary to adopt EU instruments to ensure a consistent application of the targeted sanctions across the EU territory in order to preserve the free movement of capital within the Community and to avoid distortions of competition. This reasoning was also strongly supported by some member states, such as the UK, which feared that differences in the application of the freezing of assets amongst member states would have an impact on free movement of capital in the EU, therefore leading to a risk of distortion of competition.

Counter-terrorism is one of the most complicated policy areas in the Union owing to its inherent cross-pillar character. The legal competences prior to the entry into force of the Lisbon Treaty are firmly placed in between the second and third pillar. EU legal competences for signing international agreements under the third pillar derive from Articles 24 and 38 of the Treaty on the European Union (TEU). Article 38 stipulates that agreements listed in Article 24, which falls under the second pillar, can also cover matters in the third pillar (Fletcher *et al.* 2008, p. 153). However, in relation to the EU-CTF regime, part of the EU competences are also to be found in the first pillar due to its close link to anti-money laundering measures. Both the Council Secretariat and the European Commission recognised the importance of inter-pillar and inter-institutional coordination, which are very significant conditions in order to be successful as SPEs. Both pointed to how the adoption of a comprehensive approach was undeniably the best way to address the question of CTF as well as to increase their own influence.

The Council Secretariat, in a paper submitted to COREPER on 8 March 2004,[7] observed that 'the fight against terrorism is a cross-pillar activity engaging many EU actors and instruments'. It also highlighted then that many coordination problems have posed a challenge to the EU's capacity to coherently and effectively respond to its international legal obligations. Hence, on 25 March 2004, the new Office of the EU Counter-Terrorism Coordinator (CTC) was created with the aim to improve coordination in EU counter-terrorism policy. This office was based in the Council Secretariat under the leadership of the High Representative for Foreign and Security Policy.[8] The EU CTC[9] was tasked, together with the Commission, to ensure the follow-up of the strategy on terrorist financing on a cross-pillar basis and to submit a six monthly report to the Council. The most recent version of this strategy (European Council 2008) pointed out that most actions mentioned in the 2004 Strategy have been carried out with a considerable improvement of coordination. This is a clear sign that the two institutions have been working better together.

Transposing Financial Action Task Force recommendations

This section explores the role played by the European Commission in the first pillar policy area with regards to the implementation of the FATF Special Recommendations. The FATF Nine Special Recommendations require the extension of the EU anti-money laundering regulatory framework to also include the offence of terrorist financing. As cooperation at the EU level during the 1990s focused more on fighting transnational organised crime rather than terrorism, the European actors, *in primis* the Commission, who were already in charge of anti-money laundering tasks, could largely rely on that experience.

Following Kingdon's definition (1995), SPEs stand at the policy window in order to propose, lobby for, and sell a policy proposal. They need to possess resources which they are willing to invest, such as time, energy, reputation, money and actively use these to promote a policy position in return for anticipated future gains. However, SPEs according to Kingdon (1995, p. 180) have 'one of three sources: expertise, an ability to speak for others, or an authoritative decision-making position'. The European

Commission, in particular DG Internal Market (DG Markt), utilised the expertise and competence it acquired on anti-money-laundering matters in order to initiate terrorist financing-related legislation. According to the treaties, pre- and post-Lisbon Treaty, the Commission has the exclusive right to initiate proposals on terrorist financing with regards to first pillar provisions concerning financial crime. Consequently, it used this power of initiation and then worked to persuade the Council of Ministers and the European Parliament to approve its legislative proposals. In addition, the Commission is itself, together with the EU 15 'old' member states, an FATF member. DG Markt leads the European delegation during FATF negotiations by seeking to improve coordination between EU member states, despite their obvious jealousy to protect their national prerogatives.

In Kingdon's (1995) view, political entrepreneurs are necessary for the coupling of streams. A political entrepreneur stands at the policy window in order to propose, lobby for, and sell a policy proposal. Since the 2001 attacks, especially in the initial months of major political pressure for action, the Commission managed to accelerate the adoption of some legislative measures with terrorist financing implications that were already under discussion before 9/11, including the 'Protocol to the Convention on Mutual Assistance in Criminal Matters',[10] which provides for the exchange of information between the member states concerning bank accounts whose holder is subject to criminal investigations. The protocol represents a considerable improvement of cooperation in the fight against economic and financial crime. Furthermore, the Commission pushed for the adoption of the so-called 'second anti-money laundering Directive'. While controversial negotiations on the Directive had been ongoing since the summer of 1999,[11] the Commission proved to be extremely skilful in pushing this initiative through the 9/11 'window of opportunity'. While Kingdon (1995) suggests that SPEs need to push, push and push for their proposals, they also do more than that. They need to lie in wait for a window to open and therefore seize the right moment. The Commission excelled in this regard by using the close link between money laundering and terrorist financing in order to push the European Parliament to agree on the text already approved by the Council. The second anti-money laundering Directive was adopted at the conciliation stage in December 2001, and it thereby amended the earlier 1991 Directive.

The success of this legislation has clear similarities with the Commission's policy entrepreneurship in the adoption of the European Arrest Warrant (EAW; Kaunert 2007). The eventual EAW, which in its initial state would have been difficult to swallow for most member states in the mere context of the 'fight against crime' that prevailed in the 1990s, was politically constructed to become an important instrument in the 'war on terror'. In the same way, the emerging international norm of joining in the 'war on terror' made it necessary to adopt a new CTF Directive, even though it seemed implausible to adopt these instruments in the 'fight against money laundering'.[12] In this way, the norm to participate in the war on terror (via EU mechanisms) was used strategically to convince the majority of member states of the political merits of the second anti-money laundering directive, and it allowed the Commission to use member states' peer pressure to convince the reluctant member states to participate. Thus, the Commission managed to play the role of an SPE and persuaded member states to promote European integration in CTF.

This process was pushed even more strongly when, in 2004, the Commission prepared a far-reaching Communication focused on the prevention of and the fight against terrorist financing through measures to improve the exchange of information, to strengthen transparency and enhance the traceability of financial transactions. Most of the elements included in the Communication were also inserted in the 2005 'third anti-money laundering Directive'[13] which repealed the previous two directives. The 'third directive' also made the title 'terrorist financing' more explicit, and, once again, reaffirmed the EU objective to comply with FATF standards. It clearly incorporated most of the latest version of the FATF Recommendations (as revised in 2003) into Community legislation.

In addition, it also integrated a number of associated measures aimed at implementing the FATF requirements: (1) Regulation (EC) No 1889/2005 on the control of cash entering or leaving the Community (which implements SR IX on cash couriers); (2) Regulation (EC) No 1781/2006 on information on the payer accompanying transfers of funds[14]; and (3) Directive 2007/64/EC on payment services (PSD) in the internal market, which provides the legal foundation for the creation of an EU-wide single market for payments.[15]

Finally, following the Council Decision 2000/642/JHA of 17 October 2000 concerning arrangements for cooperation between Financial Intelligence Units (FIUs) of EU member states, the Commission launched the 'FIU.Net initiative', an EU-wide network of all national FIUs aimed at sharing information on terrorist funding in a secure environment and at supporting the cooperation between the various FIUs. In addition, the Commission set-up a forum for discussion, the so-called 'EU FIUs Platform', aimed at enabling the EU FIUs to exchange views and experiences on technical issues. The FIU.NET project was co-financed by the Commission for a period of 2 years until the end of 2009. The Netherlands are the contracting party and co-financing is provided by Finland, Germany, Romania, the UK, France, Greece and Italy (Council of the European Union 2009). The Board of Partners of the projects is formed by representatives of these eight member states. By May 2009, 18 EU member states FIUs have been connected to the FIU.NET and four are in the process of being connected. The CTC expects that in total 22 FIUs will be connected before August 2009.

Transposing United Nations Security Council resolutions

As analysed previously, the regime of targeted financial sanctions foreseen by UNSC resolutions is one of the cornerstones in the international fight against terrorist financing. The EU Council of Ministers, within the second pillar intergovernmental context of the CFSP, was entrusted with the transposition of such resolutions, and the Council Secretariat actively participated in the process. Following the precedent of the UNSC Resolution 1267 concerning Al-Qaida, Osama Bin Laden and the Taliban and Associated Individuals and Entities, the EU adopted and implemented a specific set of rules to transpose UNSC Resolution 1373 in the context of the second pillar. Since the adoption in 1999 of Resolution 1267, the EU has already been applying certain sanctions on Al Qaeda and Taliban suspects in accordance with the list designed by the UN 'Al-Qaida and Taliban Sanctions Committee'. Yet, after 9/11 the implementation of Resolution 1373, whose most important component is the 'freezing of assets' provision, required imposing freezing measures against whatever terrorist group, and no longer just against Al Qaeda and Taliban.

As a consequence, the EU decided to establish its own autonomous system aimed at identifying and designating individuals and organisations under suspicion of terrorism (but not included under the 1267 sanctions regime). In order do this, the Council adopted a Common Position (2001/931/CFSP) on the joint bases of Articles 15 and 34 TEU in December 2001. The Common Position lays clearly down the criteria for listing persons, groups or entities suspected of having links with terrorism and of being involved in terrorist acts, as well as defining the actions that amount to a terrorist act.

This was complemented by a Council Regulation (EC) No 2580/2001, adopted under Articles 60, 301 and 308 TEC, implementing the EC law aspects of the foreign policy aspects of the Common Position. The EC Regulation provides for the freezing of all funds, other financial assets and economic resources belonging to the persons, groups and entities listed in the Common Position and coming from outside the EU. Furthermore, all persons, groups and entities listed in the Common Position are subject to enhanced measures taken in the field of police and judicial cooperation in criminal matters. The need to adopt a first pillar regulation alongside of a second/ third pillar common position was due to the fact that an asset freeze represents a hindrance to the Community provision for the free movement of capital. This would have been prohibited by EC law without this regulation. Hence, through the adoption of the Common Position and the EC Regulation, the EU addressed both foreign policy and criminal law matters.

The Council Secretariat-Directorate General E for EU external affairs, with the support of the European Commission-DG External Relations, was charged with the strictly intergovernmental procedures of listing and de-listing of terrorist suspects. As suggested above, SPEs according to Kingdon (1995) have to excel in expertise, need to be able to speak for other actors, or need to be in a decision-making position. Incrementally, all these factors came into being for the Council Secretariat as well. While the former is much more reliant on persuasive force, and thus potentially a less powerful SPE than the Commission, its authoritative position in the EU policy-making system is not negligible: its responsibilities include administrative work such as the drafting of agendas (and thus the gate-keeping role for proposals), keeping records (and thus one important element of persuasive power), providing legal advice (the second dimension of persuasive power) and monitoring policy decisions (Nugent 2000, pp. 152–153). Thus, the Council Secretariat can use more 'soft' tools, such as persuasion and the power of the pen in the negotiations, and thus fulfils the conditions set by Kingdon's model (1995). However, its greatest strength in the negotiations, at least for the area of CTF, is to act in unison with the Commission as allies.

While the Council Secretariat has over time acquired important functions in the intergovernmental areas of CFSP, it is equally increasing its weight also in some areas of police and criminal justice cooperation as EU member states were reluctant to empower the Commission in these sensitive fields. As a result, since 1999, the Council Secretariat has taken the lead, on behalf of the Council,[16] in the implementation of UNSC Resolution 1267 and in the update of EU legislation following relevant changes in the UN 'blacklist'. This kind of legacy presumably influenced the institutional and organisational arrangements which were chosen for managing the implementation of Resolution 1373 since 2001. In this area, the Council Secretariat plays a significant executive role and is endowed with the delicate responsibility to assist the ad hoc working group which was created within the Council and empowered with the responsibility for the EU blacklist's management.

A purely intergovernmental working group called the 'clearing house', which is composed of secret services' national delegates, was set up after 9/11 to evaluate the requests to add suspects to the EU list. A request can be submitted either by an EU member state or by a third country on the basis of a competent judicial authority's decision. This very secretive process,[5] which is not open to any political scrutiny, has been partially upgraded since March 2007. Following the verdicts by the Court of First Instance, which annulled a 2002 Council decision to freeze the funds of the People's Mujahidin Organisation of Iran (PMOI) on the basis of an EU breach of fundamental rights, the Council opted for the establishment of a more transparent procedure. It introduced the so-called 'due process' which includes statements of reasons to motivate listings and asset freezes, as well as notification procedures towards listed persons or entities. The Council also replaced the 'clearing house' with a new working group which is made up of EU member states' representatives and called the 'Working Party on implementation of Common Position 2001/931/CFSP on the application of specific measures to combat terrorism', conventionally labelled 'CP 931 WP'.[17] However, the workings of the group continue to take place in strictly confidential meetings.

Undoubtedly, the establishment of ad hoc rules and the institutional engineering constitutes an example of very successful policy innovation. Thus, it can be argued that the Council Secretariat managed to have a significant weight within the intergovernmental context of the Council of Ministers, thus facilitating the promotion of European CTF cooperation in countering terrorist financing.

Conclusions

In conclusion, the article demonstrates that European integration is possible also in 'high politics' areas which lie at the core of what the nation state is all about, such as counter-terrorism and the monopoly of force. Despite the centrality that EU member states maintain in the policy-making process, EU supranational actors, in particular the European Commission and the Council Secretariat, have been very active players in promoting increasing cooperation and in shaping the current EU-CTF regime. In fact, the EU developed a large number of legislative instruments, operational measures and institutional venues across all three pillars. The 9/11 events and the urgency to transpose UNSC resolutions and FATF recommendations into EU legislation opened an important 'policy window' which the European Commission, in particular, proved able to exploit by acting as a supranational policy entrepreneur. It contributed to member states' preference building and to embed the CTF policy into the European response to US-led 'war on terror'. It also created a political momentum that led to blurring the boundaries between anti-money laundering and anti-terrorism policy. However, it is important to note that UN reports provide the perspective that compliance within the EU, even with EU-level Directives, Regulations and Common Positions, is no better and no worse than the rest of the UN member (Cameron, 2002, 2003, 2006, Lavranos 2006, 2007, Eckes 2008a, 2008b, Klabbers, 2008). Consequently, it is important to note that events in Brussels did not happen in isolation, but were influenced by events in New York, as well as EU Member States' capitals.

Furthermore, as suggested in this article, the potential for SPE is different amongst the two EU institutions. The Commission, due to its institutional powers, has a stronger and more direct impact on EU policy negotiations. Its powers include: (1) initiating and implementing EU policy; (2) drafting of legislation; and (3) a mediating role between EU Member States. These responsibilities ensure much more clearly that it can act as an SPE. Kingdon outlines the three fundamental characteristics of a successful policy entrepreneur: (1) 'claim to a hearing'; (2) a good negotiator; and (3) persistence in waiting for a policy window to open Its legal responsibilities clearly give the Commission a good starting point to be able to fulfil these conditions. On the other hand, the Council General Secretariat is much more reliant on persuasive force, and thus potentially a less powerful SPE. Its responsibilities include: (1) the drafting of agendas (and thus the gate-keeping role for proposals); (2) keeping records (and thus one important element of persuasive power); (3) providing legal advice (the second dimension of persuasive power); and (4) monitoring policy decisions. Thus, these functions imply that it needs to resort to more 'soft' tools, such as persuasion and the power of the pen in the negotiations. But this role makes it an indispensable ally for the Commission. The findings of this article clearly suggest that European institutions can be important players in all the three pre-Lisbon pillars of counter-terrorism, in addition to the JHA pillar previously analysed (Kaunert 2007). In so doing, they contrast with intergovernmentalist arguments that dismiss the role of EU supranational actors in this process of European integration.

Although the treaties attributed a relatively limited role to the Union in the fight against terrorism in terms of legal competences, the EU contributed significantly to help its member states to work internationally with partners such as the UN, the FATF and other multilateral organisations. It clearly took advantage of the 9/11 'window of opportunity' to develop a CTF regime on a cross-pillar basis. Furthermore, inter-institutional relations between key supranational actors such as the Commission and the Council Secretariat, proved to be much more successful than might have been anticipated. The two institutions were able to cooperate well together.

However, the argument in this article has some limitations. The fact that the Commission and the Council Secretariat acquired the capacity to act as SPEs, as demonstrated by the CTF case, suggests that they can play a potentially significant role in the legislative process, even in institutionally difficult terrain such as counter-terrorism. The findings, though, are limited to the legislative process. There is still, in practice, a significant implementation deficit at the national level, which inevitably limits the argument to the legislative phase of international compliance.

In a report concerning the follow-up of the revised CTF Strategy on Terrorist Financing[18] (Council of the EU 2008), the CTC and the Commission pointed to the progress achieved in the legislative process, while remarking the lack of progress in the national implementation of EU-CTF provisions (Council of the European Union 2009). For instance, the report singles out the Directive 2005/60/EC on the prevention of the use of the financial system for the purpose of money laundering and terrorist financing (3rd CTF Directive) which entered into force on 15 December 2005. Member states had to transpose this directive before 15 December 2007. However, by May 2009, six EU member states had not finalised this transposition process (Belgium, Spain, France, Ireland, Poland and Finland). Although the Commission repeatedly emphasised the importance of speeding up the transposition process under the threat that an infringement procedure could follow, as this is a first pillar directive, this did not always result in success. Even worse, in the second and third pillar the Commission could not take member states to the ECJ for failure to transpose legislation properly or on time in the implementation process as would be the case in infringement proceedings under the TEU. As for the implementation of freezing of assets measures at national level, even officials of the Council Secretariat admitted not to know exactly to what extent such measures are actually implemented by national governments once a decision taken.[5]

However, significant changes are now expected due to the entry into force of the Lisbon Treaty, which creates a simplified decision-making procedure. One of the most important changes is the fact that the pillar structure is formally abolished, which results in the communitarisation of the areas of criminal justice, policing and counter-terrorism, and thus the abolition of the pillar duality over the JHA policy domain. While the so-called 'Community method' is now extended also to police and judicial cooperation in criminal matters, this occurred only with some differences, such as the 'break and accelerator procedure' giving each member state a de-facto opt-out from these policies. The standard decision-making procedure in the AFSJ will be co-decision between Parliament and Council and qualified majority voting (QMV) in the Council. The Commission will be given the exclusive power to propose legislation. In criminal justice and policing legislation, the latter power is shared with a quarter of the member states. As a result of these changes, the Commission will be given increased competences and will be enabled to play its traditional role of 'guardian of the treaties' also on all counter-terrorism matters.

Notes

1. The FATF is an intergovernmental body which operates in the context of the Organisation for Economic Cooperation and Development (OECD) since its creation at the 1989 July Paris Summit Meeting of the seven major industrialised nations (G7). The FATF mandate is to design and promote policies at both the national and the international level in order to fight money laundering and, after 2001, also terrorist financing.
2. Actually, only UN resolutions are binding in international law, whereas FATF standards take the form of recommendations. Nonetheless, despite this non-binding character, FATF recommendations were seen as the appropriate course of action after 9/11.
3. The Council Secretariat is here assumed to be a supranational institutional actor following the conceptualisation by Christiansen (2002, p. 35), who suggests that 'in spite of the official nomenclature, the Council Secretariat is clearly an institution, possessing a formal structure with a set of internal rules and administrative practices which regulate the work of a body of permanent staff. As it is located at the European level, possessing a high degree of institutional autonomy, it is arguably supranational in nature.
4. It is also important to note the fact that events in Brussels did not happen in isolation, but were influenced by events in New York, Luxembourg, Stockholm and the other Member States' capitals.
5. Interview, General Secretariat of the Council of the EU, Brussels, March 2009.
6. The other three priority areas include information sharing, mainstreaming counter-terrorism in the EU external relations, and improving civil protection and protection of critical infrastructures.
7. See doc. 7177/04.
8. In the field of countering terrorist financing the role of the CTC is to facilitate coordination between the EU and national CTF efforts, both internally and externally. The CTC also coordinates between and within EU institutions, specifically between the different relevant bodies in the Council (i.e. the COTER, the MDG-Multi-Disciplinary

Group on Organised Crime, the TWG – Terrorism Working Group, the 'clearing house'), and between the diverse Directorates General of the Commission which have CTF tasks (i.e. DG Justice, Liberty and Security, DG Internal Market and Services, DG External Relations).

9. The former CTC, Mr Gijs de Vries, was in office until March 2007, when his three year term finished. The incumbent CTC, Mr Gilles de Kerchove, was appointed in September 2007.

10. Council Act (2001/C 326/01) of 16 October 2001 establishing, in accordance with Article 34 TEU, the Protocol to the Convention on Mutual Assistance in Criminal Matters between the Member States of the EU, OJ C326, 21 November 2001.

11. It should be noted that there were clear difficulties in Parliament that prevented passage of the 2nd Anti-money Laundering Directive until post-9/11 norms changed the perception of decision-makers over terrorism. While this means that, intitially, there was no wide-spread recognition of a need for EU level action, it also strengthens the argument that the emerging norm to join into the 'war on terror' did bring decision-makers more in line with EU CTF priorities. It also should be noted that the subsequent passage of the 3rd Anti-money Laundering Directive has been arguably helped along by Member State lobbying, as de Goede suggests was the case on the part of the UK (de Goede 2008, p. 98).

12. However, it is worthwhile recalling that, facing the post-cold war rise of transnational organised crime, the EU succeeded to adopt money-laundering instruments, including the first directive on money-laundering in 1991.

13. Council Directive (2005/60/EC) of 26 October 2005 on the prevention of the use of the financial system for the purpose of money laundering and terrorist financing, OJ L309, 25 November 2005.

14. This establishes rules for payment service providers to send information on the payer throughout the payment chain; it serves to implement SR VII on wire transfers.

15. In combination with the third anti-money laundering directive, this directive implements SR VI on alternative remittances.

16. The Council decided to rely on the Council Secretariat for the implementation process.

17. See doc. 10826/07, 21 June 2007.

18. A revised version of the strategy was endorsed by the Council on 24/25 July 2008.

Notes on contributors

Christian Kaunert is lecturer in EU Politics & International Relations and programme leader of the Master (MA) in Terrorism and Security. He is the author of several articles on EU counter-terrorism and internal security, as well as a monograph entitled *European Internal Security? – Towards Supranational Governance* with Manchester University Press. He is currently a visiting research fellow at IBEI Barcelona, Spain, and from October 2010, a Marie Curie Research Fellow at the European University Institute in Florence, Italy.

Marina Della Giovanna is a researcher at the Tocqueville Chair on Security Policies at the University of Namur (FUNDP) and a Ph.D. candidate in Comparative and European Politics at the Centre for the Study of Political Change (CIRCaP), at the University of Siena Italy.

References

Allen, W., 2003. The war against terrorist financing. *Journal of money laundering control*, 6 (4), 306–310.

Argomaniz, J., 2009. Post-9/11 institutionalisation of European Union counter-terrorism: emergence, acceleration and inertia. *European security*, 18 (2), 151–172.

Beach, D., 2005. *The dynamics of European integration – why and when EU institutions matter*. London: Palgrave Macmillan.

Bossong, R., 2008. The action plan on combating terrorism: a flawed instrument of EU security governance. *Journal of common market studies*, 46 (1), 27–48.

Bures, O., 2006. EU counter-terrorism: a paper tiger. *Terrorism and political violence*, 18 (1), 57–87.

Bures, O., 2008. Europol's fledgling counterterrorism role. *Terrorism and political violence*, 20 (1), 498–517.

Cameron, I., 2002. *Targeted sanctions and legal safeguards*. Report to the Swedish foreign office. Available from: http://resources.jur.uu.se/repository/5/PDF/staff/sanctions.pdf [Accessed 15 January 2009]

Cameron, I., 2003. UN targeted sanctions, legal safeguards and the European convention on human rights. *Nordic journal of international law*, 72 (2), 159–214.

Cameron, I., 2006. *The European convention on human rights, due process and United Nations Security Council counter-terrorism sanctions*. Council of Europe. Available from: http://www.statewatch.org/terrorlists/terrorlists.html [Accessed 31 March 2009]

Christiansen, T., 2002. The role of supranational actors in EU treaty reform. *Journal of European public policy*, 9 (1), 33–53.

Christiansen, T., 2006. The European Commission: the European executive between continuity and change. *In*: J. Richardson, ed. *European Union: power and policy-making*. 3rd ed. Oxon: Routledge, 99–120.

Council of the European Union, 2009. *Counter-terrorism coordinator-report on the implementation of the revised strategy on terrorist financing of 5 May 2009*. Brussels, 8864/1/09 REV 1.

den Boer, M., 2006. Fusing the fragments. Challenges for EU internal security governance on terrorism. *In*: D. Mahncke and J. Monar, eds. *International terrorism. A European response to a global threat?* Brussels: Peter Lang, 83–111.

den Boer, M. and Monar, J., 2002. Keynote article: 11 September and the challenge of global terrorism to the EU as a security actor. *Journal of common market studies*, 40, 11–28.

den Boer, M., Hillebrand, C., and Nölke, A., 2008. Legitimacy under pressure: the European web of counter-terrorism networks'. *Journal of common market studies*, 46 (1), 101–124.

Deflem, M., 2006. Europol and the policing of international terrorism: counter-terrorism in a global perspective. *Justice quarterly*, 23 (3), 336–359.

de Goede, M., 2003. Hawala discourse and the war on terrorist finance. *Environment and planning D*, 21 (5), 513–532.

de Goede, M., 2007. Financial regulation and the war on terror. *In*: L. Assassi, A. Nesvetailova, and D. Wigan, eds. *Global finance in the new century: beyond deregulation*. Basingstoke: Palgrave Macmillan, 193–206.

de Goede, M., 2008. 'Risk, preemption and exception in the war on terrorist financing'. *In*: L. Amoore and M. de Goede, eds. *Risk and the war on terror*. London and New York: Routledge, 97–111.

de Moraes Ruehsen, M., 2007. Arab government responses to the threat of terrorist financing. *In*: J.K. Giraldo and H.A. Trinkunas, eds. *Terrorism financing and state responses: a comparative perspective*. Stanford: Stanford University Press, 152–170.

Dubois, D., 2002. The attacks of 11 September: EU–US cooperation against terrorism in the field of justice and home affairs. *European foreign affairs review*, 7 (3), 317–355.

Eckes, C., 2008a. Sanctions against individuals'. *European constitutional law review*, 4 (2), 205–224.

Eckes, C., 2008b. Judicial review of European anti-terrorism measures-the Yusuf and Kadi judgments of the court of first instance. *European law journal*, 14 (1), 74–92.

Edwards, G. and Meyer, C.O., 2008. Introduction: charting a contested transformation. *Journal of common market studies*, 46 (1), 1–25.

Edwards, G. and Spence, D., eds., 2005. *The European commission*. 2nd ed. London: Cartermill.

Eling, K., 2006. The EU, terrorism and effective multilateralism. *In*: D. Spence, ed. *The European Union and terrorism*. London: John Harper, 105–123.

European Council, 2001. *Conclusions and plan of action of the extraordinary European Council meeting on 21 September 2001*. Brussels, SN 140/01.

European Council, 2004a. *Declaration on combating terrorism of 29 March 2004*. Brussels, 7906/04.

European Council, 2004b. *EU joint strategy paper "The fight against terrorist financing"*. Brussels, 16089/04.

European Council, 2008. *Revised strategy on terrorist financing.* Brussels, 11778/1/08.

Financial Action Task Force, 2001. *Nine special recommendations on terrorist financing*, 30 October. Paris. Available from: http://www.fatf-gafi.org/dataoecd/8/17/34849466.pdf [Accessed 20 March 2009].

Finnemore, M., 1996a. *National interest in international society.* Ithaca, NY: Cornell University Press.

Finnemore, M., 1996b. Norms, culture and world politics: insights from Sociology's institutionalism. *International organization*, 50 (2), 325–348.

Finnemore, M. and Sikkink, K., 1998. International norm dynamics and political change. *International organization*, 52 (4), 887–917.

Fletcher, M., Lööf, R., and Gilmore, B., 2008. *EU criminal law and justice.* Cheltenham: Edward Elgar.

Friedrichs, J., 2005. *Fighting terrorism and drugs.* London: Routledge.

Gardner, K.L., 2007. Fighting terrorism the FATF way. *Global governance*, 13 (3), 325–345.

Gilmore, B., 2003. The twin towers and the third pillar. Some security agenda developments. *EUI law working papers*, 7, 1–18.

Gilmore, W.C., 2004. *Dirty money: the evolution of international measures to counter money laundering and the financing of terrorism.* 3rd ed. Strasbourg: Council of Europe.

Gregory, F., 2005. The EU's response to 9/11: a case study of institutional roles and policy processes with special reference to issues of accountability and human rights. *Terrorism and violence*, 17, 105–123.

Guild, E., 2008. The uses and abuses of counter-terrorism policies in Europe: the case of the terrorist lists. *Journal of common market studies*, 46 (1), 173–193.

Gunning, J., 2008. Terrorism, charities and diasporas: contrasting the fundraising practices of Hamas and al Qaeda among Muslims in Europe. *In*: T.J. Biersteker and S.E. Eckert, eds. *Countering the financing of terrorism.* London: Routledge, 93–123.

Haas, E., 1958. *The uniting of Europe: political, social, and economic forces 1950–1957.* Stanford: Stanford University Press.

Heng, Y.-K. and McDonagh, K., 2008. The other war on terror revealed: global governmentality and the financial action task force's campaign against terrorist financing. *Review of International Studies*, 34 (03), 553–573.

Heupel, M., 2007. Adapting to transnational terrorism: the UN Security Council's evolving approach to terrorism. *Security dialogue*, 38 (4), 477–499.

Heupel, M., 2009. Multilateral sanctions against terror suspects and the violation of due process standards. *International affairs*, 85 (2), 307–321.

Hülsse, R., 2007. Creating demand for global governance: the making of a global money-laundering problem. *Global society*, 21 (2), 155–178.

Kaunert, C., 2005. The area of freedom, security and justice: the construction of a European public order. *European security*, 14 (4), 459–483.

Kaunert, C., 2007. Without the power of purse or sword: the European arrest warrant and the role of the Commission. *Journal of European integration*, 29 (4), 387–404.

Kaunert, C., 2009. Liberty versus security? EU asylum policy and the European Commission. *Journal of contemporary European research*, 5 (2), 148–170.

Kaunert, C., 2010a. The external dimension of EU counter-terrorism relations: competences, interests & institutions. *Terrorism and political violence*, 22 (1), 41–61.

Kaunert, C., 2010b. Europol and EU counter-terrorism: international security actorness in the external dimension? *Studies in conflict and terrorism*, 33 (7), 652–671.

Keohane, D., 2008. The absent friend: EU foreign policy and counter-terrorism. *Journal of common market studies*, 46 (1), 125–146.

Kingdon, J.W., 1995. *Agenda, alternatives, and public policies.* New York: Longman.

Klabbers, J., 2008. Kadi justice at the security council? *International organizations law review*, 4 (2), 293–304.

Lavranos, N., 2006. Judicial review of UN sanctions by the court of first instance. *European foreign affairs review*, 11 (4), 471–490.

Lavranos, N., 2007. UN sanctions and judicial review. *Nordic journal of international law*, 76 (1), 1–17.

Lindberg, L., 1963. *The political dynamics of European economic integration*. Stanford: Stanford University Press.

Mitsilegas, V. and Gilmore, B., 2007. The EU legislative framework against money laundering and terrorist finance: a critical analysis in the light of evolving global standards. *International and comparative law quarterly*, 56 (1), 119–141.

Monar, J., 2007. The EU's approach post-September 11: global terrorism as a multi-dimensional law enforcement challenge. *Cambridge review of international affairs*, 20 (2), 267–283.

Moravcsik, A., 1993. Preferences and power in the European Community: a liberal intergovernmentalist approach. *Journal of common market studies*, 33 (4), 611–628.

Moravcsik, A., 1998. *The choice for Europe. Social purpose & state power from Messina to Maastricht*. Ithaca and New York: Cornell University Press.

Moravcsik, A., 1999. A new statecraft? Supranational entrepreneurs and international cooperation. *International organization*, 53 (2), 267–306.

Müller-Wille, B., 2008. The effect of international terrorism on EU intelligence co-operation. *Journal of common market studies*, 46 (1), 49–73.

Nugent, N., ed., 2000. *At the heart of the union: studies of the European Commission*. 2nd ed. London: Palgrave Macmillan.

Occhipinti, J., 2003. *The politics of EU police cooperation – towards a European FBI?* Boulder, CO: Lynne Rienner.

Pollack, M.A., 2003. *The engines of European integration*. Clarendon: Oxford University Press.

Razavy, M. and Haggerty, K.D., 2009. Hawala under scrutiny: documentation, surveillance and trust. *International political sociology*, 3 (2), 139–155.

Reinares, F., ed., 2000. *European democracies against terrorrism – government policies and intergovernmental cooperation*. Aldershot: Ashgate.

Sandholtz, W. and Stone Sweet, A., eds., 1998. *European integration and supranational governance*. Oxford: Oxford University Press.

Spence, D., ed., 2006. *The European Union and terrorism*. London: John Harper.

Sykes, R., 2007. Some questions on the FATF 40 + 9 and the methodology for assessing compliance with the FATF 40 + 9 recommendations. *Journal of banking regulation*, 8 (3), 236–243.

Thony, J.-F. and Png, C.-A., 2007. FATF special recommendations and UN resolutions on the financing of terrorism. *Journal of financial crime*, 14 (2), 150–169.

United Nations, 1999. *UN Security Council Resolution 1267*. Available from: http://daccessdds.un.org/doc/UNDOC/GEN/N99/300/44/PDF/N9930044.pdf?OpenElement [Accessed 19 March 2009].

United Nations, 2001. *UN Security Council Resolution 1373*. Available from: http://daccessdds.un.org/doc/UNDOC/GEN/N01/557/43/PDF/N0155743.pdf?OpenElement [Accessed 21 March 2009].

van Thiel, S., 2008. UN anti-terrorism sanctions and EU Human Rights: the lessons of European integration. *In*: B. Martenczuck and S. van Thiel, eds. *Justice, liberty and security – new challenges for EU external relations*. Brussels: VUB Press, Brussels University Press.

Vlcek, W., 2007. Surveillance to combat terrorist financing in Europe: whose liberty, whose security? *European security*, 16 (1), 99–119.

Vlcek, W., 2008. Development vs. terrorism: money transfers and EU financial regulations in the UK. *British journal of politics and international relations*, 10 (2), 286–302.

Vlcek, W., 2009. Hitting the right target: EU and Security Council pursuit of terrorist financing. *Critical studies on terrorism*, 2 (2), 275–291.

Wallace, H., Wallace, W., and Pollack, M.A., eds., 2005. *Policy-making in the European Union*. 5th ed. Oxford: Oxford University Press.

Zimmermann, D., 2006. The European Union and post-9/11 counterterrorism: a reappraisal. *Studies in conflict and terrorism*, 29 (1), 123–145.

Before and after Lisbon: legal implementation as the 'Achilles heel' in EU counter-terrorism?

Javier Argomaniz

Centre for the Study of Terrorism and Political Violence (CSTPV), University of St Andrews, St Andrews, UK

Implementation has often been described as a key weakness affecting European Union (EU) counter-terrorism. However, this view is often adopted as a given and there has not been so far a systematic examination of the degree to which this represents an obstacle to the effectiveness of the EU response. This paper aims to contribute towards this goal through the use of primary sources in the study of the legal transposition of counter-terror instruments into national law, a key stage in the implementation process. It shows the presence of major implementation delays in this policy sector but, importantly, also significant cross-national variation with regards transposition failure associated with the administrative endowment of the individual member states. Furthermore, the mechanisms deployed by the Union to encourage a fluid implementation of European measures are critically evaluated and the potential impact in the process of the institutional transformations brought about by Lisbon is also examined.

Introduction

This paper explores an important element in the effectiveness of the European Union (EU) response to the threat of transnational terrorism, namely, the process of domestic legal transposition of European counter-terrorism policies. Slow and/or flawed transposition of European legislation affects police and judicial operational cooperation by being a source of legal uncertainty and subsequent confusion and frustration for practitioners. As such, implementation has been mentioned in passing in previous analysis of the EU counter-terror response (Nilsson 2004, Bures 2006, Keohane 2006, Monar 2006, 2007, Zimmerman 2006, Bossong 2008) but it is contended here that it is yet to be examined in a systemic and structured manner. This article aims to contribute towards a more thorough and detailed understanding of this subject by conducting a descriptive analysis of data from EU official documents on the transposition of pertinent legal measures and interviews with national and European policy-makers on the intervening factors impacting transposition pace.

Before embarking on the analysis, it must be clarified that the implementation of EU policies is a process that encompasses both an initial stage of the transposition of the law into national legislation (legal implementation) and the subsequent application in practice of such mechanism by national administrative authorities (final implementation). Furthermore, full compliance involves the subsequent enforcement of the rules by national agencies and bureaucrats. Yet, in contrast with Common Market rules, detailed data on the national application and enforcement of EU internal security measures are generally not widely available[1] and in the counter-terrorism case this scarcity is compounded by the relative recentness of the response. As a result this study will follow the example of the large majority of studies on EU implementation (Lampinen and Uusikylä 1998, p. 233) and focus the analysis on an indirect measure of compliance, the initial transposition stage, in this case paying special attention to a selection of key legal texts that are at the core of the EU counter-terror efforts. Legal implementation is central because it represents a prerequisite, a 'necessary condition' for successful implementation, as delayed transposition negatively affects whether states will be 'in a good position to implement these directives to the best of their capabilities' (Steunenberg and Toshkov 2009, p. 966). In this regard, fluent, widespread and fast-paced transposition of EU legislation would be a positive indicator whereas slow and/or uneven national translation of the laws would signify systemic problems.

Unlike other implementation studies conducting statistical analyses on the transposition of common market policies (Toshkov 2010), this paper does not aim to provide causal models. It uses instead an exploratory approach that draws upon the findings from implementation studies in other EU areas and applies their conclusions to the interpretation of the data from the EU Counter-terror Coordinator reports. In a nutshell, it will confirm the widely held view that the transposition of EU counter-terror legislation is hampered by substantial delays that are clearly lengthier than in other EU policy areas, yet these are still fully representative of the state of affairs in the field of Justice and Home Affairs (JHA). This argument will be taken a step further to elaborate on a finding that has not received the attention it deserves in the literature and will be particularly evident in the analysis: the fact that national implementation of counter-terror policies is not uniformly poor across the EU-27. The picture instead is patchy and involves important cross-national differences. Conventional explanations for this poor implementation, such as the absence of enforcement mechanisms in the pre-Lisbon third pillar, do not account for such wide variation and need to be further refined. Thus, it will be contended here that these divergences do not lie on – as some authors and policy-makers have argued – varying national threat perceptions that lead to differences in the prioritisation of the domestic adoption of these measures. Instead, administrative culture and institutional capacity are more effective explanatory variables for the laggardness of some member states. Relevantly to the broader discussion on the implementation of EU law, evidence from reports and interviews with national and European officials supports the view that state-based approaches are more effective than preference-based perspectives in drawing attention to the factors behind the problematic transposition of counter-terrorism legislation.

In line with the above conclusions, the paper will start by reviewing the criticisms that have been directed towards this aspect of the EU response. This is followed by an exploration of some of the existing data in order to evaluate the extent to which legal implementation is a problem area in European counter-terrorism. The article then turns the spotlight on the potential factors that influence the transposal of EU counter-terror measures. It finally moves to a discussion on how the changes introduced by Lisbon Treaty impact on this matter before concluding with some summarising remarks.

The implementation of European Union counter-terrorism instruments and its critics

It is following the 11 March 2004 attacks in Madrid when domestic implementation of EU policies and legislation in the field of counter-terrorism started receiving closer attention. Counter-terrorism was until then a rapidly evolving area of European governance as a result of the energetic policy drive that followed the 9/11 attacks (den Boer and Monar 2002). Yet the first major jihadist attack on European soil brought to light the fact that although the number of internal security measures agreed in the aftermath of 9/11 was impressive, the putting in practice of these initiatives by member states may have been less so.

The 25 March 2004 European Council Declaration on Combating Terrorism stressed this matter by pointing out that 'in light of the events in Madrid, the European Council believes that full implementation of measures to combat terrorism is a matter of urgency' (European Council 2004). This was the first time that a major EU document implicitly recognised the fact that the lack of a major attack in Europe had contributed until then to camouflage implementation deficits. This statement came on the back of an 18 March 2004 Commission memorandum to the Council that emphasised how implementation of counter-terror legislative measures had been 'often slow, poor and inadequate' (European Commission 2004, p. 1).

The message was reinforced by the 15 June 2004 revised Counter-Terror Action Plan, which declared as a priority the application in practice of the policies agreed in the immediate post-9/11 period. The appointment of a Counter-terror Coordinator, tasked with the auditing of progress by national governments in this area, signalled the extent to which the Union acknowledged the need for better monitoring of the implementation process.

Nevertheless, transposition delays associated with key counter-terror decisions have continued being repeatedly flagged up by EU actors. Nilsson, director of Criminal Judicial Cooperation unit at the Council Secretariat, stressed the fact that only about 25 out of the 175 measures in the 2001 Road Map had been implemented (Nilsson 2004, p. 15). Unsurprisingly given their remit, the EU Counter-terror Coordinators have been amongst the most vocal critics. De Vries claimed in his article that national administrators often find difficult to implement properly Council decisions (de Vries 2005). His successor de Kerchove has paid significant attention to this problem in a series of discussion papers. The documents have emphasised that implementation remains a key challenge in European counter-terrorism and have singled out individual measures 'crucial to improving the prevention and combating of terrorism' for being well behind the Council's deadline (Council of the European Union 2009a, p. 15). These include inter alia the 2001 Protocol to the mutual assistance in criminal matters convention, the 2003 EU–US agreements on extradition and mutual assistance on criminal matters, the 2005 Directive on money-laundering and terrorist financing and the 2006 Directive on the retention of telecommunications data.

In this respect, the coordinator has suggested, as a tool to improve the situation, regular follow-up of the process of implementation in competent working parties, 'not only to increase awareness but also to share good practices and identify possible problems' (Council of the European Union 2007, p. 16). Although his predecessor had already made mention of these weaknesses, poor implementation has become a fundamental priority for de Kerchove, signalling a shift from the previous emphasis on policy formulation prevalent in the 2001–04 period.

It was not only EU officials who brought to the fore this emerging implementation gap, but a few external observers have also argued that this was becoming a crucial problem in European counter-terrorism. Experts have criticised the fact that member states often lacked 'the political will to align laws or making their policies work together' and even after agreeing to a policy 'EU countries can be remarkably slow in implementing' it (Keohane 2006, p. 68). For Zimmermann (2006, p. 130) 'implementation of counterterrorism measures constitutes a far second after political decision making' and Monar (2007, p. 310) concurs: EU member states are 'much better at agreeing on comprehensive packages of measures than at effectively implementing them afterwards'. A Dutch Intelligence report also depicted EU action in this area as plagued with 'delays in the ratification of conventions and protocols, and the belated incorporation of EU decisions into national law and practice' (General Intelligence and Security Service of The Netherlands [AIVD] 2005, p. 32). Implementation in sum has been described as the weak spot of European counter-terrorism, Monar going as far as calling it its 'Achilles heel' (Monar 2006, p. 155).

In this context, the explanations put forward to account for the poor state of implementation are three-fold: lack of political will, absence of enforcement capabilities and weaknesses in the policy design process. Thus, Zimmermann (2006, p. 130) contends that implementation is a 'relatively reliable indicator for the expression of political will by the Union' and therefore this reflects poorly on member states' interest to combat terrorism at the European level. Bures (2006, p. 57) agrees by claiming that negotiated political agreements have not been properly implemented 'in large part due to the absence of genuine pro-integration thinking in the area of Justice and Home Affairs (JHA)'.

In parallel Bossong (2008, p. 42) argues that problems in the policy-making stage need to be considered. In this way the Action Plan on Combating Terrorism required a context of low policy conflict and low ambiguity where it could be carefully developed. However, this was profoundly at odds with the hectic and 'chaotic' policy-making process that following the New York and Madrid attacks led to an agenda overload that 'overtaxed the decision-making and implementation capacity of the EU'.

Finally, Monar (2007, p. 310) highlights the considerable challenge that implementing these measures across 27 different systems with their 'own priorities and procedures' represents. More importantly he underlines the fact that the Commission has not had the capacity to put pressure on non-fulfilling member states because of its reduced powers on the domain of JHA. Thus, unlike the Community pillar, in the pre-Lisbon intergovernmental third pillar decision-making the Commission has lacked effective powers to launch infringement proceedings to remedy deficiencies in national implementation.

Legal implementation in European Union counter-terrorism (2004–09): an empirical analysis

Whereas there has been a general acknowledgement in the hitherto rather scarce literature on this topic that legal implementation has been far from satisfactory, we still lack a rigorous evaluation of the extent of such problem and a thorough exploration of potential explanatory factors. In order to do so and test the aforementioned authors' claims, this section examines empirically the data provided by the EU Counter-terror Coordinator reports on the Implementation of the Action Plan to Combat Terrorism. Released every 6 months, they indicate on a point-by-point basis whether countries are sticking to their agreements and publicise member states' performance in counter-terrorism (European Council 2004).

The reports document progress in the form of a scoreboard based on whether each member state has ratified or transposed to the national level those conventions and pieces of legislation that are considered key in the EU fight against terrorism. These by no means represent the entirety of the EU counter-terror response but certainly encompass measures pivotal in its institutionalisation as an area of EU governance. Therefore a descriptive analysis of these documents does offer very valuable insights on the extent of the delays. Accordingly, Table 1 displays the 14 key counter-terror mechanisms periodically monitored in these reports and charts the evolution of their implementation from the first evaluation released by the Counter-terror Coordinator office in 2004 to the latest available version in 2009.

The scoreboard measures the extent of implementation of counter-terror mechanisms in four separate categories: 'implementation completed and legislation entered into force'; 'implementation completed but legislation not entered into force yet'; 'implementation not completed'; and 'implemented in part'. In order to add clarity to the analysis questions of completeness – amount of transposition – are circumvented: only those in the first category, meaning that all the different articles of the measure have been translated to national law, will be considered to have fully implemented the measure in Table 1. As a consequence, in those cases where some but not all elements of an instrument have been transposed by the deadline specified by the respective provision the measure is still documented as not implemented. Accordingly each individual measure is categorised binarily as either delayed or transposed in a timely fashion. Therefore 'implementation' is virtually synonymous in these reports with 'legal transposition in due time' although whether it meets its second stipulation 'correctly' is not addressed. Still accounting for the fact that the precision of the analysis is not absolute, these figures offer us a detailed overall picture.

Confirming the views of analysts and policy-makers, Table 1 shows that in the 5-year period in which implementation has been monitored, the initial deadline set by the Council was never met by all member states in any of the instruments. Moreover, in a number of instances it was actually missed by a majority of EU states.

Furthermore, not only the regularity but also the length of the delays is in most cases very significant. Mechanisms that were approved in 2002 and considered essential in the European fight against terrorism are, 7 years later, yet to be translated to national law by all 27 member states: the Framework Decision on Joint Investigation Teams is still to be transposed by Italy, the Framework Decision on Combating Terrorism by Cyprus and Slovakia. Without a doubt, the worst example

Table 1. Number of countries yet to implement counter-terror measures.

	29 November 2004[a]	30 May 2005[a]	9 December 2005	19 May 2006	30 November 2006	20 May 2007	29 November 2007[b]	26 May 2008[b,c]	2 June 2009[b]	27 November 2009[b]
European Arrest Warrant (date of agreement: 13 June 2002; transposition deadline: June 2004)	1	–	–	1	–	–	–	–	–	–
Joint Investigation Teams(date of agreement: 13 June 2002; transposition deadline: June 2004)	8	4	3	2	2	4	4	1	1	1
Framework Decision on Combating Terrorism (date of agreement: 13 June 2002; transposition deadline: June 2004)	8	7	4	3	3	5	1	2	2	2
Framework Decision on money laundering and confiscation of proceeds of crime (date of agreement: 26 June 2001; transposition deadline: June 2004)	10	8	6	2	3	5	2	2	1	–
Decision establishing Eurojust (date of agreement: 28 February 2002; transposition deadline: June 2004)	6	4	4	4	2	3	2	1	1	1
Decision on the implementation of specific measures for police and judicial cooperation to combat terrorism (date of agreement 19 December 2002; transposition deadline: June 2004)	–		–	–	–	2	–			–
Convention on Mutual Assistance in Criminal Matters (date of agreement: 29 May 2000; transposition deadline: December 2004)	17	12	9	6	5	7	7	4	3	3
Protocol to the Convention on Mutual Assistance in Criminal Matters (date of agreement: 16 October 2001; transposition deadline: December 2004)	21	14	11	8	7	8	8	5	4	4

Table 1 (*Continued*)

	29 November 2004[a]	30 May 2005[a]	9 December 2005	19 May 2006	30 November 2006	20 May 2007	29 November 2007[b]	26 May 2008[b,c]	2 June 2009[b]	27 November 2009[b]
First Protocol to Europol Convention (date of agreement: 30 November 2000; transposition deadline: December 2004)	7	3	3	2	1	–	–	–	–	–
Second Protocol to Europol Convention (date of agreement: 28 November 2002; transposition deadline: December 2004)	12	6	5	4	2	–	–	–	–	–
Third Protocol to Europol Convention (date of agreement: 27 November 2003; transposition deadline: December 2004)	15	9	7	5	3	–	–	–	–	–
Framework Decision on the execution of orders freezing property or evidence (date of agreement: 22 July 2003; transposition deadline: December 2004)	25	22	17	15	14	16	11	10	6	5
Framework Decision on attacks against information systems (date of agreement: 24 February 2005, transposition deadline: March 2007)	–	–	–	–	–	–	13	13	10	7
Decision on the exchange of information and cooperation concerning terrorist offences (date of agreement: 20 September 2005, transposition deadline: June 2006)	–	–	–	–	–	–	25	16	13	11

[a]Source: EU Plan of Action on Combating Terrorism Updates (2004–2005).
[b]Includes Romania and Bulgaria.
[c]24 Nov 2008 publicly available version of the report is unreadable. See: http://register.consilium.europa.eu/pdf/en/08/st15/st15912-ad01re01.en08.pdf
Note: Implementation completed and legislation has entered into force. Source: Counter-Terror Coordinator Implementation of the Action Plan to Combat Terrorism reports (2005–2009).

continues being the 2000 Convention on Mutual Assistance in Criminal Matters; where, almost a decade later, there are three countries still to implement and four more have not transposed its 2001 Protocol. Unsurprisingly, this particular case often emerges in the Coordinator reports as an example of poor transposition.

Importantly, whereas the instruments disposed in Decisions and Framework Decisions can be put into use by member states once legislation is implemented, Conventions cannot enter into force until transposed by all signatories. In this way Europol officials have often responded to criticisms by pointing out that three protocols that would have enhanced their competences have been implemented by all member states with 3 years delay, in effect preventing them from making use of these new powers during this period.

To put these figures in context, on average Member States take 9 months to transpose internal market directives after the transposition deadline expires (European Commission 2010, p. 13). Therefore and, even if one controls for the problem of ratifying conventions, there can be little doubt that serious delays are common in the domestic adoption of counter-terror legislation regardless of the type of instrument.

It should also be noted that the post-Madrid institutional calls seemed to have had a negligible impact as the transposition of the most recent legislation reviewed in the report is still slow: one year after the deadline expired only two member states had implemented the 2005 Decision on the exchange of information concerning terrorist offences. As such the intervening factors behind the slow process of domestic legal transfer have persisted during the whole period.

It becomes abundantly clear from the above exploratory analysis that the negative picture described by other authors is backed by strong evidence from official reports. In this regard it is possible to argue that the EU's poor transposition figures in counter-terrorism should not constitute a surprise as a similar conclusion could be reached about its overall record. Hence, in the most researched area of the Internal Market, where data have been more readily available and the policy areas have a longer history, a 2001 Commission White Paper on Governance states that only five out of the 83 directives to be transposed in 2000 have been done so by all member states (European Commission 2001, p. 18). In relation to specific policy areas, only 39 per cent of the EU transport acquis from 1957 to 2004 was transposed in time in Germany, Greece, the UK, Spain and the Netherlands (Kaeding 2006, p. 229) and in maritime transport 'problems occur in 58 per cent of transposition cases' (Steunenberg and Kaeding 2009, p. 449). The figure is 42 per cent for EU social directives enacted between 1975 and 1999 in Germany, Greece, The Netherlands, Spain and the UK (Haverland and Romeijn 2007, p. 765).

Studies on individual countries' performances tend to reflect even lower levels of timely transposition: Mastenbroek (2003) showed that the Netherlands did not meet the deadline in 58 per cent of the directives adopted between 1995 and 1998 while Borghetto et al. (2006) showed that Italy's transposition of over 75 per cent of measures is delayed by an average of 2 years. In summary, and as König and Luetgert (2009, p. 170) claim, 'most scholars agree that EU member states have difficulty transposing Community law in a timely fashion'.

Notwithstanding the fact that counter-terrorism as a sector is reflective of general EU transposition trends, it is also evident that the figures reported above are still lower than the virtually 100 per cent transposition delay rate that is observed in the

Coordinator scoreboard. A figure that is in fact closer to other issue areas within police and judicial cooperation in criminal matters. Here the Commission reviews of the Hague Programme have acknowledged that 'national implementation leaves a lot of room for improvement' due to lengthy delays and the fact that transposition is often incorrect or incomplete (European Commission 2008). In fact Miettinen (2010, p. 6) has argued that 'to date no third pillar instrument has been flawlessly transposed in a timely fashion by all Member States'. In summary, whereas domestic transposition of first pillar legislation is far from perfect, national adoption of the pre-Lisbon Title VI texts, including counter-terrorism, is comparatively worse.

Monar (2007) has blamed this situation on the absence of strong enforcement powers available for the Community institutions in the pre-Lisbon period. The argument contends that, since the Commission has not had the power to initiate infringement procedures against member states, there has been no threat of sanctions and arguably no general sense of urgency. A legal mechanism[2] has been available for a particular member state to bring another state before the European Court of Justice (ECJ) in the third pillar – provided the disagreement is not ironed out at the Council – but the political costs are too high and the instrument has never been used. The result, as an official at the Council Secretariat rather colourfully has put it, is 'no formal way of challenging if one member state sends an implementation report and all the others think this is bullshit, what can they do?' (interview with Council Official, General Secretariat, DG H – JHA, January 2006).

In this context, the other instruments the EU has had to rely upon in order to encourage member states to promptly introduce counter-terror legislation have not compensated for the absence of 'hard' enforcement mechanisms. These so-called 'soft mechanisms' do not involve a legal challenge and are based on the nurturing of peer pressure by 'naming and shaming' in official documents those national governments who fail to meet their obligations. This is the rationale behind the implementation reports published by the Commission on specific security measures and the aforementioned scoreboard released by the EU counter-terror coordinator office.

On the one hand, the Commission has conducted ad hoc evaluations of particular internal security instruments such as the Joint Investigation Teams, the European Arrest Warrant, the Framework Decision on Exchange of Information or the Framework Decision on Freezing of Property. The Commission evaluation reports concentrate exclusively on the legal implementation of these measures and when the deadlines are not met the Commission issues a communication or memo. Sometimes this involves more than one round of evaluations as with the 2002 Framework Decision on combating terrorism where the Commission released reports in both 2004 and 2007 (European Commission 2007). It is worth mentioning, however, that the European Commission (2008, p. 14) has complained in their Hague programme reviews about the difficulty involved in assessing instruments concerning terrorism due to the general absence of an obligation for member states to communicate transposition.

On the other hand, the aforementioned Counter-terror Coordinator reports are considered by the Coordinator's office as reasonably effective: 'you would be quite surprised to know that we usually have a rush of people coming forward just before the implementation table is about to be done. So that shows that they do take that seriously to a certain extent' (interview with Council Official, General Secretariat, Counter-Terror Coordinator Office, January 2006). Even so evidence from the reports themselves shows that such form of persuasion can only go so far. Indeed the Counter-terror Coordinator lacks any enforcement powers complementing its activity as an auditor and no other actor at that level has the capacity to support or replace him as a strong 'encourager of action'. The Police Chiefs Task Force (PCOTF), the best candidate in paper, cannot play a role in this area because European police chiefs have little time to focus on European issues, the representatives have differing competencies depending on the member state and its organisational weakness has traditionally resulted in the overloading of its agenda and the lack of results. Therefore, these 'soft mechanisms' have not been sufficiently effective as 'encouragers of action' to enhance the poor overall performance of member states in this particular area.

Explaining cross-national differences

Yet explaining poor transposition in counter-terrorism as a product of the pre-Lisbon institutional weaknesses in the Third pillar is only part of the picture. A closer analysis of the data in the Coordinator reports sheds light on remarkable differences in member states' implementation records. This is illustrated by Table 2, which shows in the first column the number of times a member state has been reported in the 10 Counter-terror Coordinator implementation reports as not having fully transposed a particular measure and the number of those instruments where the implementation deadline has been missed by the country in the second column. Laggards are displayed at the top with the worst five 'offenders' highlighted.

Table 2 shows that the main laggards in this area are, according to the Coordinator reports, Italy, Luxembourg, Greece, Ireland and Cyprus with more than 40 instances reported. The five best implementers (Austria, Denmark, Hungary, Finland and Poland) have been reported in less than 10 occasions. It must also be noted that the 'new member states' that joined the Union after 2004 do not seem as a whole to be worse transposers than the old 15 members,[3] and this coincides with findings from research in other areas (Falkner and Treib 2008, Steunenberg and Toshkov 2009) and the Commission's own Internal Market Scoreboard (European Commission 2010).

There can be little doubt that there is substantial divergence in the national transposition records. Highlighting the gulf between the 'worst laggards' and 'best transposers' in the reports, Italy, Luxembourg and Greece have been reported almost 10 times more than Austria and Denmark. In contrast with other areas of EU law (Thomson et al. 2007, p. 706), we can observe more variation amongst countries than across different measures. This is highly relevant since the existing literature on this topic has tended to put all the EU-27 countries in the same group, proposing far-reaching explanations for a general problem. The varying implementation patterns that have been exposed above and where some member states perform systematically better than others has been rarely acknowledged.

The essential point is that although the lack of hard enforcement mechanisms may account for the overall poor record, where not a single measure has been transposed by all states in time, it cannot fully explain a patchy picture with varying degrees of implementation 'failure'. In order to interpret this puzzle, we need to turn our attention to the existing literature where experts have produced two main types

Table 2.   Laggard member states.

Countries	Number of instances reported	Number of instruments
Italy	**59**	**11**
Luxembourg	**52**	**10**
Greece	**51**	**8**
Ireland	**46**	**9**
Cyprus	**41**	**9**
Slovakia	31	8
Malta	30	7
Czech Republic	29	6
Latvia	29	6
Estonia	23	7
Portugal	23	6
Sweden	20	8
Bulgaria	19	9
UK	17	6
Germany	17	6
Romania	16	8
Belgium	15	8
France	15	6
Spain	15	5
Slovenia	12	7
Netherlands	12	5
Lithuania	10	4
Poland	9	5
Finland	8	4
Hungary	7	5
Denmark	6	6
Austria	6	6

Note: Bold values indicate the top 5 laggards.
Source: Counter-Terror Coordinator Implementation of the Action Plan to Combat Terrorism reports (2005–2009) and EU Plan of Action on Combating Terrorism updates (2004–2005). 24 November 2008 publicly available version of the report is unreadable. See: http://register.consilium.europa.eu/pdf/en/08/st15/st15912-ad01re01.en08.pdf

of explanatory models, state based and preference based, to account for cross-national variation in the transposition of EU legal texts.

Preference based

Preference-based explanations focus on the governments' policy preferences and strategic choices, the central assumption being that member states with stronger incentives to deviate from a particular EU legislative instrument take longer to transpose it. The expectation is that countries opposing a measure at the decision-making stage will be less likely to implement the measure rapidly and 'faithfully' (Thomson et al. 2007, p. 688) whereas those which have a strong preference for a particular policy to be 'downloaded' will comply faster (Toshkov 2010, p. 18). Unlike state-based explanations, this approach is effective to explain important variations in compliance across policy fields.

The emphasis put by authors such as Zimmermann, Bures, Monar and Keohane on the lack of political will by member states as a crucial factor in the implementation process shows how preference-based explanations implicitly underpin the general consensus on counter-terrorism and, more broadly, EU security policy. An interesting variation of these preference-based accounts contends that the absence of political will is directly correlated to low threat perceptions. As a consequence, threat perceptions shape the process of implementation, with those governments who feel more threatened by this problem being more willing to implement these measures in time (Bakker 2006, Meyer 2009). In this way, Bakker (2006, p. 60) has suggested that 'in general, EU Member States whose citizens do not see terrorism as an important issue lag behind in ratifying and implementing new laws and cooperation agreements, compared to countries where governments face populations that feel more threatened by terrorism'.

Bakker's analysis of threat perceptions for member states populations is based on data from the Eurobarometer[4] for the 2004–06 period and, more specifically, a question on the proportion of respondents who mentioned terrorism as one of the two most important issues affecting their country. This paper extends the period under analysis to 2009 when the country with the highest average threat perception is still Spain, affected by both Islamist and separatist terrorism following the conclusion of ETA's ceasefire on December 2006, with an average of 35 per cent of respondents considering terrorism one of the country's two main problems. Spain is followed by the UK (19 per cent), Denmark (17 per cent), The Netherlands (15 per cent), Italy (8 per cent), Germany (6 per cent) and France (6 per cent). For the vast majority of member states the percentage is 5 per cent or lower. In fact for Estonia, Lithuania, Latvia and Slovenia the proportion does not go above 1 per cent, which is in line with the view that new accession members have generally lower threat perceptions than the old 15 member states.

Table 2, however, has shown that despite displaying one of the highest threat perception rates, Italy is the most sluggish transposer. In fact, out of the four other countries with the highest threat perceptions, only Denmark is one of the top five implementers. More importantly, the five countries with the lowest threat perception do not seem to be, as a group, worse implementers than other member states: although Malta, Latvia and Estonia have missed deadlines a considerable number of times, in fact Hungary and Slovenia have a very good record. As shown in section 'Explaining cross-national differences', whereas the societies in new accession members are generally less concerned about terrorism, their governments are not as a whole slower transposers.

In summary, the exploratory analysis does not present evidence of a relationship between threat perceptions and implementation: those countries with the lowest threat perceptions do not necessarily implement measures more slowly than those member states where the public has indicated a high degree of concern. However, some EU officials interviewed seemed prepared to accept this argument, a member of the Counter-terror Coordinator office arguing that 'in general those states which think there's less of a terrorist threat in their territory are a bit slower' (interview with Council Official, General Secretariat, Counter-Terror Coordinator Office, January 2006). This is a relevant finding as the fact that some EU policy-makers agreed to this perception amounts to an important misrepresentation of the situation.

An alternative within this preference-based approach is Börzel and Risse's (2003) concept of 'goodness-of-fit'. It refers to the fact that, other things being equal, the more the EU and the national policy differ – the greater the degree of misfit – the more costly the compliance. Even if all relevant national actors approve of the EU law, delays may still occur due to the fact that 'it takes a lot of time to identify and sort out the legal "mess" created by the new piece of legislation' (Steunenberg and Toshkov 2009, p. 955). Therefore, those European rules that require less adjustments to existing national legislation and practices – 'fit better' – will be faster and better implemented.

As König and Luetgert (2009, p. 182) argue, investigation of this theory has traditionally been restricted to case studies because of the difficulty entailed in measuring compatibility between EU legislation and existing national policies and structures. We will therefore only broadly explore this factor by making reference to the fact that counter-terrorism is an area where a small number of countries (those most affected by this problem, and whose populations display the highest threat perceptions: the 'Big 5' plus the Netherlands, Denmark and Belgium) have adopted a leading role and become the most active policy generators. There is theoretically the possibility that other member states, where the risk is lower and/or expertise is lacking, would be less involved in the policy formulation, be disproportionally affected by 'misfit' and then struggle with the implementation or avoid prioritising these measures. This idea did in fact emerge in the interviews:

> Even the Danes or the Swedes they never implemented the participation to a terrorism organisation because they don't like the concept of just being incriminated for just being a member even if you have not committed any crime because it is an awkward concept for their legal system. So, sometimes why does a member state implement badly is because either it doesn't like or it's so new for its legal system that it's not easy to translate, I suppose. (Interview with Council Official, General Secretariat, DG H-JHA, January 2006)

Again this hypothesis does not seem to be strongly supported by the data as minor players with little experience in this area such as Austria, Hungary or Finland are top legal implementers. It is worth mentioning that Finland has not experienced a single high profile terrorist attack in its territory. In summary, preference-based explanations do not demonstrate much explanatory power in this policy sector.

State based

On the other hand, state-based explanations have concentrated on the administrative and institutional characteristics of member states and would suggest that, over a large number of legislative acts, countries display structural tendencies on the speed and quality of the implementation. In other words, non-compliance is voluntary, not the result of strategic choices (Börzel et al. 2007). This approach entails the notion that some member states' structures are more adequate to formally transpose European legislation than others.

Hence, national administrative constraints such as government inefficiency and corruption (Mbaye 2001) are expected to slow down transposition and compliance in some member states. Weaker state bureaucracies would have more difficulties to pool and coordinate diverse levels of government when adjusting to the demands emerging from the European stage. Some authors have also argued that more centralised nation states are better prepared to manage EU legislation than decentralised systems since they have a lower number of domestic veto players (Levy *et al.* 1995) and public support towards the UE is a positive influence in the process (Lampinen and Uusikylä 1998).

Others have called attention to cultural norms, where some member states' officials would be more inclined to transpose effectively even if it is incompatible with their national traditions (Dimitrakopoulos and Richardson 2001). The most sophisticated and influential model on the impact of national cultural factors comes from Falkner and Treib (2008) who classify member states in four categories: 'world of law observance', 'world of domestic politics', 'world of transposition neglect' and 'world of dead letters'. Falkner and Treib's typology examines final implementation, yet it is still highly relevant for this particular analysis because divergent transposition patterns receive special attention. The first category includes Denmark, Finland and Sweden, and represents a group where compliance overrides domestic concerns and transposition is 'usually both in time and correct'. The 'world of domestics politics' consists of Austria, Belgium, Germany, the Netherlands, Spain and the UK and here 'transposition is likely to be timely and correct where no domestic concerns dominate over the fragile aspiration to comply' (Falkner and Treib 2008, p. 297). The 'world of neglect' encompasses France, Greece, Luxembourg and Portugal where the cultural norm of EU law compliance is not strong with political or administrative actors so there is a tendency for 'negligence at the transposition stage' (Falkner and Treib 2008, pp. 296–297). Finally the 'world of dead letters' consists of Italy, Ireland, Czech Republic, Hungary, Slovakia and Slovenia and in these countries the pattern is of a transposition that is dependent on the 'prevalent political constellation among domestic actors' (Falkner and Treib 2008, p. 297).

Under this structural approach we would expect the laggards in the coordinator reports to broadly correspond with those countries doing badly in other areas due to their administrative weaknesses (i.e. resources, funding and expertise) and/or political culture. With this in mind, we will turn our attention to first pillar data from the 2009 Commission Internal Market Scoreboard. These reports point the finger at Greece, Luxembourg, Spain, Austria and Portugal, in that order and followed by Belgium and Italy, as the five 'worst offenders' in relation to transposition delays. Most of these are also the Union members with the highest number of long overdue directives: Greece, Luxembourg, Italy, Austria and Portugal (European Commision 2009, p. 13). This is largely in line with the typology of administrative capacity in Thomson (2009, p. 12) where Greece, Italy and Portugal have lower scores than the other 12 old member states.

As shown in Table 3, three members of the abovementioned group: Luxembourg, Italy and Greece have also been frequently admonished by the Commission evaluations of the implementation of the Hague programme. These reports have examined those legislative instruments in the programme that required transposition by the member states – Directives and Framework Decisions – and presented an overall assessment based on member states' failures to notify transposal measures and cases of incorrect transposition. They are therefore not directly comparable to the coordinator report figures but still give us a snapshot of those countries that have struggled in the 2005–07 period with the transposition of Freedom, Security and

Justice (FSJ) legislation in the fields of justice, security, citizenship, immigration, asylum and borders.

Even though the three sources use widely different indicators to evaluate transposition, cover separate periods and the table should not be interpreted as a direct comparison, some important commonalities are still noticeable. Thus, the five worst laggards in transposing counter-terror laws are also 'named and shamed' in the Commission reports whereas Malta does poorly in both set of evaluations. Therefore the worst laggards in the coordinator reports not only poorly transpose key counter-terror laws but, more broadly, FSJ legislation and, in some cases, also first pillar *acquis*.[5] Interestingly, those same member states are classified as either part of 'the world of transposition neglect' or the 'world of dead letters' in Falkner and Treib's model.[6]

This state-based approach is also supported by evidence gathered during fieldwork. EU officials interviewed see slow implementation as structural in some countries: 'those member states who are usually slow in implementing European law are usually also slow in implementing counter-terrorist legislation. The problems are structural in those member states: no interest in the parliament, no interest in the government, slow legislative procedure, confusion, etc' (interview with Council Official, General Secretariat, DG H – JHA, January 2006). In this way, a state with a real terrorist problem, such as Italy, was singled out in a number of interviews as a country where implementation of some anti-terror legislation has been problematic, whereas 'there are some member states who have never had a problem with terrorism and have implemented everything in real time like Finland' (interview with Council Official, General Secretariat, DG H – JHA, January 2006). In fact Scandinavian countries were praised for their performance in this field based on the existing domestic procedures set in place to transpose European legislation (interview with National Official, Article 36 Committee, January 2006).

Some officials put the emphasis on broader, more prosaic factors such as a fragmented electoral system that leads to coalition governments, occasional collapses of minority governments and elections called during transposition periods (i.e. Italy; interview with National Official, Member State Permanent Representation, January 2006). On balance, however, evidence on the impact of type of government (minority or not) in compliance of EU legislation has been conflictive and unclear in other studies (Toshkov 2010, p. 26). Others have put the accent on the cultural dimension such as the low profile of European legislation in some national parliaments. As a Council official remarked:

> Because it is not, I suppose, interesting for bureaucracy at home to spend time in parliament on that, first. Because the minister of justice has already a lot to do in parliament, they don't put implementation of EU legislation as a top priority (…)., no political gain, so a minister won't spend much time because they don't have anything to gain at home. (Interview with Council Official, General Secretariat, DG H – JHA, January 2006)

Accordingly, and based on evidence from interviews and figures from official reports, although state-based explanations face deviations and do not fully explain national variation single-handedly, they are still fundamental to understand the root causes behind the difficulties that some countries find in the transposal of counter-terror

Table 3. Five worst transposition laggards.

Counter-terrorism (2004–2009)	FSJ 2007	FSJ 2006	FSJ 2005	Internal Market 2009
Italy	Greece	Malta	Luxembourg	Greece
Luxembourg	Malta	Greece	Greece	Luxembourg
Greece	Luxembourg	Italy	Malta	Spain
Ireland	Cyprus	Luxembourg	Cyprus	Austria
Cyprus	Ireland	Cyprus	Italy	Portugal

Sources: Counter-Terror Coordinator Implementation of the Action Plan to Combat Terrorism reports (2005–2009), EU Plan of Action on Combating Terrorism updates (2004–2005), European Commission Internal Market Scoreboard 2009, Report on the implementation of The Hague Programme (2005–2007).

legislation. In this regard, the abovementioned factors of national political culture and institutional capacity have a much stronger explanatory value than threat perceptions and other preference-based explanations. In general, member states transposing counter-terror laws comparatively slowly, do so, not because they *choose to,* but mostly due to the lack of institutional and bureaucratic resources to meet their obligations.

The impact of Lisbon

The relevance of structural factors in explaining implementation deficits by some member states is important when ascertaining the potential that institutional transformation at the European level has to alleviate these problems. Hence, it is argued here that the ratification of the Lisbon Treaty will have a lesser impact on this matter than initially expected. In principle, following the conventional infringement procedures argument, implementation should greatly benefit from the dissolution of the pillars and the communitarisation of police and judicial cooperation. This will result, after a 5 years transition period, in the ECJ extending its jurisdiction to the interpretation and review of the validity of JHA legislation, enhancing in the process the judicial oversight and legitimacy of EU's internal security policies. More specifically, this will allow the Commission to initiate infringement proceedings against member states and, in theory, the threat of being brought before the ECJ may persuade laggards to transpose EU laws adequately and on time to avoid penalties and/or censure.

On the other hand, the involvement of the ECJ will not be extended to 'internal law and order and security responsibilities' (Council of the European Union 2010, p. 11), excluding in this way a sizeable section of future counter-terror legislation. In addition, some member states such as the UK have not accepted the ECJ jurisdiction in this area. Moreover, the fact formal powers are being endowed does not necessarily entail their future employment. Thus, it remains to be seen whether the Commission, who has required years to build its credibility in this field and earn member states' trust, would be willing to compromise its present position by often taking this politically charged step. In relation to this, a Commission official working in this area summarised their current views by reminding this author: 'we are not public prosecutors (...) I don't believe in adversarial procedures, this is not the internal market. I would advise against using infringement procedures too often after Lisbon' (interview with Commission Official, DG JLS, April 2008).

Hence, the political sensitivity of these policies will make them less susceptible to interference by European institutions. More importantly, when facing strong cultural and institutional capacity problems, legal reform at the European level may not make a substantial difference in a number of cases. This is illustrated by the persistent and significant differentials in transposition records in first pillar policy fields, indicative of the fact that state-based factors may be too important in some member states to be significantly affected by the threat from the application of 'hard' enforcement mechanisms by the Commission.

Even more so since some institutional changes from Lisbon are not necessarily conducive to speedier transposal. Indeed, Kaeding (2006, p. 241) has shown that the introduction of QMV for Transport policies caused more transposition delay and Franchino (2006, p. 287) has posited that the involvement of the European Parliament 'leads to a decline in national administrative discretion', although empirical evidence on whether this may lead to further domestic reluctance to compliance has been mixed (Toshkov 2010, p. 34).

On the other hand, the stronger role outlined in the Treaty for national parliaments in European decision-making would mean that they can take responsibility for this type of measures at an earlier stage. This may lead to the prevention of situations where national parliaments were consulted regarding European decisions, which they did not initially oppose, but then procrastinated in their transposition for a number of years. It should also be noted that quantitative analyses of this question have found a positive significant relationship between the extent of parliamentary scrutiny and compliance (Toshkov 2010, p. 35).

In summary, whilst some institutional transformations from Lisbon are likely to prove beneficial, there are doubts about the practical impact of others, and, in the case of QMV, they might well affect negatively the speed of the process. It could be argued that positive changes may be reinforced by the release of the Stockholm Programme, which prioritises the matter of better implementation and the role of the Counter-Terrorism Coordinator and the Internal Security Strategy in obtaining such a goal. There is a clearly enhanced political interest in the document and a stronger rhetoric that turns the spotlight on national authorities: 'without prejudice to the role of the Commission and the Court of Justice, implementation is primarily a matter for the Member States' (Council of the European Union 2009c, p.27). Nonetheless, it is an open question whether vigorous political declarations in Brussels will be sufficient to overcome the structural domestic deficiencies characteristic of some member states institutional systems.

Conclusion

By focusing in the initial stage of transposition to national legislations, this paper has addressed an important part of the picture and sheds light on clear problems existing early in the implementation process. It has also argued that we need a more nuanced understanding of the problem since previous explanations have failed to recognise that transposition delays have been prevalent for some member states but much rarer for others. Although differences in threat perceptions are an important dimension of national and European counter-terror responses (Meyer 2009, Bures

2010), they fail to be of much use in the understanding of differentials in transposition. On the other hand, structural administrative and cultural aspects, although facing deviations and not saying much about transposition leaders, constitute an effective framework to explain cases where laggardness is severe. Those instances are more a matter of 'skill' than 'will'.

A next step, and an apparent suggestion for future research, would be to move beyond the transposition stage of compliance to observe changes in the practices of government agencies and actors in response to EU legislation in this area. In this regard, it would be necessary to ascertain whether the stronger rhetoric in Stockholm towards a lesser emphasis on new policies but a closer focus on ensuring their implementation has worked in practice. There has certainly been a streamlining of the policy response reflected in a reduction of the number of measures in the EU Counter-terror Action Plan (from 138 in 2007 to 49 in 2009; Council of the European Union 2009b) but it remains to be seen whether swifter and less flawed implementation will be the outcome. The threat perception vs. state capacity hypothesis presented in this contribution could well be retained as an analytical framework for such analyses.

Acknowledgements

Previous versions of this paper were presented at University of Salford in January 2010 and ECPR-SGIR Stockholm in September 2010. I am grateful to the participants and audience for their suggestions. I am also thankful to the anonymous reviewers for their comments.

Notes

1. The European Arrest Warrant being an exception (UK House of Lords 2006).
2. Article 35.7 of the Treaty referred to the legislative acts stated at Article 34.2 (i.e. Framework Decisions, Decisions, Joint Actions...,).
3. Bulgaria and Romania are obviously excluded from the comparison since they joined the Union in 2007 halfway through the analysis period.
4. A periodic – two 'waves' per year – survey of public opinion in the European Union carried out by the Directorate-General for Communication of the Commission.
5. Whereas commonalities are strong, variation is also present: Spain, Austria and Portugal, three of the worst laggards in the 2009 internal market evaluation, are average transposers in the FSJ reports. They show widely varying patterns in counter-terrorism: Austria is a top implementer, Spain's record is above average and Portugal's is ordinary.
6. Falkner and Treib's model does not encompass all EU-27 and Cyprus was not included.

Notes on contributor

Javier Argomaniz is a member of the St Andrews Centre for the Study of Terrorism and Political Violence (CSTPV). He has undertaken research at a variety of national and international projects and has published in the areas of European Studies, Criminology and International Security.

References

Bakker, E., 2006. Differences in terrorist threat perceptions in Europe. *In*: D. Mahncke and J. Monar, eds. *International terrorism. A European response to a global threat?*. Brussels: P.I.E Peter Lang, 47–62.

Borghetto, E., Franchino, F., and Giannetti, D., 2006. Complying with transposition deadlines of EU directives: evidence from Italy. *Rivista italiana di politiche pubbliche*, 1, 7–38.

Bossong, R., 2008. The action plan on combating terrorism: a flawed instrument of EU security governance. *JCMS: journal of common market studies*, 46, 27–48.

Börzel, T.A. and Risse, T., 2003. Conceptualising the domestic impact of Europe. *In*: K. Featherstone and C. Radaelli, eds. *The politics of Europeanization*. Oxford: Oxford University Press, 55–78.

Börzel, T.A., *et al.*, 2007. *Recalcitrance, inefficiency, and support for European integration: why member states do (not) comply with European law*. Working Paper 151. Harvard: Center for European Studies.

Bures, O., 2006. EU Counterterrorism policy: a paper tiger? *Terrorism and political violence*, 18, 57–78.

Bures, O., 2010. Perceptions of the terrorist threat among EU member states. *Central European journal of international and security studies*, 4 (1), 51–80.

Council of the European Union, 2007. *Implementation of the EU counter-terrorism strategy – discussion paper*. Brussels, 23 November, 15448/07.

Council of the European Union, 2009a. *EU counter-terrorism strategy – discussion paper*. Brussels, 14 May, 9717/09.

Council of the European Union, 2009b. *EU action plan on combating terrorism*. Brussels, 26 November, 15358/09.

Council of the European Union, 2009c. *The Stockholm programme – an open and secure Europe serving and protecting the citizens*. Brussels, 2 December, 17024/09.

Council of the European Union, 2010. *Draft internal security strategy for the European Union: "towards a European security model"*. Brussels, 23 February, 5842/2/10.

de Vries, G., 2005. The European Union's role in the fight against terrorism. *Irish studies in international affairs*, 16, 3–9.

den Boer, M. and Monar, J., 2002. Keynote article: September and the challenge of global terrorism to the EU as a security actor. *Journal of common market studies*, 40, 11–28.

Dimitrakopoulos, D. and Richardson, J., 2001. Implementing EU public policy. *In*: J. Richardson, ed. *European Union. Power and policy-making*, (2nd ed.). London: Routledge, 335–356.

European Commission, 2001. *European governance: a white paper*. Brussels, 25 July, COM 428 final.

European Commission, 2004. *Existing legislative instruments relevant to the fight against terrorism, and draft measures already on the Council table*. Brussels, 18 March, Memo/04/63.

European Commission, 2007. *Report from the Commission based on Article 11 of the Council Framework Decision of 13 June 2002 on combating terrorism*. Brussels, 6 November, COM (2007) 681 final.

European Commission, 2008. *Report on the implementation of the Hague Programme 2007*. Brussels, 2 July, COM(2008) 373 final.

European Commission, 2009. *Justice freedom and security in Europe since 2005: an evaluation of the Hague programme and action plan*. Brussels, 10 June, COM(2009) 263 final.

European Commission, 2010. *Internal market scoreboard*. Brussels, 1 March, December 2009 n 20. Available from: http://ec.europa.eu/internal_market/score/docs/score20_en.pdf [Accessed 2 April 2010]

European Council, 2004. *Declaration on Combating Terrorism*. Brussels, 25 March.

Falkner, G. and Treib, O., 2008. Three worlds of compliance or four? The EU-15 compared to new member states. *Journal of common market studies*, 46 (2), 293–313.

Franchino, F., 2006. *The powers of the union: delegation in the EU*. Cambridge: Cambridge University Press.

General Intelligence and Security Service of The Netherlands (AIVD), 2005. *Annual report 2004. General intelligence and security service*. The Hague: AIVD.

Haverland, M. and Romeijn, M., 2007. Do member states make European policies work? Analysing the EU transposition deficit. *Public administration*, 85, 757–778.

Kaeding, M., 2006. Determinants of transposition delay in the European Union. *Journal of public policy*, 26, 229–253.

Keohane, D., 2006. Implementing the EU's counter-terrorism strategy. Intelligence, emergencies, and foreign policy. *In*: D. Mahncke and J. Monar, eds. *International Terrorism. A European response to a global threat?*. Brussels: P.I.E Peter Lang, 63–72.

König, T. and Luetgert, B., 2009. Troubles with transposition? Explaining trends in member-state notification and the delayed transposition of EU directives. *British journal of political science*, 39, 163–194.

Lampinen, R. and Uusikylä, P., 1998. Implementation deficit – why member states do not comply with EU directives? *Scandinavian political studies*, 21 (3), 231–251.

Levy, M., Young, O., and Zurn, M., 1995. The study of international regimes. *European journal of international relations*, 1, 267–330.

Mastenbroek, E., 2003. Surviving the deadline. The transposition of EU directives in the Netherlands. *European Union politics*, 4, 371–395.

Mbaye, H., 2001. Why national states comply with supranational law? Explaining implementation. Infringements in the European Union, 1972–1993. *European Union politics*, 2, 259–281.

Meyer, C., 2009. International terrorism as a force for homogenization? A constructivist approach to understanding cross-national threat perceptions and responses. *Cambridge review of international affairs*, 22 (4), 647–666.

Miettinen, S., 2010. Third pillar instruments and national implementation: a 'virtual criminal law?', *Policing and European Studies Conference*, University of Abertay, Dundee, UK, 26 February 2010.

Monar, J., 2006. Conclusions. International terrorism – a 'European response' to a global threat? *In*: D. Mahncke and J. Monar, eds. *International terrorism. "A European response to a global threat?* Brussels: P.I.E Peter Lang, 151–158.

Monar, J., 2007. Common threat and common response? The European Union's counter-terrorism strategy and its problems. *Government and opposition*, 42 (3), 292–313.

Nilsson, H.G., 2004. Judicial co-operation in the European Union. *In*: O. Horvath and T. Bremmers, eds. *European co-operation against terrorism*. Nijmegen: Wolf, 15–22.

Steunenberg, B. and Kaeding, M., 2009. As time goes by: Explaining the transposition of maritime directives. *European journal of political research*, 48, 432–454.

Steunenberg, B. and Toshkov, D., 2009. Comparing transposition in the 27 member states of the EU: the impact of discretion and legal fit. *Journal of European public policy*, 16 (7), 951–970.

Thomson, R., 2009. Same effects in different worlds: the transposition of EU directives. *Journal of European public policy*, 16, 1–18.

Thomson, R., Torenvield, R., and Arregui, J., 2007. The paradox of compliance: infringements and delays in transposing European Union directives. *British journal of political science*, 37, 685–709.

Toshkov, D., 2010. *Taking stock: a review of quantitative studies of transposition and implementation of EU law.* Working Paper 01/2010. Vienna: Institute for European Integration Research.

UK House of Lords, 2006. *European arrest warrant – recent developments.* Paper 156. London: HMSO.

Zimmermann, D., 2006. The European Union and post-9/11 counterterrorism: a reappraisal. *Studies in conflict & terrorism*, 29, 123–145.

The iron curtain revisited: the 'Austrian way' of policing the internal Schengen border

Alexandra Schwell

Institut für Europäische Ethnologie der Universität Wien, Hanuschgasse 3, A-1010 Wien, Austria

Since 1990 draftees of the Austrian army have been stationed at the border to Hungary, and later to Slovakia, as a reaction to both the system change in Eastern Europe as well as the expected increase in cross-border crime. This so-called 'support deployment' was initially planned to last no longer than 10 weeks, but soon it became apparent that the military's border security deployment could also serve other ends than mere security goals. Since then it has been prolonged numerous times. In scrutinising the strategies of the various actors involved, the paper shows that the support deployment can be considered an act of securitisation and is as such almost entirely decoupled from the actual policing of the Schengen internal border. Furthermore, it argues to 'bring the audience back in' and to recognise the audience's agency in the analysis of securitisation processes.

Introduction

As has been argued by numerous authors, the end of the cold war and the break-up of the bipolar system left the armed forces, as a result of their vanished enemy, with an identity crisis and led to a merging of internal and external security (see e.g. Lutterbeck 2005, Bigo 2006, Eriksson and Rhinard 2009). The police increasingly take over tasks that traditionally have been reserved for the armed forces, such as deployments on foreign soil, and the military tends to conceive the domestic context as yet another field of manoeuvre. While the army's temporarily limited assistance in cases like flooding or disaster management is hardly contested, the military participation in internal security is subject to constant debate where fundamental principles of the nation state are at stake. What these debates all have in common is the notion of 'exceptionality' (cf. Guittet 2006). Furthermore, the *policisation* of the armed forces is a process that does not take place in isolation, but rather carries meaning that goes beyond the immediate confines of the nation state. One prominent example for the militarisation of the police in Western Europe is the policing of the external border of the European Union. Interestingly, a 'policisation' of the military has taken place in this respect as well. Austria is the 'European country in which the armed forces have become the most deeply implicated in securing the country's frontiers and preventing irregular immigration' (Lutterbeck 2005, p. 242). Since

175

1990, soldiers in the Austrian army, the *Bundesheer*, have been stationed at the border to Hungary and later to Slovakia. The deployment was initiated as a reaction to the system change in Eastern Europe. When the borders opened in 1990, Austria was suddenly confronted with a huge influx of migrants not only from Eastern Europe, but also with refugees fleeing the war in former Yugoslavia.

The paper will elaborate on a case where an issue – undocumented migration from and via Eastern Europe – has become successfully and sustainably securitised by political actors and security professionals by equating migration with cross-border crime. Extraordinary measures have been put in place to fight this threat: the deployment of the Austrian army. I will argue that this extraordinary measure, having by now virtually become institutionalised as a part of the Austrian normal social world, is no longer considered legitimate, due to new socio-political realities. The method of deploying the army is not regarded as being adequate to combat the threat effectively. The more the referent object moves from the national to the local level, the less the wider public is willing to accept the securitisation. The paper concludes, firstly, by arguing that the deployment over the years has become almost entirely decoupled from the initial threat and, secondly, that the actors promoting the deployment are becoming less and less credible to the public, since the discrepancy between the threat and the efficiency of the counter-measures becomes too obvious. Thus the truth about the threat scenarios the field produces, which must link agents with the audience in a given context, is no longer capable of establishing itself as the hegemonic way of interpreting the social world.

The first section of the paper introduces the theoretical concepts on which the analysis is based. This framework is provided by the notion of securitisation as a strategic practice, as well as on the idea of a security field, where actors constantly negotiate their strategies. In a second step, the strategies of the actors in the security field will be scrutinised. This empirical part of the paper will draw on three types of sources: interviews with officials of the ministry of the interior and the Austrian lands,[1] media discourse, and research in an internet forum frequented by soldiers.[2] By embedding the case in a wider framework and context, the paper employs the *Extended Case Method* which '[...] takes the social situation as the point of empirical examination and works with given general concepts and laws about states, economies, legal orders, and the like to understand how those micro situations are shaped by its wider structures' (Burawoy 1991, p. 282).[3]

Securitisation as a practice

This paper approaches the concept of security from an anthropological point of view. Although 'security' plays an important role in much anthropological research, as has been argued by Goldstein (2010), it is rarely addressed as a relevant category of research; consequently anthropology has not yet developed a unique disciplinary theoretical approach. The insights of security and securitisation studies developed within the field of IR are particularly suitable for an anthropology of security, since they treat security not as an objective fact, but as socially constructed. Furthermore, as Kent contends, '[b]y taking indigenous perspectives seriously, the anthropological approach relativizes academic constructions of referent objects of security' (Kent 2006, p. 347). Thus I contend that anthropology, which predominantly deals with phenomena of everyday culture that are framed by the wider context of the macro level, assuming that both are being mutually constitutive of each other, does not only fit very well with these approaches, but can make a valuable contribution.

The concept of securitisation

The so-called Copenhagen School's (CS) concepts for many students of security studies and securitisation theory are a starting point for critical discussions about how to deal theoretically and empirically with security issues. The CS developed a constructivist model of security that locates security somewhere between a purely military notion on the one hand, and everything people can worry about on the other. Their focus lies on the speech act that turns an issue into a security issue, if several 'facilitating conditions' are met (Buzan *et al.* 1998, p. 33). A securitisation occurs when something 'is presented as an existential threat: if we do not tackle this, everything else will be irrelevant (because we will not be here, or not be free to deal with future challenges in our way)' (Wæver 1996, p. 106). Securitisation thus is described as 'the move that takes politics beyond the established rules of the game and frames the issue either as a special kind of politics or as above politics' (Buzan *et al.* 1998, p. 23). By declaring something a security issue, the speaker calls for the legitimation of unusual and extreme measures to fight this threat and thus achieve a higher aim, such as 'survival'. If the audience accepts and supports this so-called 'securitising move', and legitimises emergency measures, the securitisation can be considered successful. Security is thus intersubjectively constructed, and it is self-referential.

The CS, however, argues that 'security should be seen as negative, as a failure to deal with issues as normal politics' (Buzan *et al.* 1998, p. 29). Instead it favours the opposite and makes a plea for desecuritisation, to take the securitised issue out of the level of 'panic politics' (Buzan 1997, p. 14) and back into the normal political process. 'Security' and 'politics' thus are opposed concepts, with the former imposing itself as the dominant, strategic and intentional way of interpreting the social world. Wæver (1995, p. 57) argues that 'security is articulated only from a specific place, in an institutional voice, by elites', producing a field effect that does not even spare researchers of security issues: 'The problematique locks people into talking in terms of "security" and this reinforces the hold of security on our thinking, even if our approach is a critical one. We do not find much work aimed at desecuritizing politics which, I suspect, would be more effective than securitizing problems' (Wæver 1995, p. 57). Effectiveness and democratic accountability are keywords for Wæver's normative preference of desecuritisation. Alternatively, one should avoid 'security dilemmas' or at best 'try to keep issues de-securitized' (Wæver 2000, p. 253). In this case, the issue is framed and perceived as being political, not as an issue relating to security, since the threat may have been handled or disappeared completely.

The CS's rather static model has faced critiques from a number of authors (see e.g. *Cooperation and Conflict* 1999, 34 (3)), but also inspired many studies that attempt to critically and constructively review, adapt and modify the original concept. Four points of critique are particularly relevant for the purpose of this paper: the importance of (1) the context; (2) the temporal aspect of the securitisation process; (3) the strategies and practices of actors; and (4) audiences.

(1) The context

A frequently voiced objection is the centrality of the speech act as an essential element of the CS concept. The relation between the speech act and the audience is considered to be simplifying in nature and thus particularly problematic by several authors. In the literature an externalist approach is opposed to an internalist approach (Stritzel 2007, Balzacq 2009): the latter, CS concept, focuses on the speech act and argues that the act of securitisation itself modifies the context: '[...] it is the utterance itself that is the act. By saying the words, something is done (like betting, giving a promise, naming a ship)' (Buzan *et al.* 1998, p. 26). The externalist approach, however, argues that successful securitisation can only occur within a wider context supportive to it: '[...] an actor cannot be significant as a social actor and a speech act cannot have an impact on social relations without a situation that constitutes them as significant. It is their embeddedness in social relations of meaning and power that constitutes both actors and speech acts' (Stritzel 2007, p. 367). Salter supports this assumption, but goes beyond it, adding that securitisation processes, actors and audiences may differ depending on the specific (sociological, bureaucratic, political, scientific,...) context. Following Goffman (1959/1990), he emphasises the importance of the respective setting of the narrative for a securitisation process, which he sees ignored in speech act models. Instead he proposes a dramaturgical analysis which '[...] argues that the setting of a securitizing move is determined by the actors and their roles, the rules of the discourse permissible within that space, and the expectations of the audience' (Salter 2008, p. 328). Who has the authority in which setting to speak? And who will listen and grant legitimacy?

Likewise the following analysis of the *Bundesheer* deployment supports the assumption that speech acts certainly can be important elements of a securitisation process, but that a mere discourse analysis is not sufficient to encompass the dynamics inherent to the securitisation process, as Buzan *et al.* (1998, p. 25) presumed, and hence to answer the questions this paper poses. Instead we should understand securitisation as a strategic and pragmatic practice (Balzacq 2005, 2009) and focus on the strategies and motives of various actors for supporting or rejecting securitisation in a given context and setting.

(2) The temporal dimension

If securitisation should be not reduced to a speech act, but rather must be analysed as a process, then the temporal dimension has to be taken into account. Long-term processes are subject to different dynamics than the CS's dramatic states of emergency. The acceptance of a securitisation can change over time, and it can change differently in different audiences and different settings. Furthermore, securitisation over time involves a certain habituation effect. What may have seemed extraordinary in the beginning, may become 'normal' soon. Therefore '[...] two temporal dimensions must be added to considerations of securitization and desecuritization: the duration of the securitization and the entropy of the public imagination' (Salter 2008, p. 324).

(3) The actors in the security field

The role of actors for the securitisation process is considered undertheorised by several authors, an argument fitting neatly with the aforementioned critique. Accordingly, Stritzel proposes three 'layers of securitisation' as a framework for analysis: '(1) the performative force of an articulated threat text, (2) its embeddedness in existing discourses and (3) the positional power of securitizing actors' (Stritzel 2007, p. 377). Bigo focuses on the securitising actors and their strategies in a 'security field': a social space where different actors are competing for hegemony, resources and influence (cf. Bourdieu 1984). Simultaneously, both actors and organisations are part of their respective social, cultural and political environment and their specific national control culture and tradition: 'The field is thus established between these "professionals", with specific "rules of the game", and rules that presuppose a particular mode of socialization or habitus. This habitus is inherited from the respective professional trajectories and social positions, but is not strongly defined along the lines of national borders' (Bigo 2008, p. 14).

The actors claim to be in possession of a hidden and privileged knowledge they derive from data that are only 'readable' for and accessible to the insider. Hence, a strict boundary between security professionals on the one hand and the population and 'naïve' (because they are unknowing) critics on the other hand is constructed. This professional knowledge does not exist on the security-political and professional backstage alone, but it goes beyond the limits of the security field and aims at establishing itself in the wider society. The field hence produces a 'truth' (cf. Foucault 1980, p. 131), a privileged knowledge of professional and political actors, which ideally is accepted almost unquestioned in a given audience (cf. Bigo 2000, p. 90). It is considered legitimate exactly because it is produced inside the security field of experts. Thus the process of securitisation cannot be reduced to a speech act, but its analysis has to include the practices that are informing and are informed by it; it rather works through 'everyday technologies, through the effects of power that are continuous rather than exceptional, through political struggles, and especially through institutional competition within the professional security field in which the most trivial interests are at stake' (Bigo 2002, p. 73).

The focus on the practices of security professionals and bureaucrats is important, for it enables us to envisage bureaucratic, organisational and other daily practices that are largely invisible to the public and do not produce as much noise as the CS's 'existential threat', but which nevertheless in effect might prove much more useful for securitisation than speech acts about exceptionality and 'survival'. The notion of the 'field' proves particularly helpful in an attempt to map the actors involved in the securitisation. However, while I am sympathetic to the concept of the security field of 'managers of unease', I contend that, like most theoretical approaches, it tends to underestimate the role and importance of the audience. The audience is ascribed a rather passive role, as it seems to be simply under the influence of the 'truth' the security field sends.

(4) Bringing the audience back in

The role of the audience as agents receives inadequate attention in most approaches. This is particularly, but not only, the case with the CS focus on state elites, '[...]

presenting [the powerless] at best as part of an audience that can collectively consent to or contest securitizing moves, and at worst as passive recipients of elite discourse' (McDonald 2008, p. 574). Since Hall's (1993) deliberations about the mechanisms of encoding and decoding of mass media it has become widely accepted that the relation between the sender and the receiver is not a one-way street, since a message can be interpreted by the recipient in a different (and sometimes even subversive) way than the sender originally had intended. Additionally, the same applies to the process of constructing or sustaining a security issue. Therefore to understand why a securitising move is successful (or fails) we have to include the underlying motifs of both actors and audience into our considerations. Why an audience supports a securitising move cannot be simply deducted from the historical and actual context relating to the security issue, but has to embrace other context factors and include the audience's own strategies of action.

Sociologist Swidler (1986) coined the concept of 'culture in action' which proves particularly useful for the purpose of this paper. She departs from the assumption that it is not abstract values that structure human behaviour, as Weber and Parsons assumed, but that culture shapes strategies of action, it forms the way actions are organised. Culture provides us with a dynamic 'tool-kit' from which actors choose to deal with familiar and unfamiliar situations, and which at the same time constantly incorporates new knowledge. The 'tool-kit' builds upon deeply rooted imaginations and stereotypes, on historical narratives about Self and Other, on current social, political and economic factors, but it also captures defining issues like class, gender and race. This idea of culture as 'a whole way of life' (Williams 1963) is not static, but dynamic and heterogeneous. Furthermore, in applying Swidler's approach to securitisation theory, we can avoid seeing the audience as predominantly passive, but recognise agency on the part of the audience, without underestimating the power relations that govern the social field: 'A realistic cultural theory should lead us to expect not passive "cultural dopes" [...], but rather the active, sometimes skilled users of culture whom we actually observe' (Swidler 1986, p. 277).

Thus it can be expected that what actors consider a security issue, and what they think how and by whom it might best be handled in a given context and setting, is to a large degree contingent upon their 'tool-kit'. Simultaneously, the incorporation and habituation effect of the tool-kit approach accounts for the temporal aspect of the securitisation process and helps explain why security issues can be evaluated differently over a particular length of time. Therefore I agree with Stritzel's critique on the actor–audience- relationship when he writes: '[...] the stronger one emphasizes the idea that "some actors are placed in positions of power", the more problematic it becomes to uphold a split between the securitizing actor and the audience where the audience is placed in the position of "having the power to define security"'' (Stritzel 2007, p. 365). This is not to say that the audience is in the same power position as the securitising actors; the respective audiences may subvert the original message and interpret it according to their own preferences, but the security experts nevertheless have to a large degree the authority to determine the agenda.

Other studies show that the audience '[...] may not simply accept securitization but also initiate an expansion of government powers' (Salter 2008, p. 337). However, his examples of widening securitisation by a concerned audience only refer to issues that are restricted to the security discourse, while I contend that we have to broaden our view and keep our eyes open for strategies and motives of actors and audiences to support or reject securitisation that go beyond this discourse and may include other issues than security, like economic well-being. Securitisation in this sense is not just a discursive practice, which is expressed only verbally and in extreme situations. It is institutionalised in practical actions by repetition and habituation and thus becomes less and less questioned, both by the public as the audience of securitisation and by the securitising actors themselves. Occasionally, it happens the other way round, as the following case study will show.

The border security support deployment

The border security support deployment of the Austrian army provides an excellent case of securitisation, as it was an extreme response to the influx of migrants after the fall of the Iron Curtain. In 1990 about 1000 irregular border crossings per week began to overburden the Austrian authorities, and a simultaneous increase in cross-border crime led the government to alter the receptive and open-hearted strategy they had employed in the past decades and rather direct their attention to inventing public-oriented counter-measures. Hence the support deployment was created: from September 1990 to December 2007 soldiers were stationed at the green border to Hungary and later to Slovakia at a length of 470 km. The operational area was gradually enlarged, finally encompassing the whole of Burgenland and parts of Lower Austria (see Figure 1).

Figure 1.   Map of the support deployment.
Source: http://www.mapcruzin.com and author.

The operation was specifically declared a *support* deployment, due to the fact that the army does not decide on the deployment independently, but acts only on the request of the ministry of the interior. One rotation comprises 1500–2000 soldiers and lasts 6 weeks; in total 334.903 soldiers, predominantly draftees, guarded the border from 1990 to 2007. From 1990 to 2007 approximately 90,000 irregular border-crossers from 110 states were apprehended. After the mandatory military service was reduced from 8 to 6 months in 2006 the support deployment increasingly has been relying on militiamen, whose share rose from 1% in 1995 to 15% in 2007 (Roth 2008).[4] The border security support deployment was initially planned to last no longer than 10 weeks, but, as a representative of the army proudly puts it in the *Bundesheer's* own magazine: 'Initially only a provisionary arrangement, the deployment evolved into an indispensable Austrian measure to secure the external EU and Schengen border' (Gröbming 2005).[5] Ten weeks in the end became more than 17 years. Over the years this led numerous jurists to question the doubtable transitional character of the deployment, and thus its lawfulness.

The soldiers' tasks were defined as follows: to prevent illegal migrants from crossing the border, to apprehend those who already have crossed illegally and, finally, to contribute to an increase in the feeling of safety in the border region. The police (and until May 2004 the customs officers) controlled border crossing points and the hinterland, while the *Bundesheer* accounted for the surveillance between the crossing points. Thus police and military tasks were strictly separated, but complemented one another. The soldiers had exactly the same rights and duties as the border police, e.g. they had also the right to stop and search, and to arrest suspects. Nevertheless both draftees and militiamen were sent to the border only after a very short preparatory period of two (until 2007), respectively, 1 week (BHI-Wiki 2009a). This is a blatant disparity in comparison to the 2 years training every border guard has to go through. The question, however, to what extent draftees and militiamen are qualified at all to exercise police powers has not been adequately answered. The support deployment every year has been prolonged for another year upon the request of the minister of the interior. Therefore every year an explanation had to be found for the deployment of the armed forces in the interior of the country to be prolonged, whose personnel was not properly qualified and that was considered unconstitutional by many observers.

The creation and implementation of the support deployment in 1990 clearly was a securitising move that was widely accepted at the time: The government identified the influx of migrants from Eastern Europe as a security threat for the Austrian population, and the support deployment appeared to be an adequate, albeit extreme, solution. The indispensability of this measure countering the threat from Eastern Europe has been confirmed every year by prolonging the deployment. Securitisation in this case is obviously not limited to a single speech act, but is a practice that has to be analysed taking into account its processual and temporal aspect. Thus it has to be asked if and how the securitisation, its proponents, and its reception have changed over time.

The post-2007 deployment

With the accession of the East-European neighbouring countries to the Schengen area on 21 December 2007 and the simultaneous abolishment of border checks, the bell should have finally tolled for the army at the border. Furthermore, the Schengen enlargement would have provided an excellent opportunity to finally end the deployment, maybe even with reference to the EU as a higher power and thus delegating responsibility to a scapegoat the Euro-sceptic Austrians are all too familiar with (cf. Pelinka 2005). But this was not the case. Already long before December 2007, claims were pushed forth from different sides for measures to compensate for the putative security deficit that would inevitably accompany the abolishment of the border controls. Tabloid newspapers warned that the opening of borders would be almost irresponsible, that asylum-seekers were about to 'flood' the country, and that the so-called 'Eastern criminals' ('Ostkriminelle') were just waiting to cross the Austrian border and break into Austrian houses and steal Austrian cars (cf. Schwell 2009).

Thus, it came as no surprise to many observers that the support deployment continued beyond 2008, despite of potential legal complications. The ministry's experts were well aware of this fact, as a protocol of a preparatory meeting in the ministry of the interior before the enlargement illustrates: 'Since the hitherto existing justification (obviation of illegal border crossings by executing the law on controlling borders) ceases to apply due to the abolition of the Schengen external border, a support deployment of the *Bundesheer* that goes beyond this point in time has to be put on a different legal footing' (Bundesministerium für Inneres n.d., p. 3). Accordingly, the 'new' support deployment had to undergo several important changes: the soldiers now do not have any executive authority anymore, but simply report their observations to the local police. The government on 7 November 2007 officially decided that the *Bundesheer* should support the police in surveilling the frontier region until the end of 2008. Since then the support deployment was again extended until the end of 2009 and, finally, until 31 December 2010. It can be assumed that the deployment will see more 'last' prolongations in the future.

'Security folklore' – critical voices

While the pre-2007 deployment had been able to justify its existence by enumerating the number of apprehensions, pointing towards a 'countable' increase in public safety, the post-2007 deployment has a hard time to prove its efficiency statistically. A recent report by the ministry of the interior revealed that in 2009 the soldiers filed 1269 reports to the security agencies in charge; 79 of these observations concerned criminal offences, and only nine of these reports resulted in apprehensions of irregular migrants. This obvious disparity led critics to calculate the army's efficiency, arguing that every arrest cost the taxpayer €2.4 million (Bauer 2010). Likewise, the Austrian Court of Audit in March 2010 considered 'the *Bundesheer's* contribution to actively combating crime in the operational area [...] in relation to the resources employed as extremely small' (Rechnungshof 2010, p. 30), concluding that the deployment is not appropriate to combat cross-border crime.

Critique of the deployment does not only arise from the inside perspective. Austria joined the EU in 1995, hence from that point in time on it also was hardly compatible with EU regulations. Although, as a confidential report authored by a joint working group of the ministries of the interior and of defence acknowledges, there are no immediate barriers to the deployment in its current shape in EU law; nevertheless 'EU commission officers in charge have been expressing over and over again to Austrian representatives of various Council Working Groups that the EU Commission judges the *Bundesheer*'s support deployment along the interior border as politically questionable' (cited in Bauer 2010). It is expensive, it is inefficient, it contradicts Austrian law and makes the EU feel uneasy. The deployment's raison d'être – a journalist angrily called it a 'security folklore' without any substance (Fritz 2009) – is increasingly put in doubt.

Apparently the securitisation that had been proven successful and had functioned for years without significant opposition becomes difficult to maintain as the political context changes and the hitherto predominantly unquestioned adequacy of the deployment is suddenly under scrutiny. The following section argues that this change cannot be explained only by reference to the different circumstances, but that the strategies of actors and audiences play a pivotal role.

The actors in the security field

In light of the concept of the cultural 'tool-kit', this section argues that while actors have particular motivations and pursue specific aims, they also construct their strategies on the basis of the tool-kit at their disposal, which frames what is considered a security issue and how it is dealt with. It will focus on the actors who are part of the 'security field', the social space where the deployment is negotiated, defended and disputed, and where knowledge about the deployment is produced and disseminated to the wider public. Bigo has explicitly used the concept of the security field to identify an inter- and transnational network of 'managers of unease', but for the present purpose I will apply it exclusively to a national field, that nevertheless relates to, is informed and determined by events, actions and knowledge that take place and are generated outside the Austrian context. Furthermore, the field is not restricted to security experts, but includes actors from different backgrounds who are relating to the support deployment and pursue specific aims. Every actor inside the security field is constrained by his/her *habitus*, by restrictions and expectations that often are beyond his/her immediate control. Various interests and variables play a role in this process, like the historical and political context or organisational and control culture (cf. Bigo 2000, p. 71).

Thus there is no objective truth to the deployment that can be unravelled, but in focusing on those actors who define and maintain the interests of the security field and in analysing the motives guiding the actors and the strategies and practices they employ, we can grasp some of the dynamics governing the security field; we can, in short, analyse the actors' strategies and the subjective 'truth' the field produces directed at a given audience.[6] Sketching and analysing the motifs and strategies of these actors who are competing and negotiating in the security field allows us to see securitisation not merely as a discursive, but as a strategic practice, embedded in 'a historical process that occurs between an antecedent influential set of events and their impact on interactions' (Balzacq 2005, p. 193). These groups of actors are not homogenous, and strategies concerning the deployment can contradict within the groups. Although the different actors conceive of the social world through the lens of their respective position in the social field and their *habitus*, all of them are part of the overarching context that, one way or another, shapes their experiences, world-views and perception of Self and Other.

(1) The local population

The Austrian population is both the referent object and audience of the securitisation, exerting, however, over time a considerable influence on the fate of the support deployment. The audience is decisive, since 'securitizing moves occur within the universe of the *audience* imagination. It is not simply a power relationship – but a knowledge-authority game' (Salter 2008, p. 330, emphasis in original). The perception of both local border populations and the national population is framed by Austria's geopolitical position and historical legacy. Austria's relationship with its immediate neighbours is charged with historical, social and symbolic meaning. The East/West-asymmetry and a feeling of superiority over the East-European neighbours are of powerful historical consequence not only due to geopolitical reasons. The concept of the backward 'East' as opposed to a civilisational progressive 'West' (cf. Wolff 1994) is reinforced by a specifically Austrian paternalism that derives from its hegemonic position in the Habsburg Empire. Furthermore, in discussing Said's (1979) concept of 'Orientalism', Gingrich describes the case of Austria as a particular type of 'Frontier Orientalism' which is strongly intertwined with the heritage of the Habsburg Empire:

> First, the 'Oriental' was portrayed not as a distant, backward, and deviant underling but rather as a close, dangerous, potential intruder of almost equal, albeit very different, skills. Second, this dangerously close 'Oriental' was a pervasive topic not only in court and 'elite' cultures, but even more so in 'folk' cultures of all varieties. [...] Third, this type of (folk and elite) frontier Orientalism fed directly into the rise of those nationalisms that had competed in Austria since the late 19th century: pan-Germanic nationalism (leading up to Nazism) and Habsburg imperial-loyalist patriotism (transformed after the 1918 imperial collapse into clerical republican nationalism) (Gingrich 2004, p. 169ff.).

Even though (or because) all East-European neighbouring countries have been part of the Habsburg Empire, and political actors (albeit frequently in a patronising way) like to refer to this historical bond, the idea of Austria as a frontier did not disappear after 1945. In fact it was reinforced by the strict separation of the Iron Curtain and remained fertile after the end of the cold war. Likewise the idea of 'Mitteleuropa' is still part of the Austrian cultural discourse on 'Austro-nostalgia' (Vidmar-Horvat and Delanty 2008).

Until the demise of Communism, Austria's Eastern part was almost completely surrounded by state-socialist countries: Czechoslovakia, Hungary, and Yugoslavia. With the Iron Curtain separating Austria from the countries of the Warsaw Pact, Austria's Eastern and Northern border regions were degraded to periphery; these frontier zones are frequently referred to as 'dead' regions at the time of the cold war, as rural areas where virtually nothing happened, where there was few population and high unemployment. However, nowadays the border population imagines the pre-1989 era as a time when nobody had to lock his bike, car or even house. The era of the 'dead' region for many people is idealised as a time of peace and silence, a time where contact with the other side did virtually not take place.[7] Following Martínez' (1994) typology, the borderlands at that time can be described as *alienated*.

Accordingly, the local population, being suddenly confronted with an over-whelming amount of 'East' in the backyard, greeted the soldiers with enthusiasm for two reasons: Firstly, the soldiers were perceived as generally increasing safety in the region. Their presence, the locals believed, would help decrease not only illegal border-crossings, but scare off petty crime, thefts and burglary, all of which were believed to come exclusively from behind the border. The locals here were in line with large parts of the wider population that felt under siege and threatened not only by criminals, but also by the war in neighbouring Yugoslavia. This, however, is only one side of the coin, and only a partial explanation of why the local population was such a grateful audience for the securitising move.

Secondly, and almost equally significant, the soldiers contributed significantly to the local economy. The soldiers are important economic features in a formerly 'dead' rural region. Shops, bakeries, and pubs do not want to lose the soldiers and the business they bring to the area. Furthermore, not all soldiers live in barracks, but some are also accommodated in private housing whose owners would lose a reliable income source in case the deployment came to an end. It has also been argued that the support deployment fosters tourism in the long run, since it supposedly had a publicity effect not only for the *Bundesheer* itself, but also for the border regions. The author of a nostalgic historical review of the support deployment notes: 'Some [soldiers] have come to detest it, but many have become fond and came back. They came to show their parents, their girlfriend, children or grandchildren where they "froze their arse off" or where they bravely apprehended a group of illegal border crossers' (Roth 2008).

While public assent to the deployment decreased considerably with the enlargement of the Schengen area, it remained remarkably high in border areas. We can explain this difference by drawing on the role of the local population as a referent object, actor and audience; and it has several implications. On the one hand we can expect a long-term involvement of the armed forces in the interior to transform the way a population conceives and interprets the social world, since 'whilst security promises to enhance subjective feelings of safety its pursuit often entails increased insecurity' (Zedner 2003, p. 163). The soldiers may provide for a subjective feeling of safety, but their mere presence and their heavily armed patrols, coupled with widespread fears of downward social mobility, add to and reproduce a feeling of subjective insecurity in large parts of the borderland population. Secondly, the borderland population as a referent object is presented by securitising actors in an essentialising way as an invariable constant that the proponents of the deployment can draw on. The subjective feeling of safety of an ideal and imagined borderland population (of voters) is the first and foremost point of reference for almost all supporters of the support deployment. The public's desire for safety and security is portrayed as the ultimate goal by the deployment's advocates to which all other issues have to be subordinated.

However, thirdly, the question of why the local population approves of the support deployment and the ubiquitous presence of soldiers along the border cannot be reduced to mere security issues, but includes questions of economy and rural development, emphasising the role of the audience as actors. Large parts of the borderland population support the ongoing securitisation, because they bring prosperity. Without this 'added value' use, the costs of the support deployment would probably be much more contested in the border region as well. Thus not only do different audiences in different settings have different backgrounds which influence how they evaluate a securitisation, but they also have different motives why they should support (or even demand) a securitisation. These motives and strategies do not always have to be related to security issues.

(2) The command level

The *Bundesheer* itself in the beginning clearly was an important securitising actor, and it had a vital interest in the support deployment. After the end of the cold war, the army was desperately in need of new tasks, and the border security deployment provided justification for the army's existence. This development has been argued to have taken place all over Western Europe, when the military, having focused exclusively on the Warsaw Pact and the Soviet Union, had suddenly lost its enemy and was in search for new fields of manoeuvre. In Austria, parts of the political class and the media strove for a dismantlement of the army in its current structure and organisation and argued for a '*Bundesheer* light' that would fully suffice the new realities (Gröbming 2005). Border guarding certainly was a most welcome opportunity to save the army and improve its reputation. Austria had based its (security) identity on the issue of neutrality, and has continued to insist upon it even after it joined the EU in 1995 (cf. Koìan 2006). Since Austria might be better described as a 'post-neutral state' (Höll 2001, p. 456), the role of the military, its size, assignments and duties are subject to constant debate (cf. Frank 2005, p. 118).

Large parts of the army's command level, however, now appear to be no longer interested in continuing the support deployment. Draftees serving at the border could be better utilised in other areas of the army. Furthermore, the money is desperately needed for investments such as equipment, munitions or simply housing facilities. Until 2007 the deployment incurred additional costs up to the sum of €661.4 million that had to be paid out of the army's own pocket (Bauer 2010). Therefore resistance comes from a number of sides, particularly from soldiers' lobby groups. A representative of the *Austrian Militia Association* in 2009 protested in an open letter: 'All experts reject this measure as a fig leaf and senseless appeasement; on the other hand there is an enormous price to pay, namely the capability of national defence in our own country which is being lastingly endangered in its existence'.[8] The *Officers Society* (self-marketing: 'The security-political conscience of the Republic of Austria') rejected the deployment, arguing that there was too little value for too much money.[9] Likewise the military command level deplores that the deployment of draftees happens at the expense of the overall training, leading to demotivation on the part of soldiers and instructors (Rechnungshof 2010, p. 28).

While the support deployment in 1990 provided an excellent opportunity to justify the existence of the Austrian army, the *Bundesheer* command level has changed its opinion. The advantages no longer outweigh the disadvantages; hence the command level ceases to take part in the continuing securitisation. Thus a considerable part of security experts who are constitutive of the security field and the dissemination of 'truth' about security threats leaves the common ground and refuses to uphold the argument.

(3) The ordinary soldiers

While parts of the army's command level have already publicly rejected the continuing support deployment, the ordinary soldiers are ambivalent. On the one hand, depending on one's rank, a soldier can get €500–3000 bonus in addition to his monthly salary; thus many soldiers might be loath to give up this extraordinary subsidy. While on duty at the border, the soldiers can beat the boredom by choosing from a variety of leisure activities. There are reduced entrance fees for football matches, spas and cinemas. The soldiers frequent the local pubs as well, although, as one soldiers' Wiki warns: 'One should be cautious. Many people get provoked by the uniform' (BHI-Wiki 2009b). Apparently not everybody in the border region seems to be enthusiastic about the support deployment and the soldiers' presence.

On the other hand the deployment, with shrunken authorities and rights in its present form, impedes the soldiers' self-respect. Judging from the discussions about the prolongation of the support deployment after the Schengen enlargement in the internet forum BHI.at, one gets the distinct impression that many soldiers, who have been on duty at the border before, are missing the 'old days' of the pre-2007 deployment. The soldiers argue that the current circumstances, under which the post-2007 support deployment has to operate, render it impossible to actually behave like what they would consider a 'soldier'. One contributor describes the soldiers' daily routine as follows: 'to sleep in bus stops, flirt with the pretty young women of the village, inspect shop windows and if you are lucky (I hope so) to prevent a burglary, resp. report it to the police [...]. I just forgot: to hang around at gas stations, get plastered with beer and then accost civilians!'[10] 'Boring' is a frequently used word. Yet another soldier complains that '[...] it is not the army's task to compensate for the job centre!' He suspects that in times of economic crisis the militia system allows for a partial relaxation of the labour market, artificially reducing unemployment rates.

Before the Schengen enlargement, however, when the soldiers had executive power, reputedly everything was 'better'. In retrospect, border guarding is described by the soldiers in the forum like a 'game': soldiers vs. irregular migrants, with an unclear outcome for both sides. The notion of 'gaming' I employ here is similar to Andreas' account of border policing at the US–Mexico border. He argues that 'Calling it a "game" is meant not to belittle or trivialize border policing and its consequences but rather to capture its performative and audience-directed nature' (Andreas 2001, p. x). The 'game' as a performative act, however, is not only directed at an audience, but it functions inwards as well: it reassures those who are guarding the border of the significance of their work. Accordingly, many soldiers in the forum exchange their favourite anecdotes ('The top level deployment was at Berg. There we had 483 apprehensions and 356 rejections!'). This perspective focuses solely on the adventure aspect, and it is completely neglecting the perspective of the irregular migrant crossing the border, who unwillingly has to engage with the soldier in the 'game'.

We can consider this ignorance an institutional effect, built into the border guarding or, to put it in a wider framework, the policing function. Generally, the occupation plays a huge role in securing an individual's self-respect and dignity, while at the same time the professional culture frames the way a person (soldier, police officer) sees and evaluates his/her everyday life. Similarly Reiner with reference to the police has observed that 'Cop culture has developed as a patterned set of understandings that help officers cope with and adjust to the pressures and tensions confronting the police' (Reiner 2000, p. 87). Naturally this mechanism applies to soldiers, draftees and militiamen, as well, although they only spend a comparably short amount of time at the border. Now, devoid of all executive authority, many feel that since the deployment has become meaningless, so have they. As one soldier in the forum put it: 'the only ones profiting are pubs and brothels'.

Although the soldiers are minor voices in the debate about the support deployment they are important actors in the field, since their presence in the borderland and their strategies as how to use and give meaning to their job influences the way it is perceived and evaluated by other actors.

(4) Politicians and governors

With the exception of the Green Party, the support deployment enjoys cross-party support on all political levels. Several ministers, both of the interior and of defence, and the governors of the Eastern lands have made their marks as protectors of the allegedly crime-ridden borderlands. The governors of the lands Burgenland and Lower Austria, where the deployment is located, constitute the only group to unambiguously support the deployment, emphasising the economic factor of the deployment for the poor and rural regions. Some even display creative interpretations of political and legal regulations, like governor Niessl of Burgenland who argued in 2006 that the *Bundesheer* was indispensable to enforce a Schengen-compliant external border (Burgenländischer Landtag 2006, p. 589).

Political actors who are not directly linked to the border regions are also strong supporters. Most of them are not impressed by the doubtable lawfulness of the deployment at all. Former minister of the interior Günther Platter called it 'a nice Austrian constitutional interim solution that has been in place for 17 years' (Mayr and Weißensteiner 2007). Maria Fekter, current minister of the interior, is also a supporter of the deployment. Her ministry in December 2009 submitted a survey that was part of the evaluation on the necessity of prolonging the deployment. It found out that more than 70% of the respondents are of the opinion that the support deployment contributed to both their personal and the overall Austrian safety, while more than 80% wished for a prolongation. The survey comes to the conclusion 'that in the interest of the border population's subjective feeling of safety it is necessary to continue the support deployment' (Bundesministerium für Inneres 2009). Accordingly, Chancellor Faymann, when asked why soldiers should only be patrolling in the border region, and not in the comparably crime-ridden city of Vienna, refers to the 'public will' of a frightened border population: 'that is because I care for the citizens' subjective feeling of safety' (Hämmerle 2010).

Apparently the point of reference is not the security threat, but this ominous 'public will'. Already in 1990 more than 80% of the electorate had been in favour of the support deployment, hence both the social democrats and the conservatives found they could benefit and show themselves in a favourable light if they publicly supported the deployment (Zuser 1996, p. 33). Approval rates of the deployment have been high in the border regions ever since. Therefore most politicians representing the parties in government are competing in a race for the highest possible feeling of safety in the border regions, while any correlation with criminal statistics is carefully avoided.

Not all politicians, however, take part in this race. A representative of the Green Party called the support deployment 'a security-political horseplay and economic-political foolishness'. According to him, Austria did not need any 'heavily armed special unit that would guard shopping trolleys and note car numbers in the border region' while robbing young men of their precious lifetime (Simoner 2008). The last mentioned aspect in particular should be taken literally: some of the soldiers are unable to cope with their lonely task of observing the border, and a disproportio-nately high number of suicides by draftees using a service weapon has been reported. Reinhold Lopatka, a conservative state secretary, made waves when in an interview he compared the low success rate with the soldiers' extraordinarily high suicide rates: 'Not to put too fine a point on it, we count more suicides of young soldiers than we count apprehensions'. When asked why he deliberately ignores the frequently mentioned 'public will' of the border population, he replied: 'if politics always did what the people want, we would immediately have to abolish taxes' (Winkler-Hermaden 2010).

Political actors occupy a favourable vantage point for the securitisation of issues, as they 'hold influential positions in the security field based on their political capital, and have privileged access to mass media' (Balzacq 2005, p. 190). In the Austrian case most political actors defend the support deployment as ultimately necessary, referring to an ominous public will of an imagined borderland population, thus constantly reinforcing the securitisation.

Conclusion

One might wonder why the security threats that should be at the centre of such an analysis have not been mentioned so far. In the end, that is what the support deployment was all about in the first place: fear of the influx of cross-border crime, irregular migration, and organised crime, in short, of everything unwanted, into Austria. Thus, should not the focus of the analysis be on the question of how the actors effectively and sustainably construct and discuss these threats? When recalling the actors' positions, arguments, strategies and intentions, it appears that the initial reason that was given for the deployment of the Austrian army at the border has disappeared from the discourse over the past several years. The focus moved to the subjective feeling of safety of an imagined borderland population, leaving behind the initial threat only to emphasise the counter-measures and the ones who put them in place. The security threat that stood at the beginning of the debate is now almost entirely decoupled from the actions that have been taken to fight it.

It is this imbalance that in the end endangers the securitisation which had proven successful since 1990. Both the military lobby and most of the critical political actors do not deny a security threat, but they do object to the support deployment as an efficient counter-measure. In challenging the so far narrative they leave the common ground that enabled the 'regime of truth' about security issues to develop in the first place. Following Bigo's argument, both security professionals and political actors should promote an issue as posing a security threat in order to increase resources and hegemonic interpretative authority. The army's command level, however, has ceased to fuel anxieties that would justify its extraordinary involvement and has virtually left the political actors on their own. Concerning public opinion, such a constellation is apt to challenge the political actors' credibility with regards to the threat in question: 'Should the professionals of politics and the (in)security professionals come to clash directly, keeping this sort of knowledge secret is no longer considered proof of a hidden truth accessible only to the politicians. On the contrary, it casts doubt on the possibility that they might even *have* access to this truth, and can create a belief inside the population that politicians' truth could very well be a misrepresentation or an outright falsity' (Bigo 2008, p. 13, emphasis in original).

When it becomes too obvious that the counter-measures and the actors who represent and benefit from them have become more important than the initial reason for implementing them, then the equilibrium that produces the knowledge for the management of insecurities becomes unstable and, in the end, untrustworthy. Nevertheless, the support deployment is still in place, even though numerous security experts as well as large parts of the (national) audience have since come to reject it. This leads us to two important findings: the first finding supports Salter's (2008) emphasis on the importance of the setting: in the border region the support deployment is evaluated differently than in regions that are more distant from the Eastern border. The salience of the threat is not that obvious in Western and Central Austria, thus the threat remains largely abstract, and the audience's foremost interest is not the call for an immediate response. The border population in contrast has practical experiences to draw upon with regards to support deployment. Further-more, since 1990 the border regions have not only become accustomed and habituated to the presence of soldiers, but they have profited in a double sense as well: being 'protected', but also in terms of living conditions. The support deployment virtually nourishes the border regions. Finally, actors and audience cannot in every case be clearly distinguished; differences are blurred. Some parts of the audience may prompt the government to continue the securitisation because they deem it indispensable or they are pursuing their own agenda. This illustrates that the audience is not only a passive recipient who supports or rejects a securitising move, but that these actors can develop their own strategies and lines of action, drawing on their cultural 'tool-kit'.

The army's border security deployment was often described by interview partners as the 'Austrian way' of handling security issues. Advocates of this 'Austrian way' argue that one should not take the support deployment too seriously. Firstly, the deployment of the *Bundesheer* has been an interim solution from the beginning and is thus temporarily limited, even though temporarily limited events apparently last longer in Austria than in other countries. Secondly, the deployment was first and foremost intended to provide a subjective feeling of safety to a population that until the demise of the Iron Curtain had lived in a more or less crime-free area and that accordingly longed for the army. Beyond the subjective feeling of safety, the support deployment is not perceived to have any practical benefit relevant for security. And, as one proponent put it, 'why bother? After all, they are not hurting anybody'.[11]

Notes

1. The empirical research was collected in 2008 during four months of field research in the Austrian Ministry of the Interior, the Federal Criminal Police Office and other police and security units in the Austrian lands. I conducted qualitative interviews and informal conversations with political actors and practitioners, all of whom were concerned with different aspects of the 2007 Schengen enlargement.
2. 'Bundesheer-Infoecke (BHI)'. Available from http://www.bhi.at/ [Accessed 21 April 2010], complemented by the private 'BHI-Wiki'. Available from http://www.floriankollmann.at/wiki_bhi/doku.php [Accessed 21 April 2010].
3. I am most grateful to Guido Tiemann, Linda Jakubowicz, Patrick Pasquet and the anonymous referee for valuable suggestions and most helpful comments on previous drafts of this article.
4. Militiamen in the Austrian armed forces are part of the Bundesheer, but are civilians and only become militarily active for training and deployment purposes.

5. All quotations from German sources are the author's translations.
6. For the purpose of this analysis I have chosen not to treat the media as a separate actor. I have elaborated on this issue elsewhere (Schwell 2009).
7. Last year's anniversary of 1989 has spurred ethnographically informed research along the former Iron Curtain that supports this finding; see the contributions in Lozoviuk 2009.
8. Open Letter of the Austrian Militia Association to Federal Chancellor Faymann, 27 May 2009, emphasis in original.
9. Open letter of the Officers Society to General Mag. Edmund Entacher, 15 February 2010.
10. All quotes are taken from BHI.at; screenshots and documentation are available upon request.
11. Interview with ministry official, Vienna, 18 November 2008.

Notes on contributor

Alexandra Schwell is an assistant professor (Universitätsassistentin) at the Department of European Ethnology at the University of Vienna. She obtained her Ph.D. in Comparative Cultural and Social Anthropology in 2007 from the European University Viadrina in Frankfurt (Oder). Currently she is working on a comparative analysis of the construction of security threats in Austrian and Polish state institutions. Research interests include border studies, Eastern Europe, anthropology of security and European integration.

References

Andreas, P., 2001. *Border games: policing the U.S.-Mexico divide.* Ithaca, NY: Cornell University Press.
Balzacq, T., 2005. The three faces of securitization: political agency, audience and context. *European journal of international relations,* 11 (2), 171–201.
Balzacq, T., 2009. Constructivism and securitization studies. *In*: M. Dunn Cavelty and V. Mauer, eds. *The Routledge handbook of security studies.* London: Routledge, 56–72.
Bauer, G., 2010. Peinliche Divisionen. *Profil,* 7, 16 January 28–29.
BHI-Wiki, 2009a. *Asse_grue,* Available from: http://www.floriankollmann.at/wiki_bhi/doku.php?id = sonstiges:asse_grue [Accessed 21 April 2010].
BHI-Wiki, 2009b. *Asihpolasse_sche,* 10 March. Available from: http://www.floriankollmann.at/wiki_bhi/doku.php?id = sihpolasse_sche [Accessed 21 April 2010].
Bigo, D., 2000. Liaison officers in Europe. New officers in the European security field. *In*: J.W.E. Sheptycki, ed. *Issues in transnational policing.* London, New York: Routledge, 65–99.
Bigo, D., 2002. Security and immigration: toward a critique of the governmentality of unease. *Alternatives,* 27 (Special Issue), 63–92.
Bigo, D., 2006. Internal and external aspects of security. *European security,* 15 (4), 385–404.
Bigo, D., 2008. Globalized (in)security: the field and the ban-opticon. *In*: D. Bigo and A. Tsoukala, eds. *Terror, insecurity and liberty. Illiberal practices of liberal regimes, the (in)security games.* London, New York: Routledge, 10–48.
Bourdieu, P., 1984. *Distinction. A social critique of the judgement of taste.* Cambridge, MA: Harvard University Press.
Bundesministerium für Inneres, 2009. *Fekter: Assistenzeinsatz wird bis Ende 2010 verlängert.* Press release nr. 6101. Wien.
Bundesministerium für Inneres, o.J., n.d. Möglicher Assistenzeinsatz des Bundesheeres nach Abbau der Schengen Außengrenze – Grundsätze für den militärischen Aufgabenbereich.
Burawoy, M., 1991. The extended case method. *In*: M. Burawoy, A. Burton, A.A. Ferguson, K.J. Fox, J. Gamson, N. Gartrell, L. Hurst, C. Kurzman, L. Salzinger, J. Schiffman, and S. Ui, eds. *Ethnography unbound. Power and resistance in the modern metropolis.* Berkeley. CA: University of California Press, 271–287.
Burgenländischer Landtag, 2006. Dringlichkeitsantrag der Landtagsabgeordneten Christian Illedits, Johann Tschürtz Kolleginnen und Kollegen auf Fassung einer Entschließung betreffend die Aufrechterhaltung des Assistenzeinsatzes in unverminderter Stärke bis zur Einrichtung der Schengen-konformen Grenzsicherung in den EU-Nachbarstaaten des

Burgenlandes. Wortprotokoll der 5. Sitzung der XIX. Gesetzgebungsperiode des Burgen-ländischen Landtages. Available from: http://www.burgenland.at/media/file/15_5PRO.pdf [Accessed 3 November 2010].

Buzan, B., 1997. Rethinking security after the cold war. *Cooperation and conflict*, 32 (1), 5–28.

Buzan, B., Wæver, O., and Wilde, J.d., 1998. *Security: a new framework for analysis*. Boulder, CO: Lynne Rienner.

Eriksson, J. and Rhinard, M., 2009. The internal–external security nexus: notes on an emerging research agenda. *Cooperation and conflict*, 44 (3), 243–267.

Foucault, M., 1980. Truth and power. *In*: C. Gordon, ed. *Power/knowledge. Selected interviews and other writings 1972–1977*. New York: Pantheon, 109–133.

Frank, J., 2005. A neutral's perspective: the role of the Austrian armed forces in homeland security. Connections. *The quarterly journal*, 4 (3), 97–120.

Fritzl, M., 2009. Grenzeinstz als Sicherheitsfolklore. *Die Presse*, 20 November, p. 31.

Gingrich, A., 2004. Concepts of race vanishing, movements of racism rising? Global issues and Austrian ethnography. *Ethnos*, 69 (2), 156–176.

Goffman, E., 1990 [1959]. *The presentation of self in everyday life*. Harmondsworth: Penguin.

Goldstein, D.M., 2010. Security and the culture expert: Dilemmas of an engaged anthropology. *PoLAR: political and legal anthropology review*, 33 (s1), 126–142.

Gröbming, W., 2005. 15 Jahre Assistenzeinsatz zur Grenzraumüberwachung. *Truppendienst* (Folge 285, Ausgabe 4).

Guittet, E.-P., 2006. Military activities within national boundaries. The French case. *In*: D. Bigo and A. Tsoukala, eds. *Terror, insecurity and liberty. Illiberal practices of liberal regimes after 9/11*. London, New York: Routledge, 121–145.

Hall, S., 1993. Encoding, decoding. *In*: S. During, ed. *The cultural studies reader*. London, New York: Routledge, 90–103.

Hämmerle, W., 2010. Sicherheitspolitik der Gefühle. *Wiener Zeitung*, 17 February, p. 5.

Höll, O., 2001. European evolution and the Austrian security perspectives. *In*: P. Luif, ed. *Security in central and eastern Europe. Problems-perceptions-policies*. Wien: Braumüller, 447–476.

Kent, A., 2006. Reconfiguring security: Buddhism and moral legitimacy in Cambodia. *Security dialogue*, 37 (3), 343–361.

Koìan, M., 2006. Austrian neutrality: burden of history in the making or moral good rediscovered? *Perspectives*, (26), 23–45.

Lozoviuk, P., ed. 2009. *Grenzgebiet als Forschungsfeld. Aspekte der ethnografischen und kulturhistorischen Erforschung des Grenzlandes* [Border region as a field of research. Aspects of ethnographical and cultural-historical research in the border region]. Leipzig: Leipziger Universitätsverlag.

Lutterbeck, D., 2005. Blurring the dividing line: the convergence of internal and external security in Western Europe. *European security*, 14 (2), 231–253.

Martínez, O.J., 1994. *Border people: life and society in the U.S.-Mexico borderlands*. Tucson, AZ: University of Arizona Press.

Mayr, P. and Weißensteiner, N., 2007. *Ein schönes österreichisches Provisorium*. 21 December 2007, 10.

McDonald, M., 2008. Securitization and the construction of security. *European journal of international relations*, 14 (4), 563–587.

Pelinka, A., 2005. Austrian euroscepticism: the shift from the left to the right. *In*: R. Harmsen and M. Spiering, eds. *Euroscepticism. Party politics, national identity and European integration*. Amsterdam, New York: Rodopi, 207–224.

Rechnungshof 2010. Assistenzeinsatz des Bundesheeres im Grenzgebiet. Bund 2010/4, 08 March 2010. Available from: http://www.rechnungshof.gv.at/fileadmin/downloads/2010/berichte/teilberichte/bund/bund_2010_04/Bund_2010_04_1.pdf [Accessed 3 November 2010].

Reiner, R., 2000. *The politics of the police*. Oxford: Oxford University Press.

Roth, M., 2008. 902 Wochen und ein Tag (I). Der Assistenzeinsatz zur Grenzraumüberwachung (1990–2007). *Truppendienst*, (5).

Said, E., 1979. *Orientalism*. New York: Vintage.

Salter, M.B., 2008. Securitization and desecuritization: a dramaturgical analysis of the Canadian air transport security authority. *Journal of international relations and development*, 11, 321–349.

Schwell, A., 2009. De/securitising the 2007 Schengen enlargement: Austria and 'the East'. *Journal of contemporary European research*, 5 (2), 243–258.

Simoner, M., 2008. Streit um Schützenhilfe an Grenzen. *Der Standard*, 17 July, p. 10.

Stritzel, H., 2007. Towards a theory of securitization: Copenhagen and beyond. *European journal of international relations*, 13, 357–383.

Swidler, A., 1986. Culture in action: Symbols and strategies. *American sociological review*, 51, 273–286.

Vidmar-Horvat, K. and Delanty, G., 2008. Mitteleuropa and the European heritage. *European journal of social theory*, 11 (2), 203–218.

Wæver, O., 1995. Securitization and desecuritization. *In*: R. Lipschutz, ed. *On security*. New York: Columbia University Press, 46–86.

Wæver, O., 1996. European security identities. *Journal of common market studies*, 34 (1), 103–132.

Wæver, O., 2000. The EU as a security actor: reflections from a pessimistic constructivist on post-sovereign security orders. *In*: M. Kelstrup and M.C. Williams, eds. *International relations theory and the politics of European integration. Power, security and community.* London: Routledge, 250–294.

Williams, R., 1963. *Culture and society 1780–1950*. Harmondsworth, New York, Ringwood u.a.: Penguin.

Winkler-Hermaden, R., 2010. DerStandard.at-Interview. *Der Assistenzeinsatz sollte beendet werden*. derStandard at 14 February. Available from: http://derstandard.at/1265852065687/derStandardat-Interview-Der-Assistenzeinsatz-sollte-beendet-werden [Accessed 3 November 2010].

Wolff, L., 1994. *Inventing eastern Europe: the map of civilization on the mind of the enlightenment*. Stanford, CA: Stanford University Press.

Zedner, L., 2003. Too much security? *International journal of the sociology of law*, 31 (3), 155–184.

Zuser, P.,1996. Die Konstruktion der Ausländerfrage in Österreich. Eine Analyse des öffentlichen Diskurses 1990. *Institut für Höhere Studien (IHS)/Institute for Advanced Studies, Vienna, Reihe Politikwissenschaft/Political Science Series*, (35). Available from: http://www.ihs.ac.at/publications/pol/pw_35.pdf [Accessed 3 November 2010].

Index

Page numbers in *Italics* represent tables.
Page numbers in **Bold** represent figures.

For Product Safety Concerns and Information please contact our EU
representative GPSR@taylorandfrancis.com
Taylor & Francis Verlag GmbH, Kaufingerstraße 24, 80331 München, Germany

www.ingramcontent.com/pod-product-compliance
Lightning Source LLC
Chambersburg PA
CBHW080238270326
41926CB00020B/4283